魔法遣いに大切なこと SOMEDAY's DREAMERS

VOLUME 1

CREATED BY NORIE YAMADA

D0103461

HAMBURG // LONDON // LOS ANGELES // TOKYO

Someday's Dreamers Vol. 1
Story By Norie Yamada
Art By Kumichi Yoshizuki

Translation - Jeremiah Bourque
English Adaptation - Hope Donovan
Copy Editor - Eric Althoff
Retouch and Lettering - James Dashiell
Production Artist - Jennifer Carbajal and Lucas Rivera
Cover Design - Gary Shum

Editor - Paul Morrissey
Digital Imaging Manager - Chris Buford
Production Manager - Jennifer Miller
Managing Editor - Lindsey Johnston
VP of Production - Ron Klamert
Publisher and E.I.C. - Mike Kiley
President and C.O.O. - John Parker
C.E.O. and Chief Creative Officer - Stuart Levy

A 🔴 **TOKYOPOP**® Manga

TOKYOPOP Inc.
5900 Wilshire Blvd. Suite 2000
Los Angeles, CA 90036

E-mail: info@TOKYOPOP.com
Come visit us online at www.TOKYOPOP.com

ISBN: 1-59816-178-4

First TOKYOPOP printing: March 2006
10 9 8 7 6 5 4 3 2 1
Printed in the USA

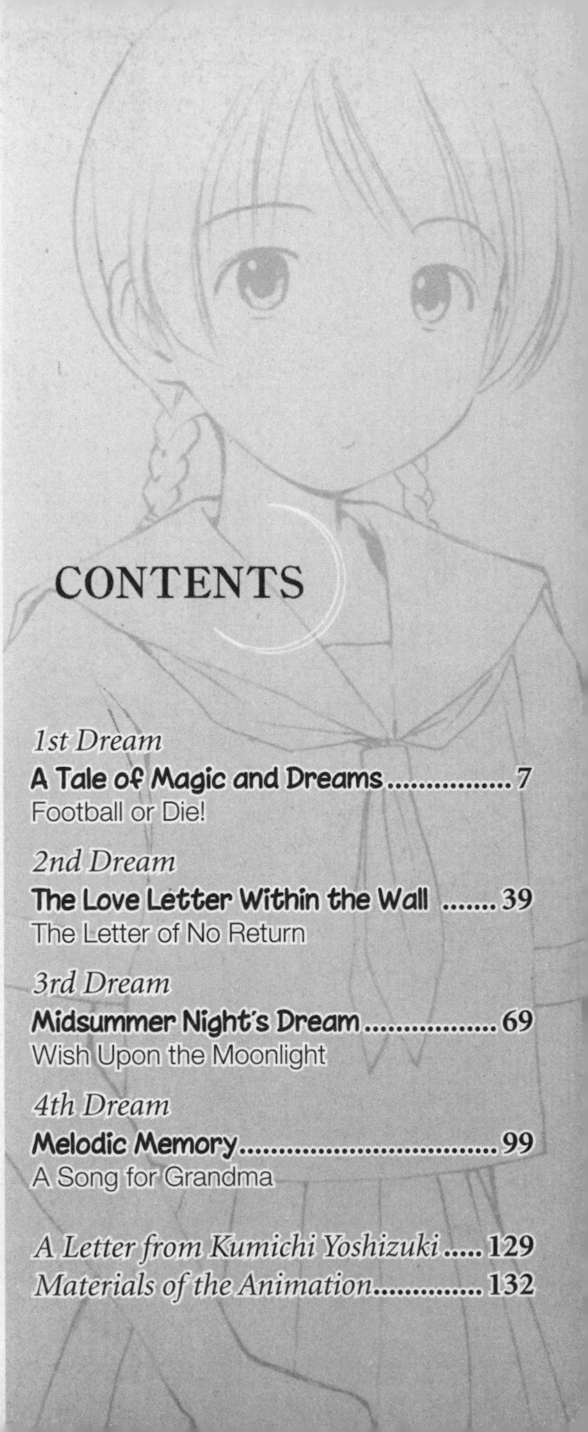

CONTENTS

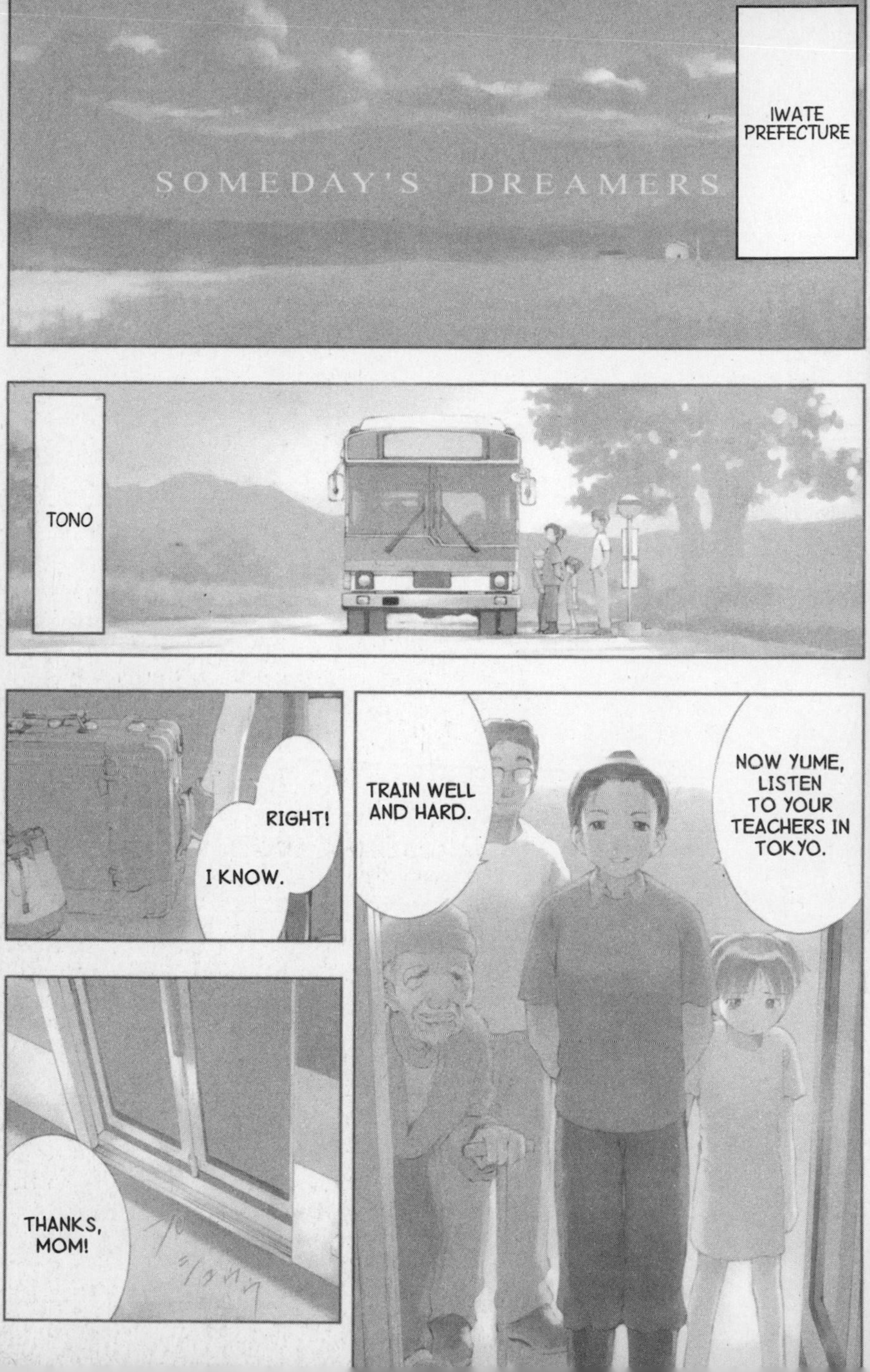
IWATE PREFECTURE
SOMEDAY'S DREAMERS
TONO
NOW YUME, LISTEN TO YOUR TEACHERS IN TOKYO.
TRAIN WELL AND HARD.
RIGHT! I KNOW.
THANKS, MOM!

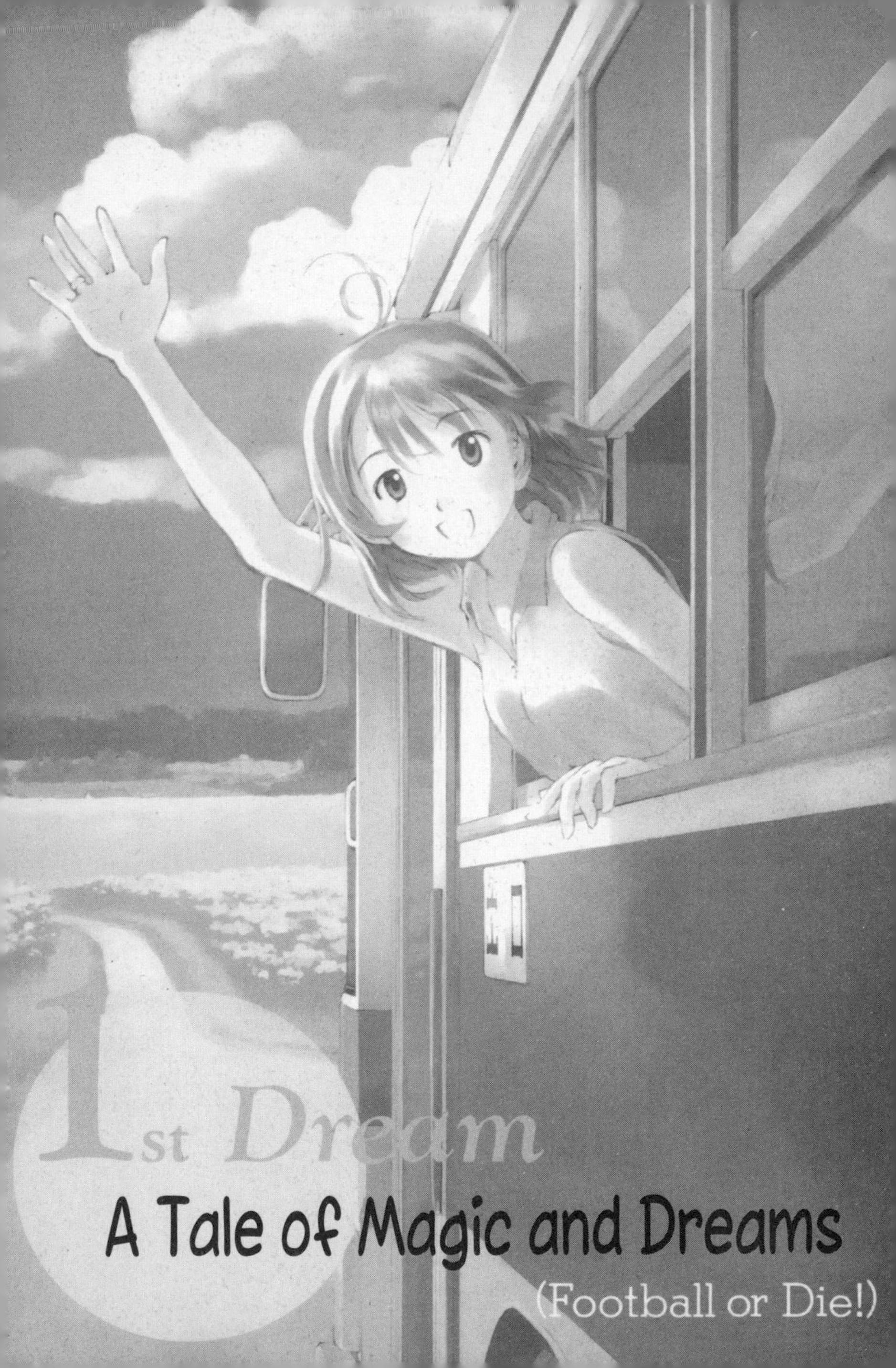
1st Dream
A Tale of Magic and Dreams
(Football or Die!)

魔法遣いに大切なこと
SOMEDAY'S DREAMERS

Story by
Norie Yamada

Art by
Kumichi Yoshizuki

You are suffering 'cause you just can't forget about your dream......
the important something you've locked up in your heart.
This is the story of a girl who's after her dream.
Why don't you look for that "something" with her,
still so precious to you.....

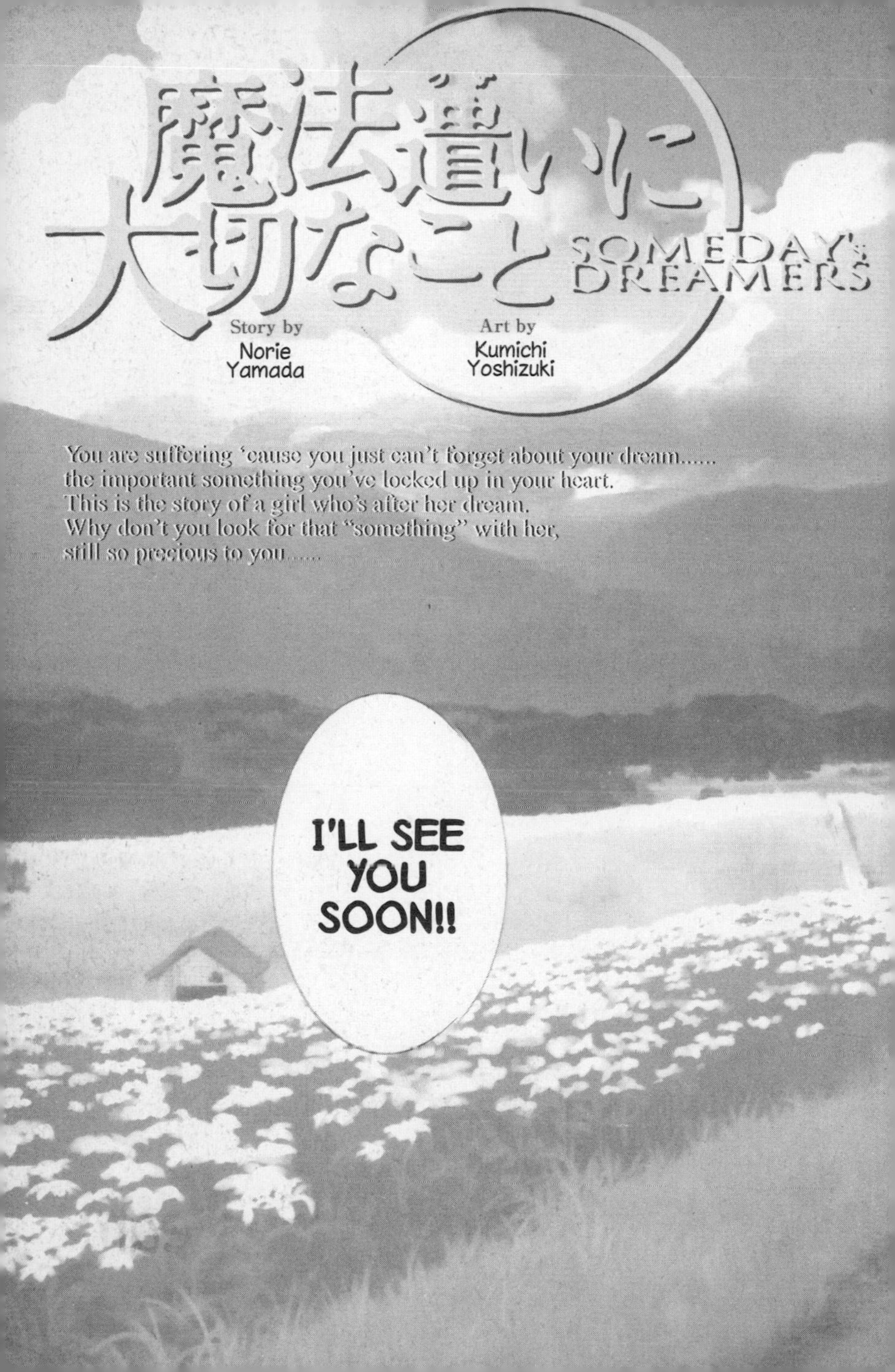
I'LL SEE YOU SOON!!

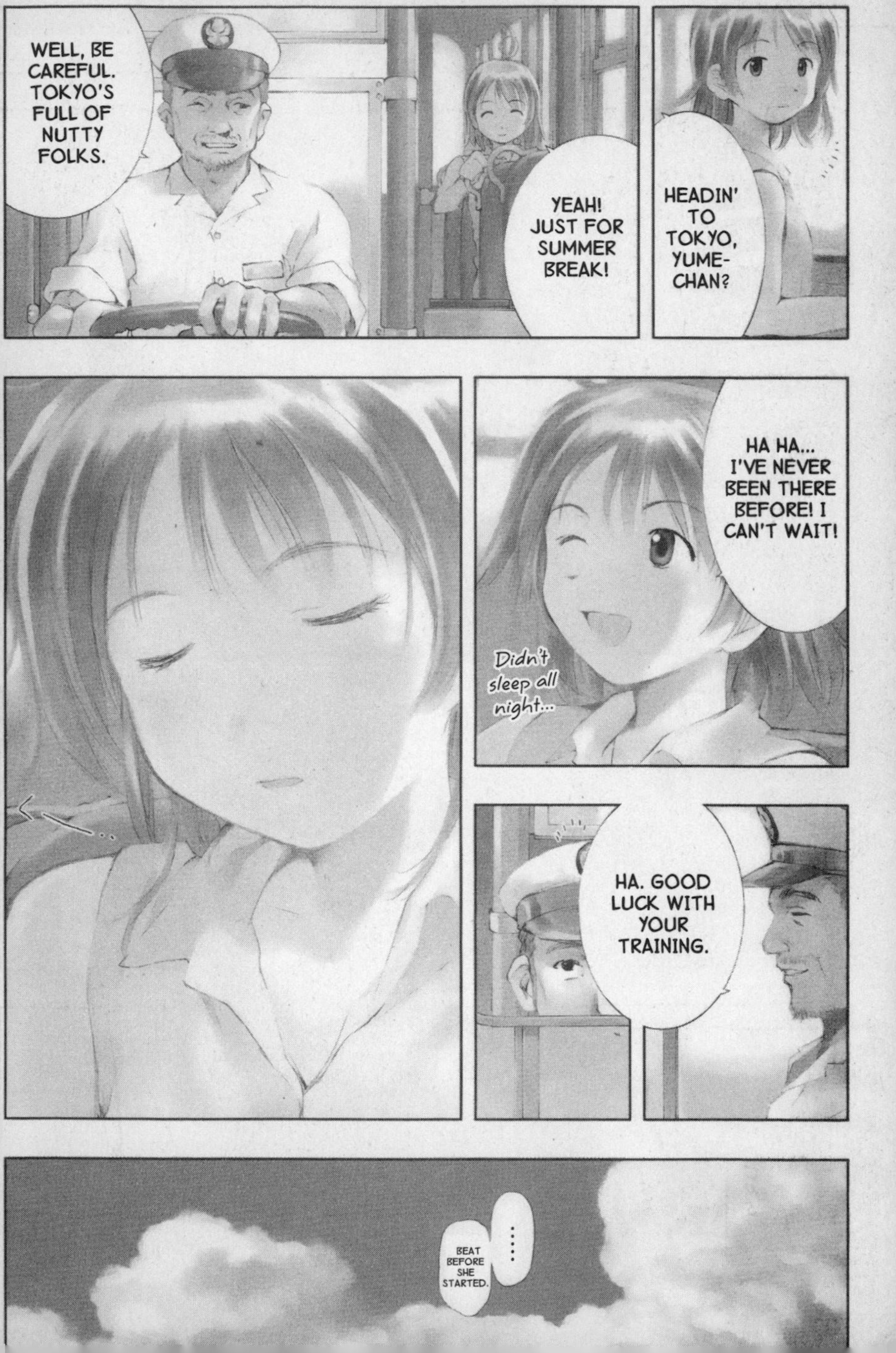
HEADIN' TO TOKYO, YUME-CHAN?
YEAH! JUST FOR SUMMER BREAK!
WELL, BE CAREFUL. TOKYO'S FULL OF NUTTY FOLKS.
HA HA... I'VE NEVER BEEN THERE BEFORE! I CAN'T WAIT!
Didn't sleep all night...
HA. GOOD LUCK WITH YOUR TRAINING.
......
BEAT BEFORE SHE STARTED.

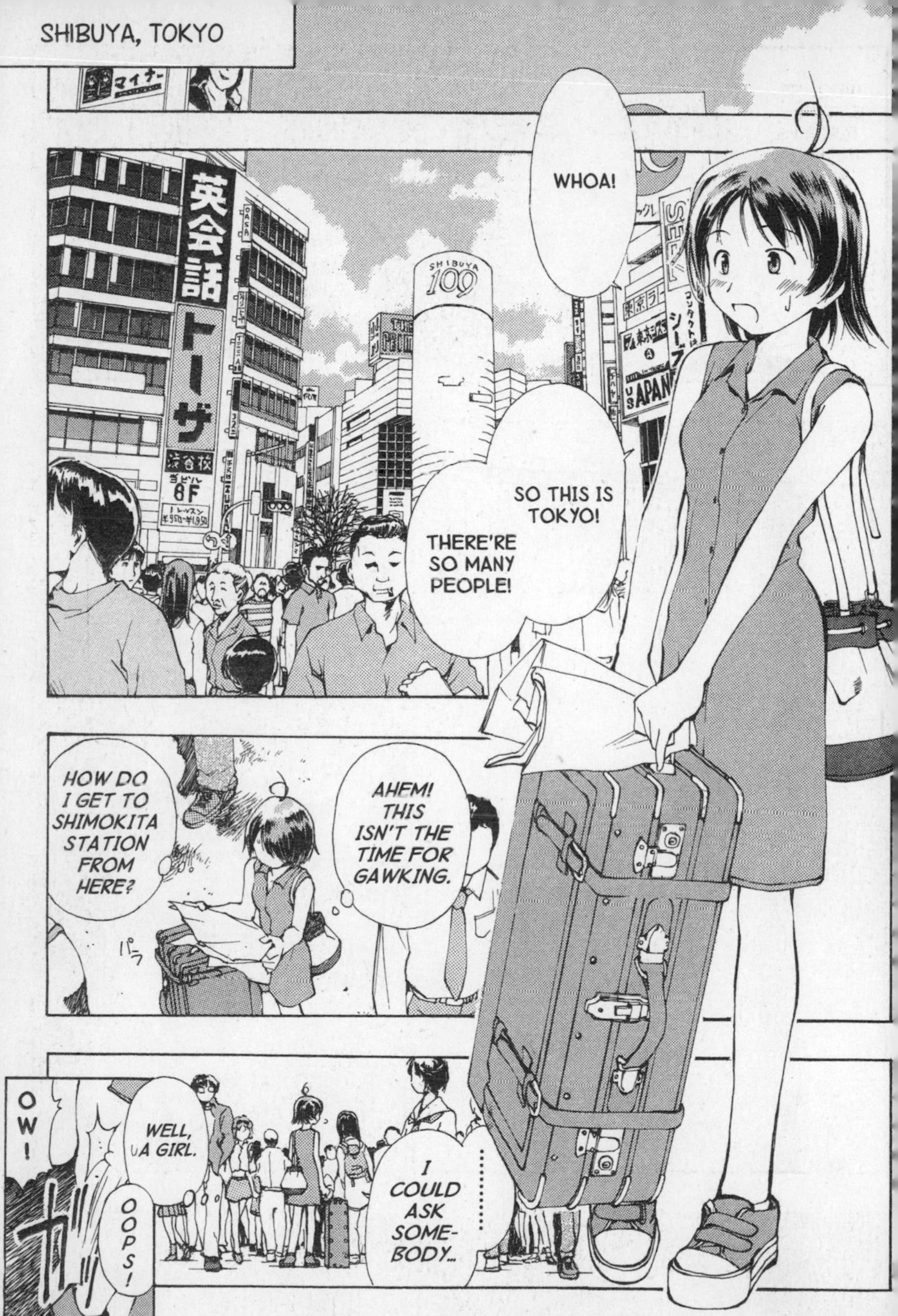

SHIBUYA, TOKYO
WHOA!
SO THIS IS TOKYO!
THERE'RE SO MANY PEOPLE!
AHEM! THIS ISN'T THE TIME FOR GAWKING.
HOW DO I GET TO SHIMOKITA STATION FROM HERE?
I COULD ASK SOME-BODY...
WELL, A GIRL.
OOPS!
OW!

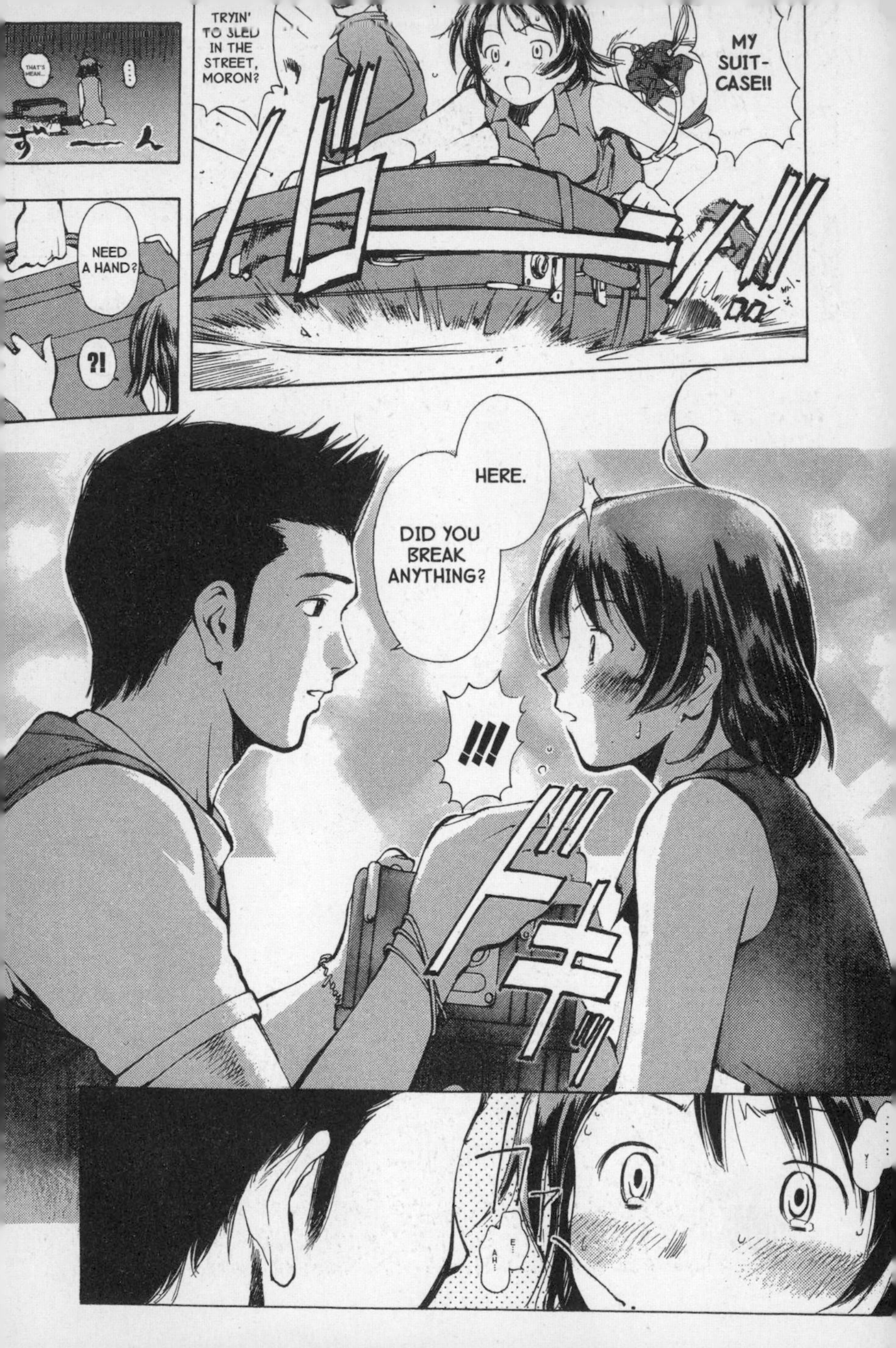
MY SUIT-CASE!!
TRYIN' TO SLED IN THE STREET, MORON?
THAT'S MEAN...
....
NEED A HAND?
?!
HERE.
DID YOU BREAK ANYTHING?
!!!

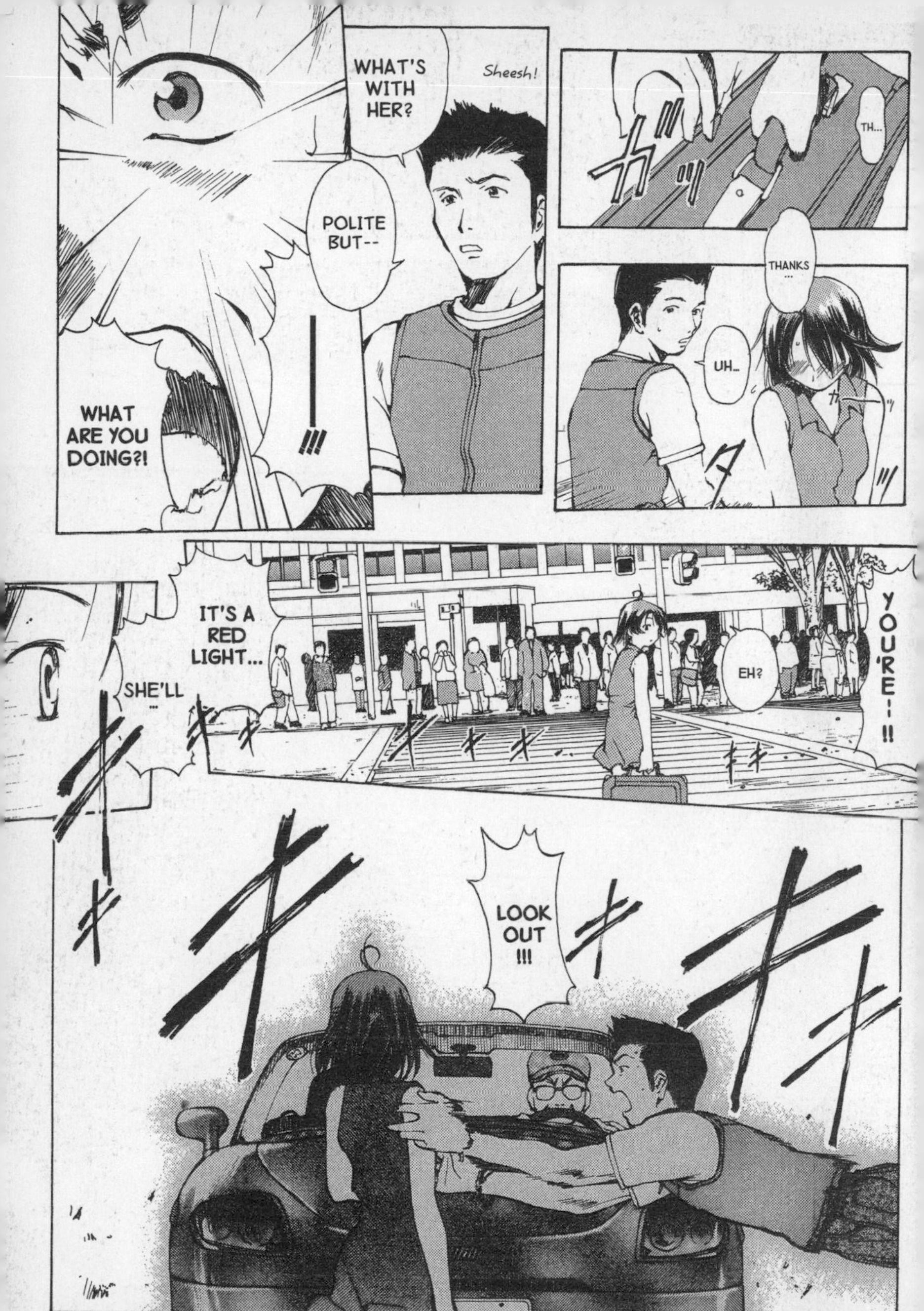
TH...
THANKS ...
UH...
WHAT'S WITH HER?
Sheesh!
POLITE BUT--
WHAT ARE YOU DOING?!
YOU'RE--!!
EH?
IT'S A RED LIGHT...
SHE'LL ...
LOOK OUT !!!

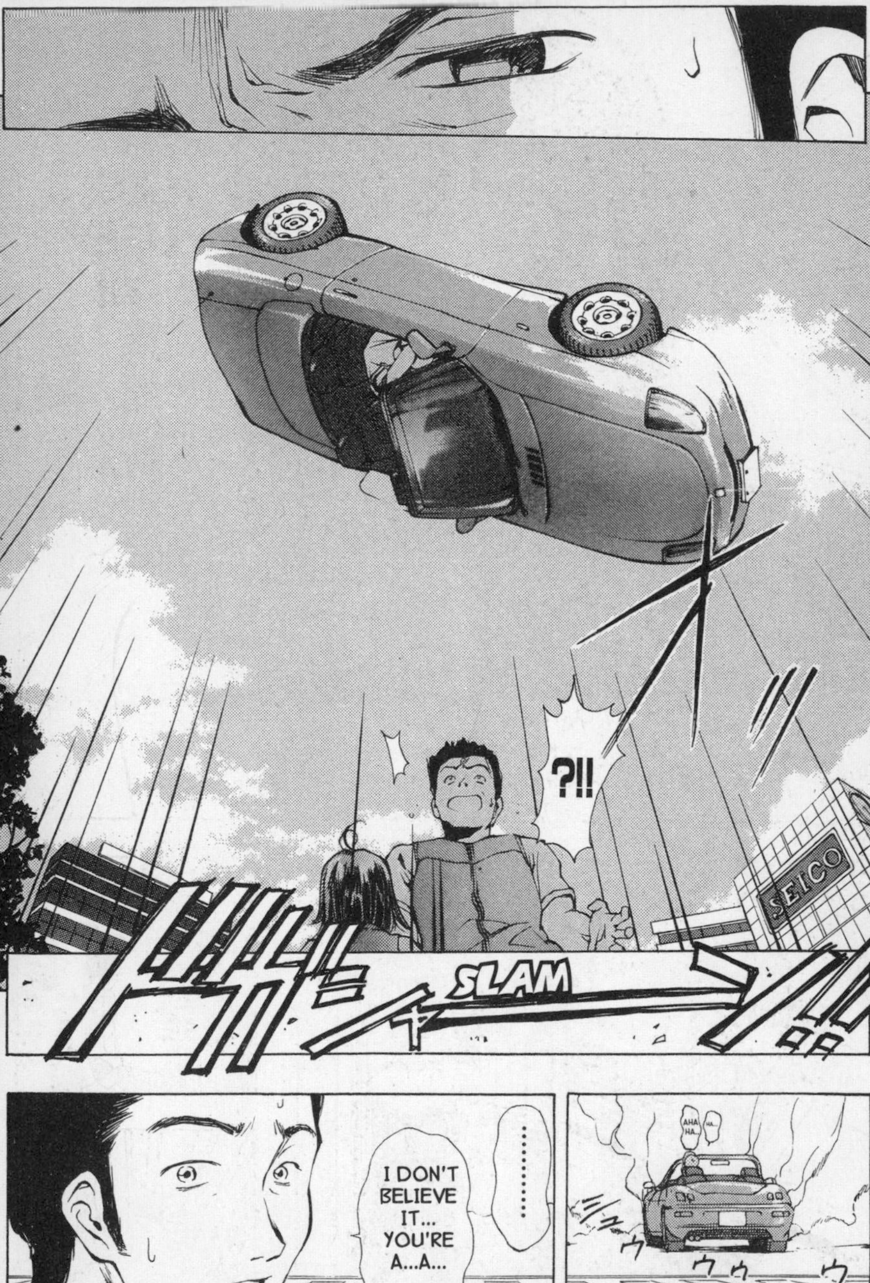
?!!
SLAM
AHA HA...
HA...
......
I DON'T BELIEVE IT... YOU'RE A...A...

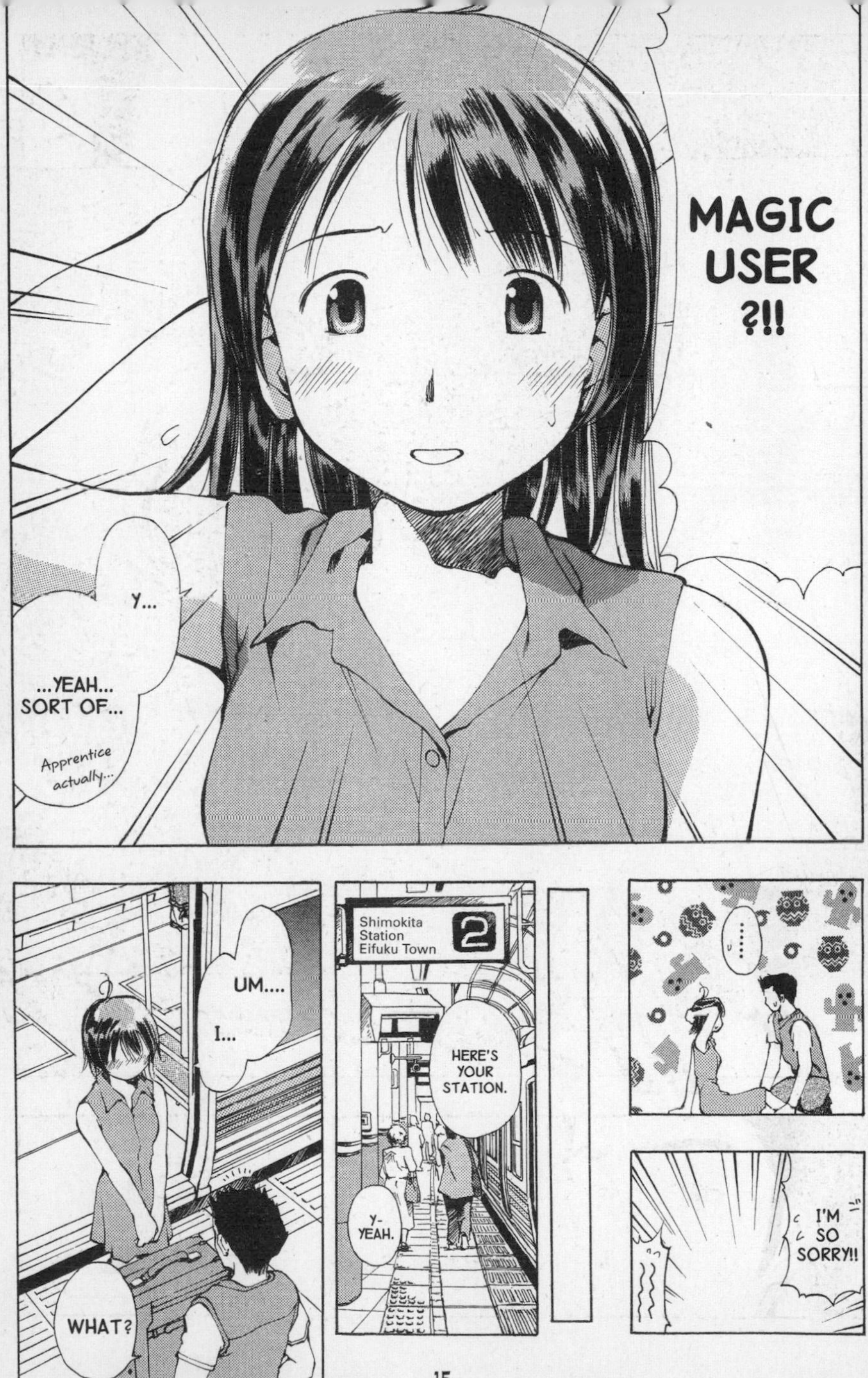
MAGIC USER ?!!
Y...
...YEAH... SORT OF...
Apprentice actually...
......
I'M SO SORRY!!
Shimokita Station Eifuku Town
2
HERE'S YOUR STATION.
Y-YEAH.
UM.... I...
WHAT?

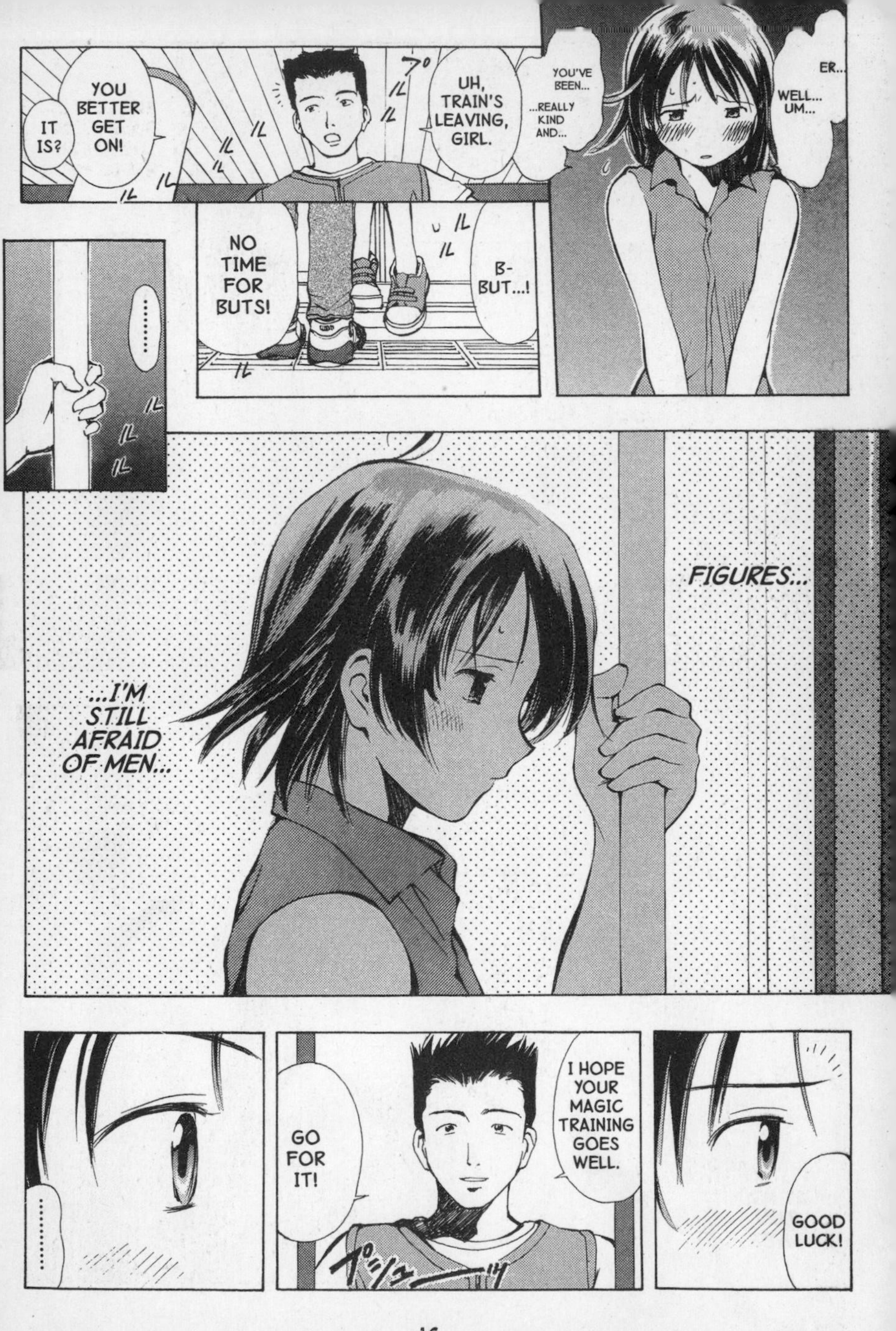
ER...
WELL... UM...
YOU'VE BEEN... ...REALLY KIND AND...
UH, TRAIN'S LEAVING, GIRL.
YOU BETTER GET ON!
IT IS?
B-BUT...!
NO TIME FOR BUTS!
......
FIGURES...
...I'M STILL AFRAID OF MEN...
GOOD LUCK!
I HOPE YOUR MAGIC TRAINING GOES WELL.
GO FOR IT!
......

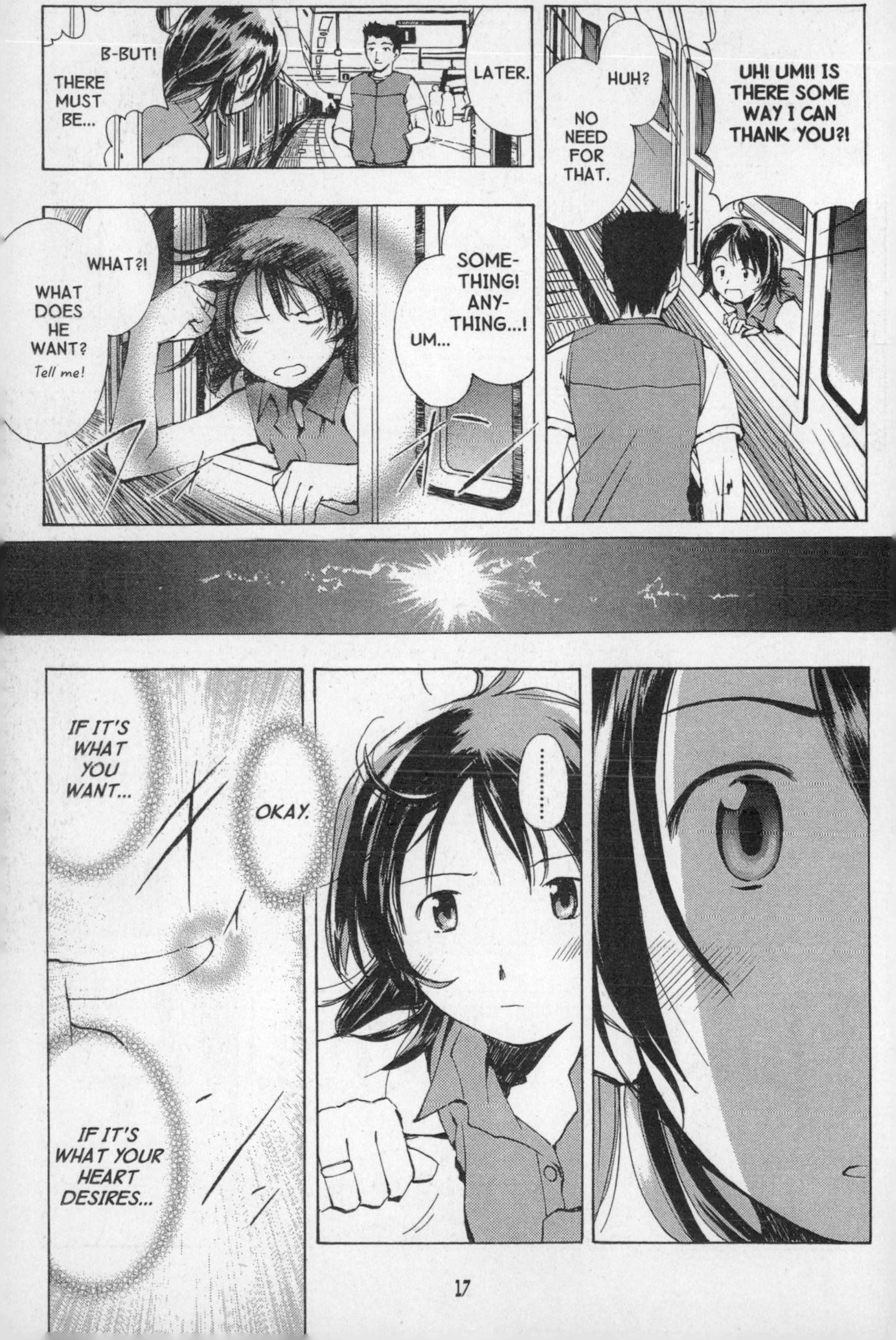
UH! UMI!! IS THERE SOME WAY I CAN THANK YOU?!
HUH?
NO NEED FOR THAT.
LATER.
B-BUT!
THERE MUST BE...
SOME-THING! ANY-THING...!
UM...
WHAT?!
WHAT DOES HE WANT?
Tell me!
......
IF IT'S WHAT YOU WANT...
OKAY.
IF IT'S WHAT YOUR HEART DESIRES...

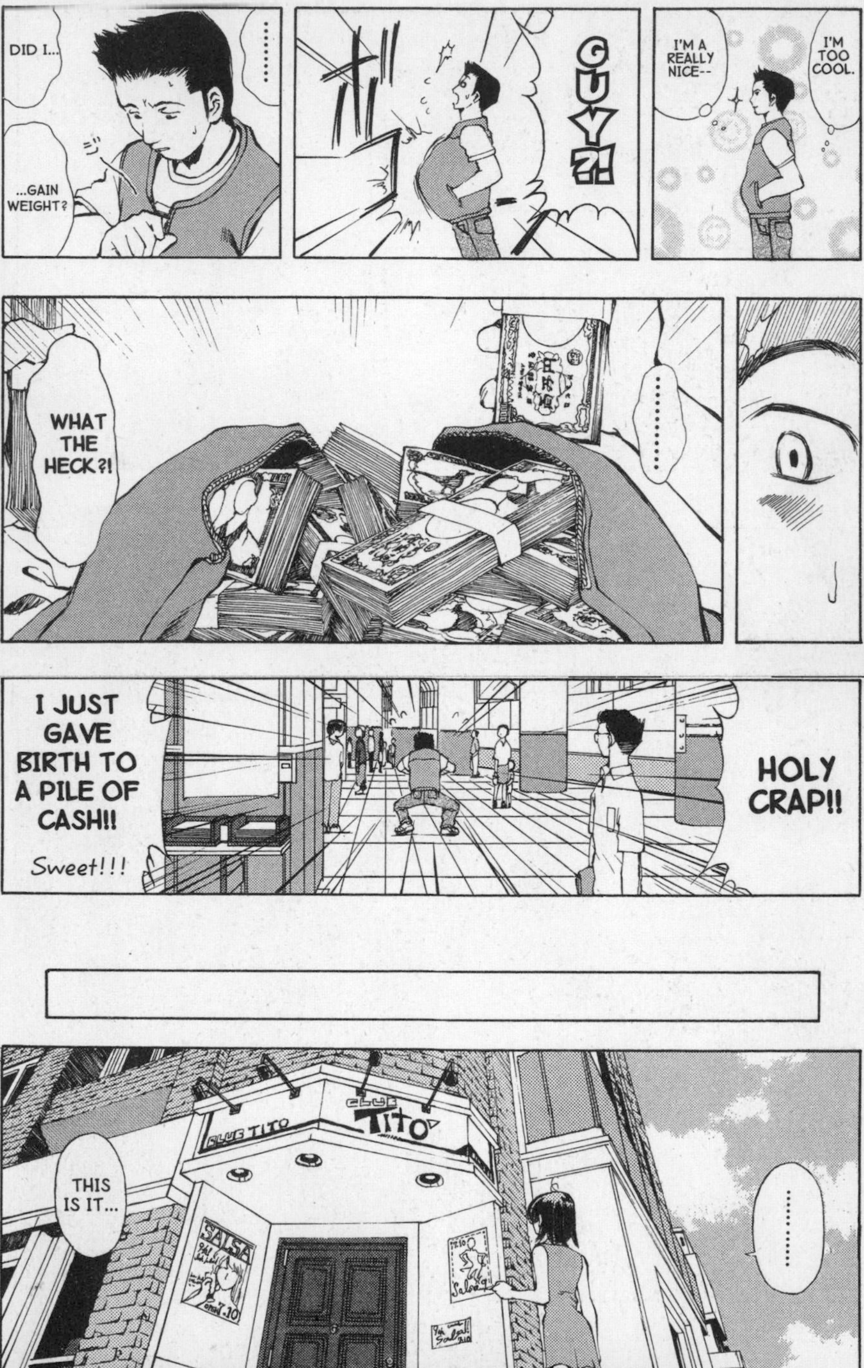
I'M TOO COOL.
I'M A REALLY NICE--
GUY?!
......
DID I...
...GAIN WEIGHT?
......
WHAT THE HECK?!
HOLY CRAP!!
I JUST GAVE BIRTH TO A PILE OF CASH!!
Sweet!!!
......
THIS IS IT...

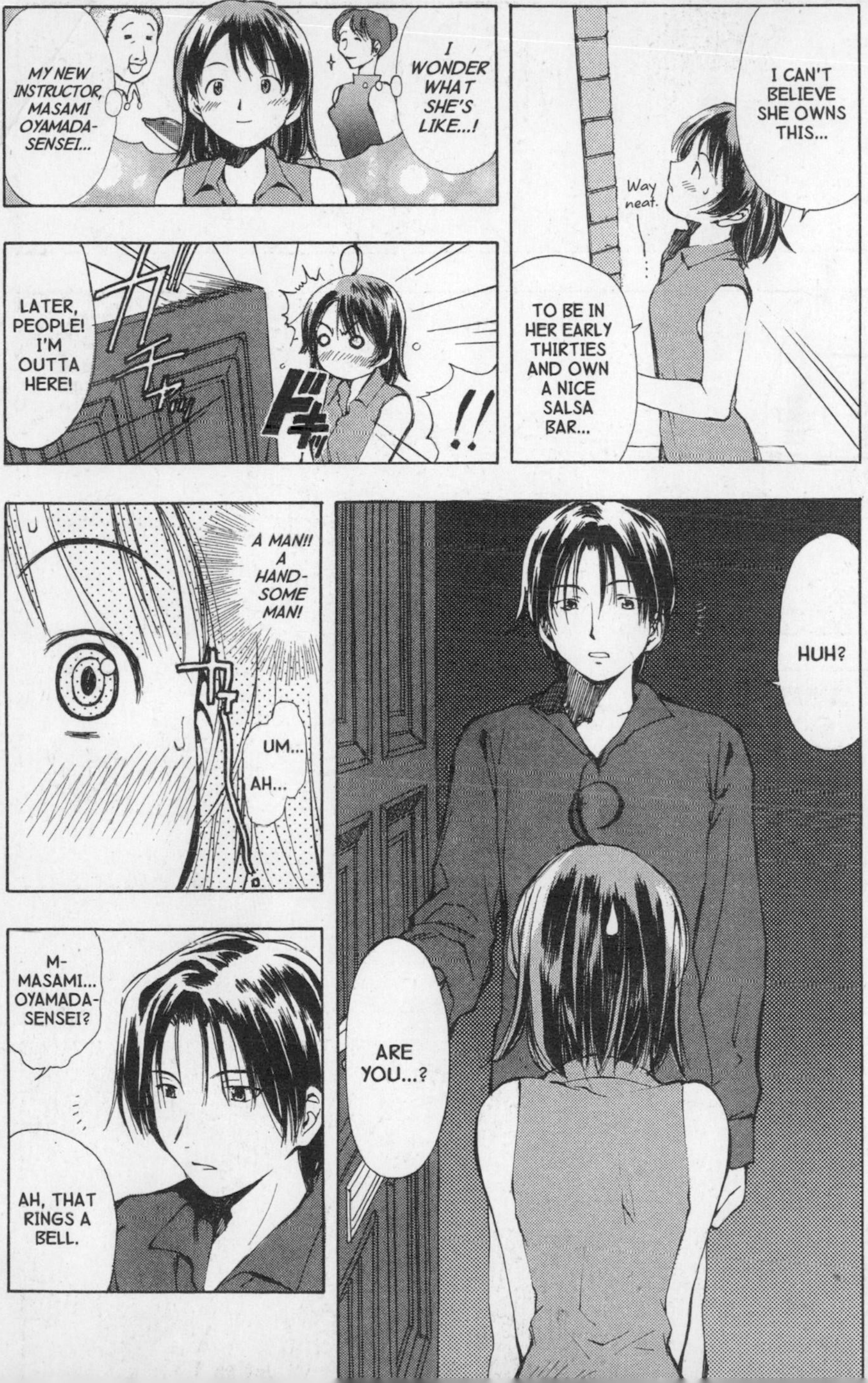
I CAN'T BELIEVE SHE OWNS THIS...
Way neat.
TO BE IN HER EARLY THIRTIES AND OWN A NICE SALSA BAR...
I WONDER WHAT SHE'S LIKE...!
MY NEW INSTRUCTOR, MASAMI OYAMADA-SENSEI...
!!
LATER, PEOPLE! I'M OUTTA HERE!
HUH?
ARE YOU...?
A MAN!! A HANDSOME MAN!
UM...
AH...
M-MASAMI... OYAMADA-SENSEI?
AH, THAT RINGS A BELL.

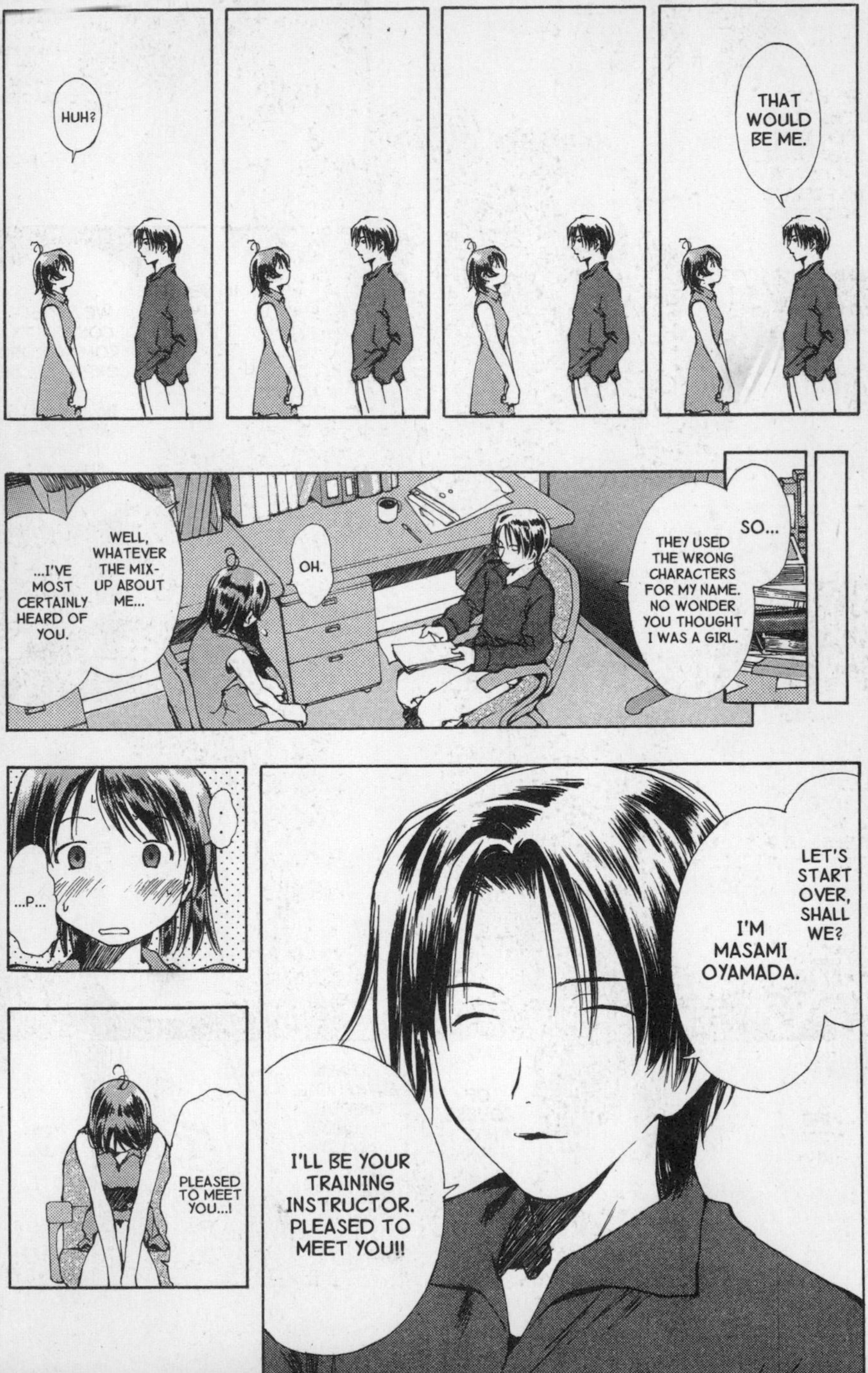

THAT WOULD BE ME.
HUH?
SO...
THEY USED THE WRONG CHARACTERS FOR MY NAME. NO WONDER YOU THOUGHT I WAS A GIRL.
OH.
WELL, WHATEVER THE MIX-UP ABOUT ME...
...I'VE MOST CERTAINLY HEARD OF YOU.
LET'S START OVER, SHALL WE?
I'M MASAMI OYAMADA.
I'LL BE YOUR TRAINING INSTRUCTOR. PLEASED TO MEET YOU!!
...P...
PLEASED TO MEET YOU...!

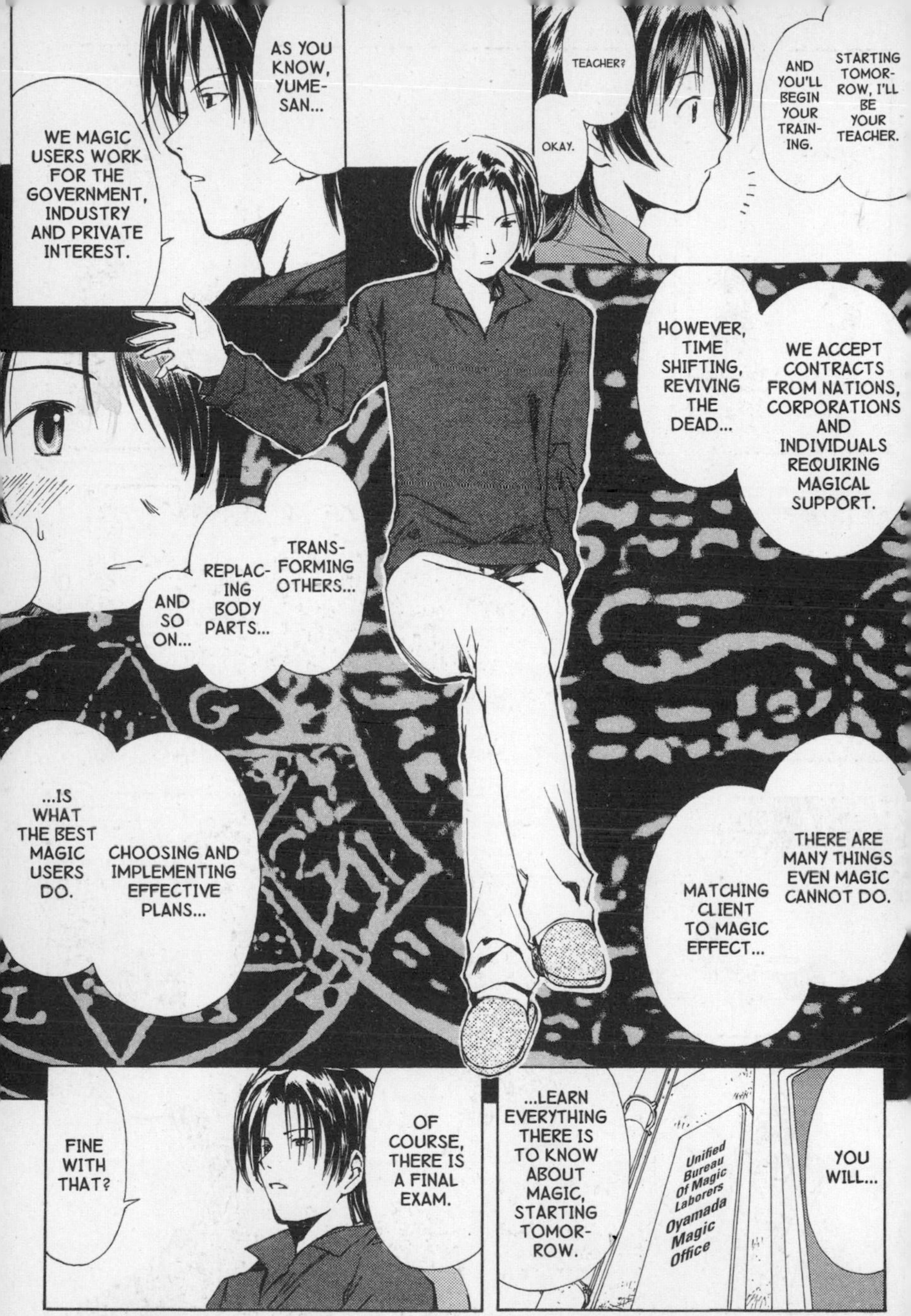
STARTING TOMORROW, I'LL BE YOUR TEACHER.
AND YOU'LL BEGIN YOUR TRAINING.
TEACHER?
OKAY.
AS YOU KNOW, YUME-SAN...
WE MAGIC USERS WORK FOR THE GOVERNMENT, INDUSTRY AND PRIVATE INTEREST.
WE ACCEPT CONTRACTS FROM NATIONS, CORPORATIONS AND INDIVIDUALS REQUIRING MAGICAL SUPPORT.
HOWEVER, TIME SHIFTING, REVIVING THE DEAD...
TRANSFORMING OTHERS...
REPLACING BODY PARTS...
AND SO ON...
THERE ARE MANY THINGS EVEN MAGIC CANNOT DO.
MATCHING CLIENT TO MAGIC EFFECT...
CHOOSING AND IMPLEMENTING EFFECTIVE PLANS...
...IS WHAT THE BEST MAGIC USERS DO.
YOU WILL...
Unified Bureau Of Magic Laborers Oyamada Magic Office
...LEARN EVERYTHING THERE IS TO KNOW ABOUT MAGIC, STARTING TOMORROW.
OF COURSE, THERE IS A FINAL EXAM.
FINE WITH THAT?

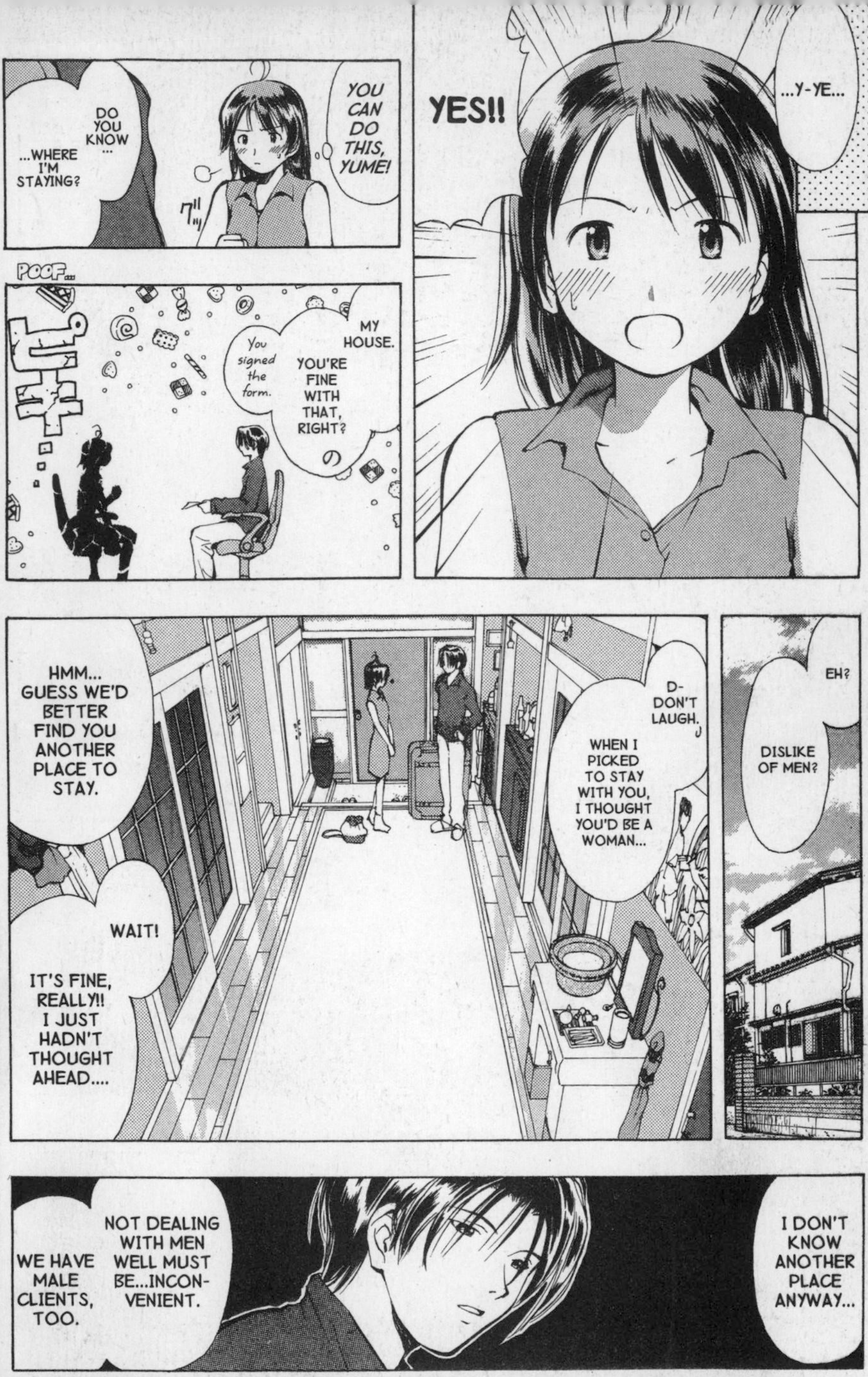
...Y-YE...
YES!!
YOU CAN DO THIS, YUME!
DO YOU KNOW ...
...WHERE I'M STAYING?
POOF...
MY HOUSE.
YOU'RE FINE WITH THAT, RIGHT?
You signed the form.
EH?
DISLIKE OF MEN?
D-DON'T LAUGH.
WHEN I PICKED TO STAY WITH YOU, I THOUGHT YOU'D BE A WOMAN...
HMM... GUESS WE'D BETTER FIND YOU ANOTHER PLACE TO STAY.
WAIT!
IT'S FINE, REALLY!! I JUST HADN'T THOUGHT AHEAD....
I DON'T KNOW ANOTHER PLACE ANYWAY...
NOT DEALING WITH MEN WELL MUST BE...INCON-VENIENT.
WE HAVE MALE CLIENTS, TOO.

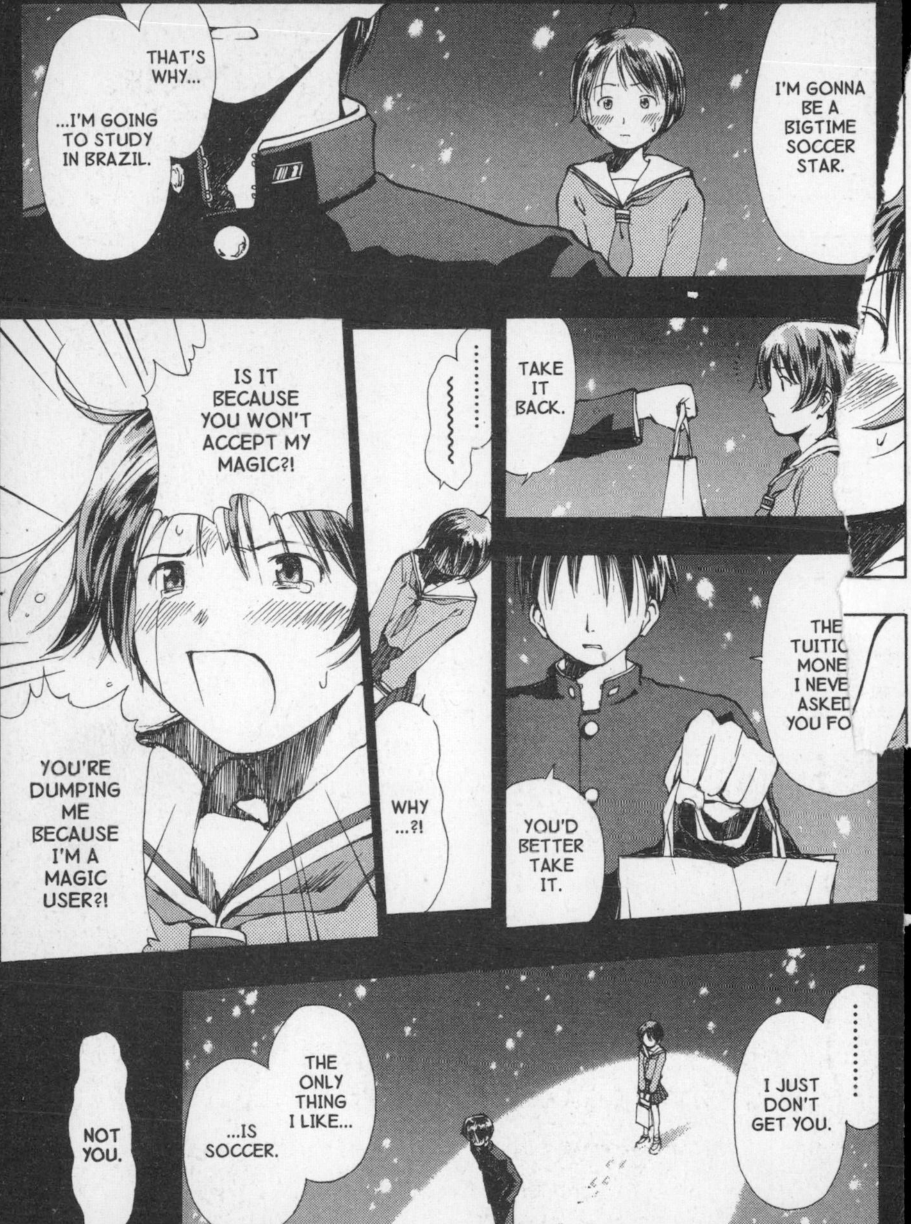
I'M GONNA BE A BIGTIME SOCCER STAR.
THAT'S WHY...
...I'M GOING TO STUDY IN BRAZIL.
TAKE IT BACK.
THE TUITIO MONE I NEVE ASKED YOU FO
YOU'D BETTER TAKE IT.
......
WHY ...?!
IS IT BECAUSE YOU WON'T ACCEPT MY MAGIC?!
YOU'RE DUMPING ME BECAUSE I'M A MAGIC USER?!
......
I JUST DON'T GET YOU.
THE ONLY THING I LIKE...
...IS SOCCER.
NOT YOU.

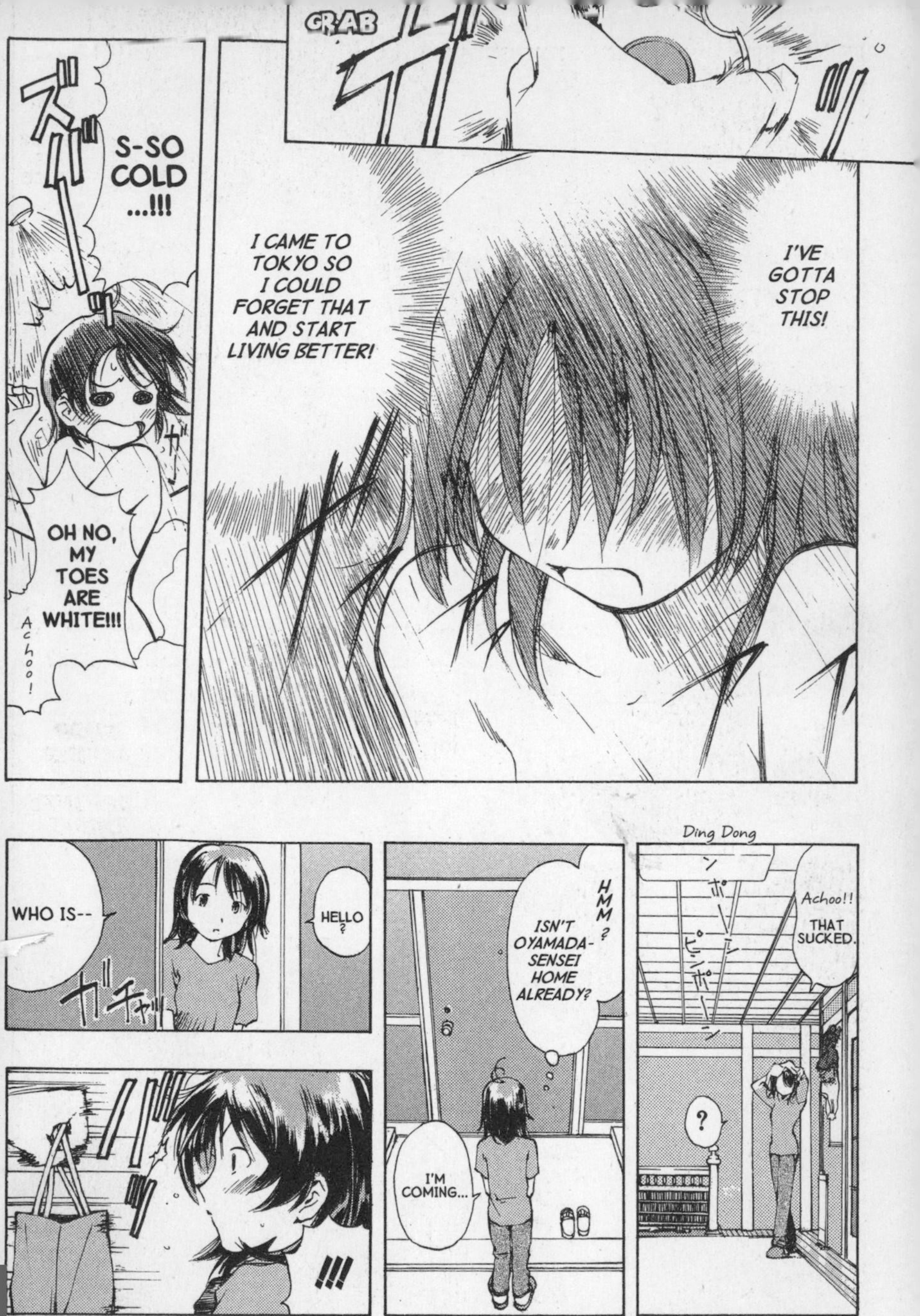
GRAB
I'VE GOTTA STOP THIS!
I CAME TO TOKYO SO I COULD FORGET THAT AND START LIVING BETTER!
S-SO COLD ...!!!
OH NO, MY TOES ARE WHITE!!!
Achoo!
Ding Dong
Achoo!! THAT SUCKED.
?
HMM?
ISN'T OYAMADA-SENSEI HOME ALREADY?
I'M COMING...
HELLO?
WHO IS--
!!!

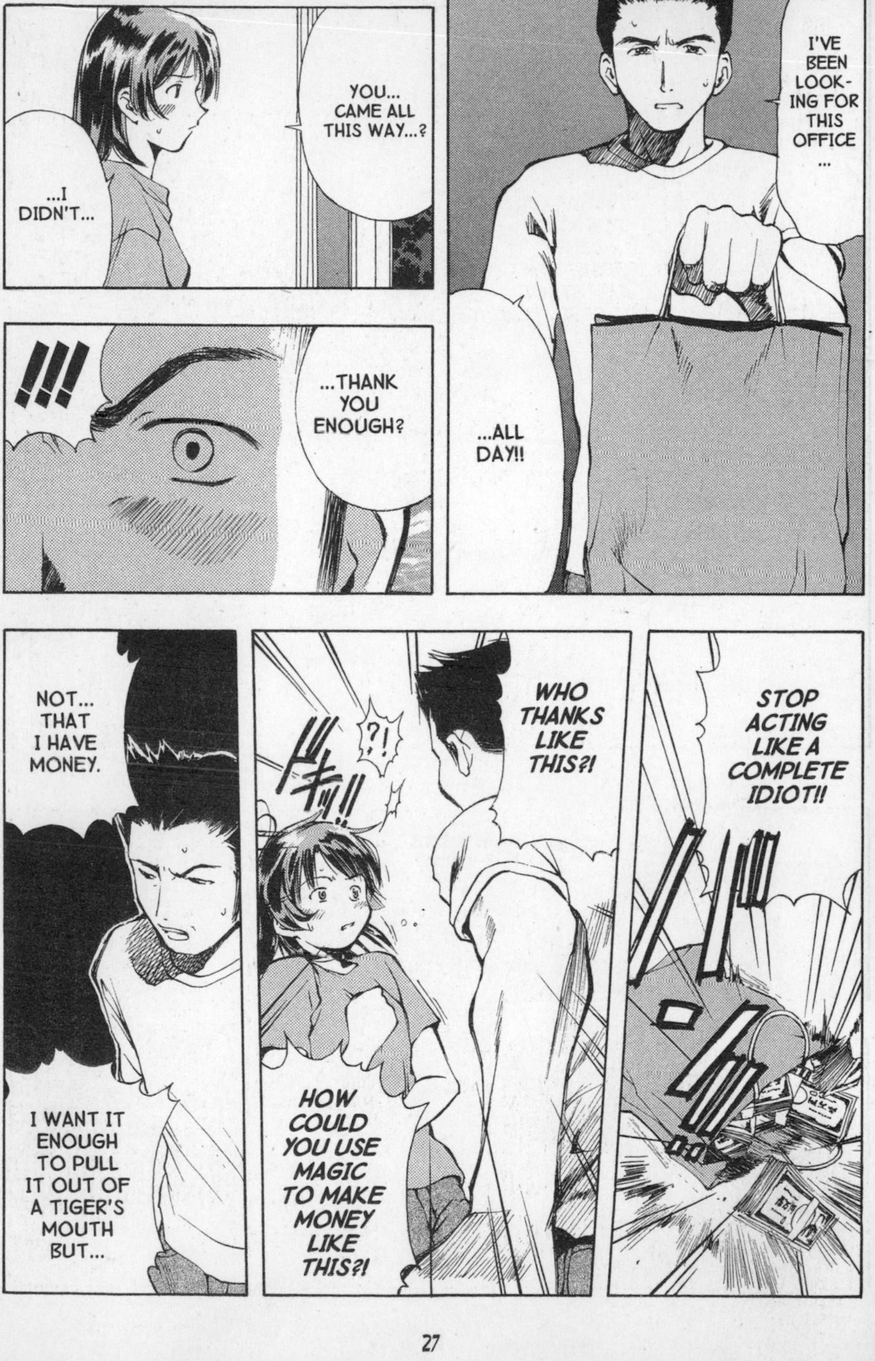

I'VE BEEN LOOKING FOR THIS OFFICE ...
...ALL DAY!!
YOU... CAME ALL THIS WAY...?
...I DIDN'T...
...THANK YOU ENOUGH?
!!!
STOP ACTING LIKE A COMPLETE IDIOT!!
WHO THANKS LIKE THIS?!
?!
HOW COULD YOU USE MAGIC TO MAKE MONEY LIKE THIS?!
NOT... THAT I HAVE MONEY.
I WANT IT ENOUGH TO PULL IT OUT OF A TIGER'S MOUTH BUT...

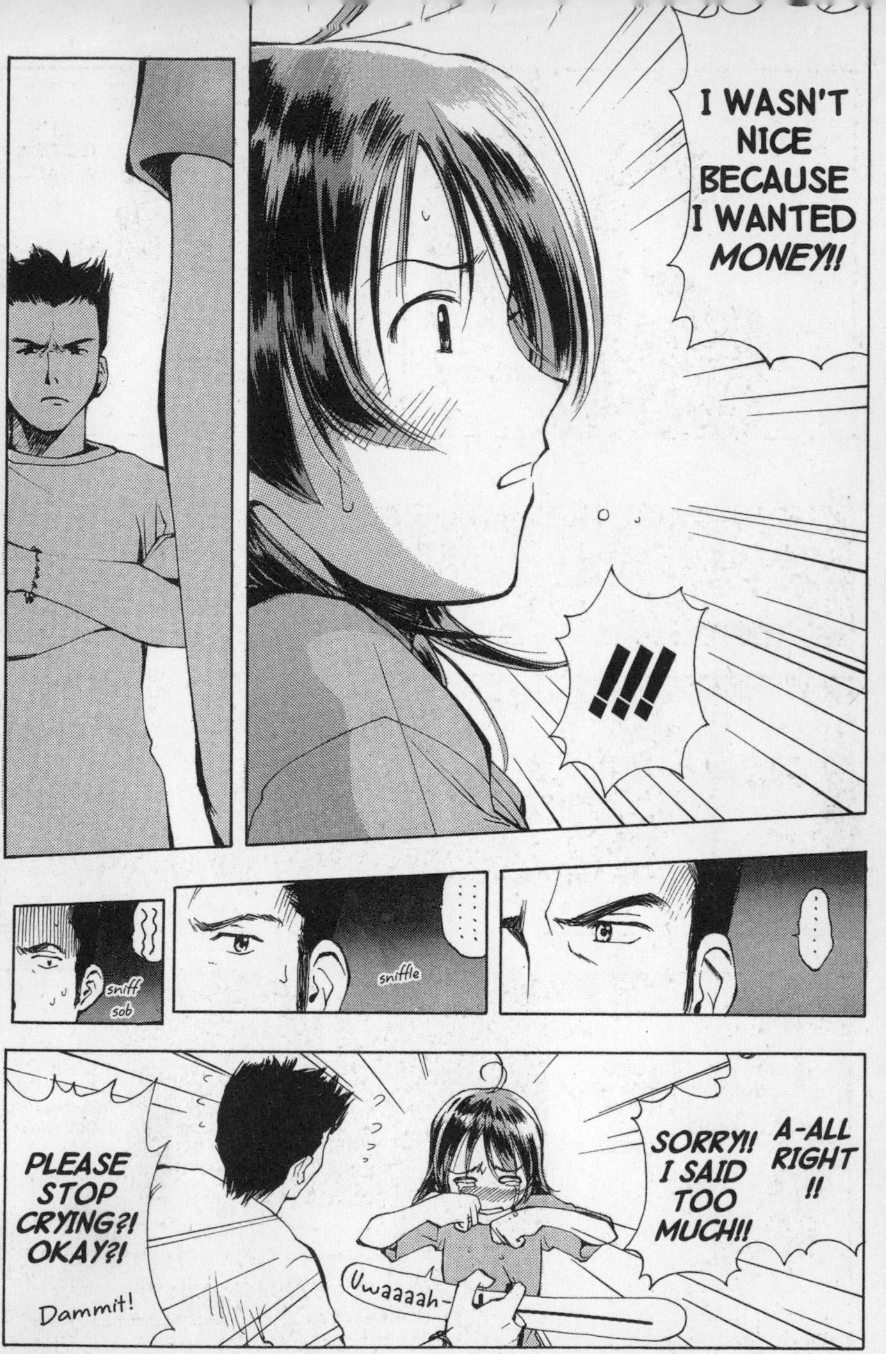
I WASN'T NICE BECAUSE I WANTED MONEY!!
!!!
......
......
sniffle
sniff sob
A-ALL RIGHT!!
SORRY!! I SAID TOO MUCH!!
Uwaaaah-
PLEASE STOP CRYING?! OKAY?!
Dammit!

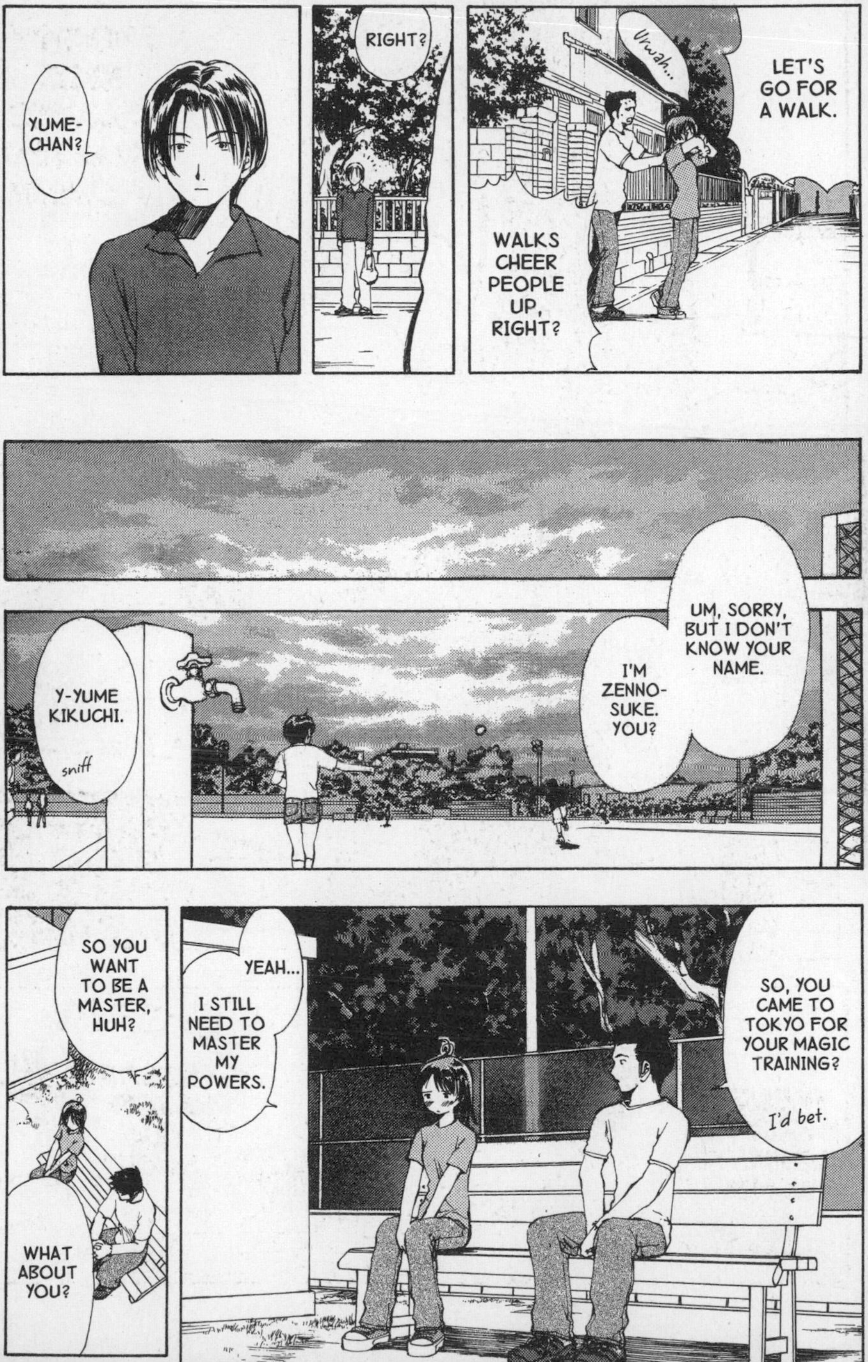
Urwah...
LET'S GO FOR A WALK.
WALKS CHEER PEOPLE UP, RIGHT?
RIGHT?
YUME-CHAN?
UM, SORRY, BUT I DON'T KNOW YOUR NAME.
I'M ZENNO-SUKE. YOU?
Y-YUME KIKUCHI.
sniff
SO, YOU CAME TO TOKYO FOR YOUR MAGIC TRAINING?
I'd bet.
YEAH...
I STILL NEED TO MASTER MY POWERS.
SO YOU WANT TO BE A MASTER, HUH?
WHAT ABOUT YOU?

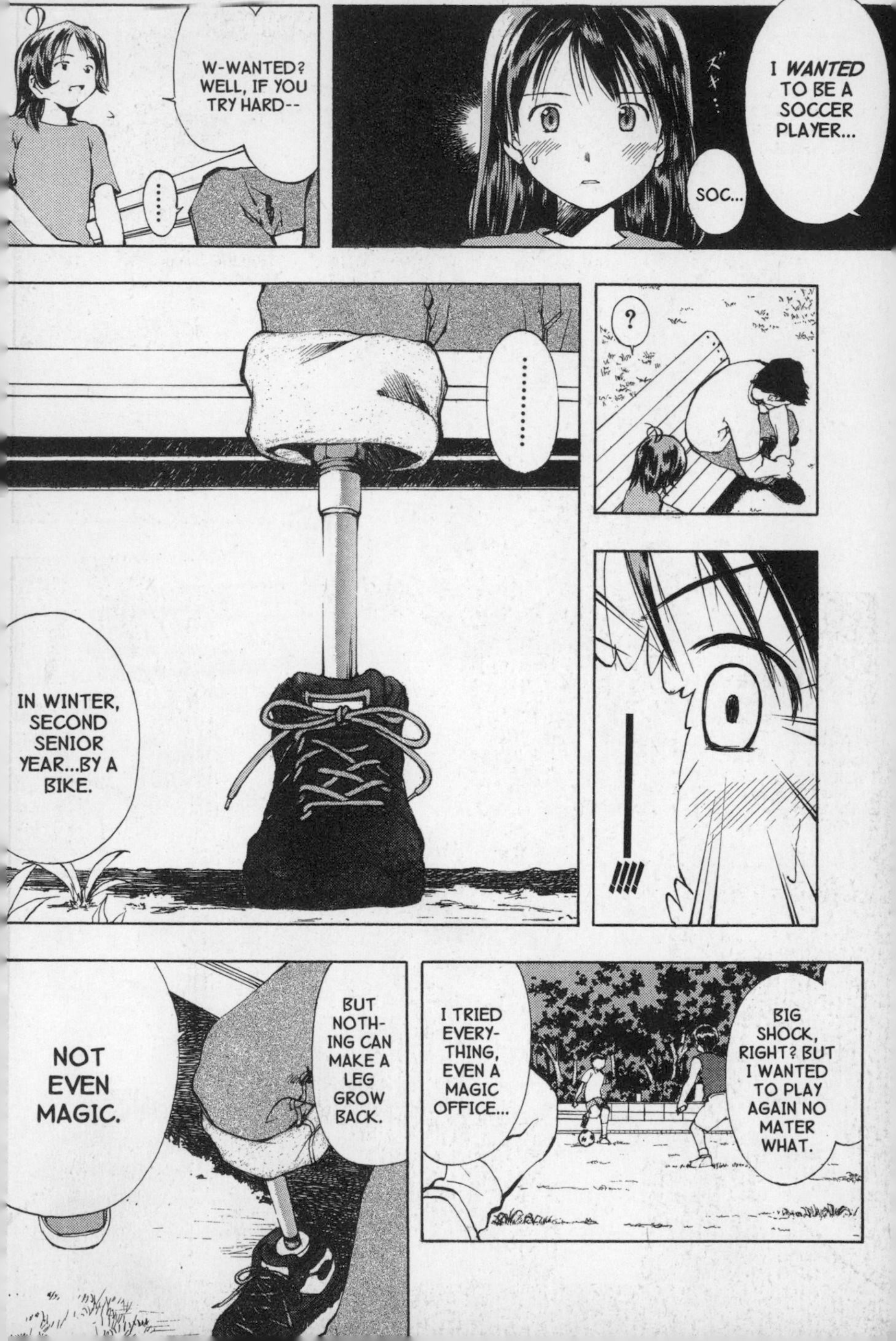
I *WANTED* TO BE A SOCCER PLAYER...
ズキ…
SOC...
W-WANTED? WELL, IF YOU TRY HARD--
......
?
......
IN WINTER, SECOND SENIOR YEAR...BY A BIKE.
BIG SHOCK, RIGHT? BUT I WANTED TO PLAY AGAIN NO MATER WHAT.
I TRIED EVERY-THING, EVEN A MAGIC OFFICE...
BUT NOTH-ING CAN MAKE A LEG GROW BACK.
NOT EVEN MAGIC.

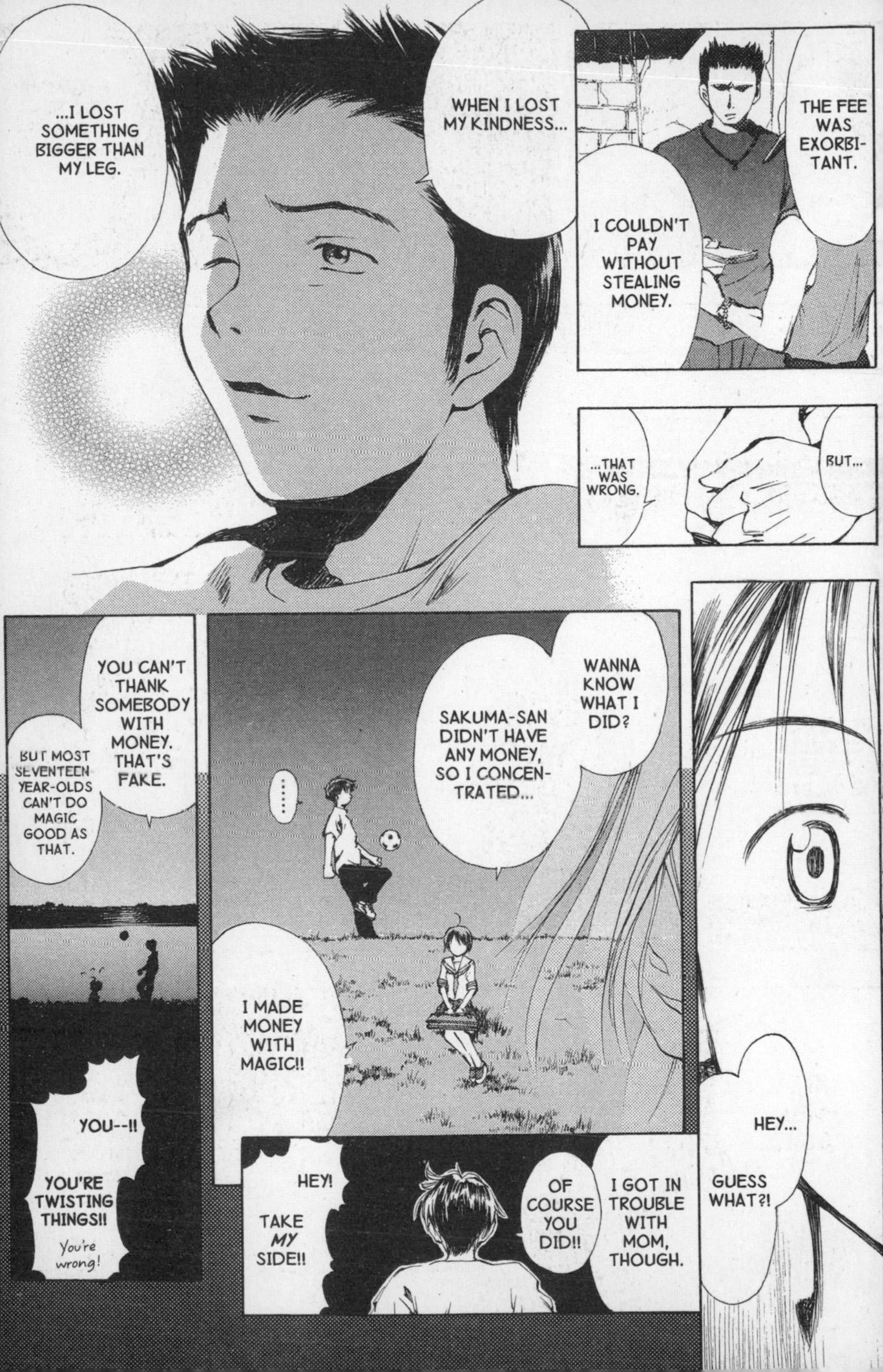

THE FEE WAS EXORBITANT.
I COULDN'T PAY WITHOUT STEALING MONEY.
BUT...
...THAT WAS WRONG.
WHEN I LOST MY KINDNESS...
...I LOST SOMETHING BIGGER THAN MY LEG.
HEY...
GUESS WHAT?!
WANNA KNOW WHAT I DID?
SAKUMA-SAN DIDN'T HAVE ANY MONEY, SO I CONCENTRATED...
......
I MADE MONEY WITH MAGIC!!
I GOT IN TROUBLE WITH MOM, THOUGH.
OF COURSE YOU DID!!
HEY!
TAKE *MY* SIDE!!
YOU CAN'T THANK SOMEBODY WITH MONEY. THAT'S FAKE.
BUT MOST SEVENTEEN-YEAR-OLDS CAN'T DO MAGIC GOOD AS THAT.
YOU--!!
YOU'RE TWISTING THINGS!!
You're wrong!

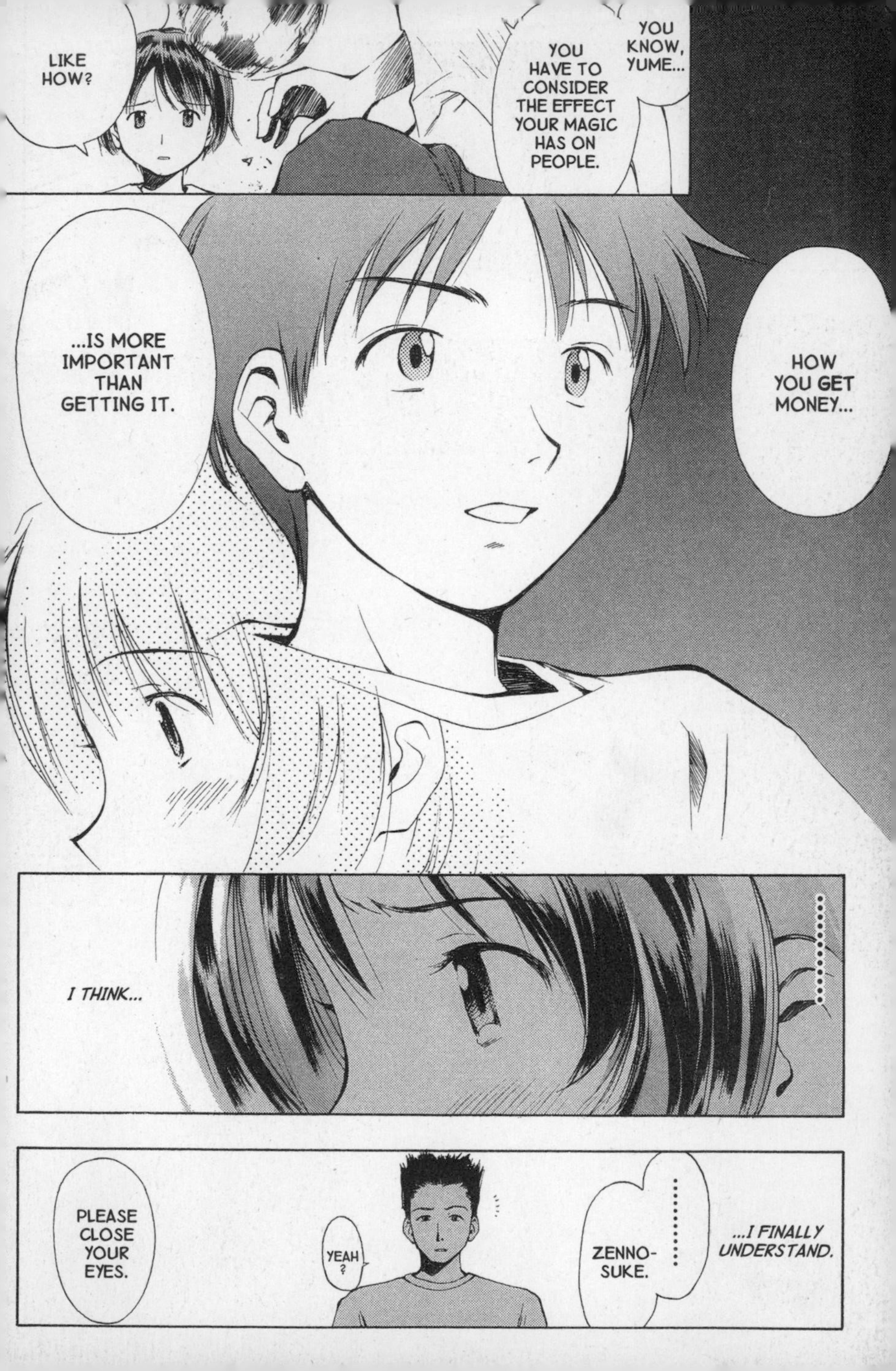
YOU KNOW, YUME...
YOU HAVE TO CONSIDER THE EFFECT YOUR MAGIC HAS ON PEOPLE.
LIKE HOW?
HOW YOU GET MONEY...
...IS MORE IMPORTANT THAN GETTING IT.
......
I THINK...
...I FINALLY UNDERSTAND.
......
ZENNO-SUKE.
YEAH?
PLEASE CLOSE YOUR EYES.

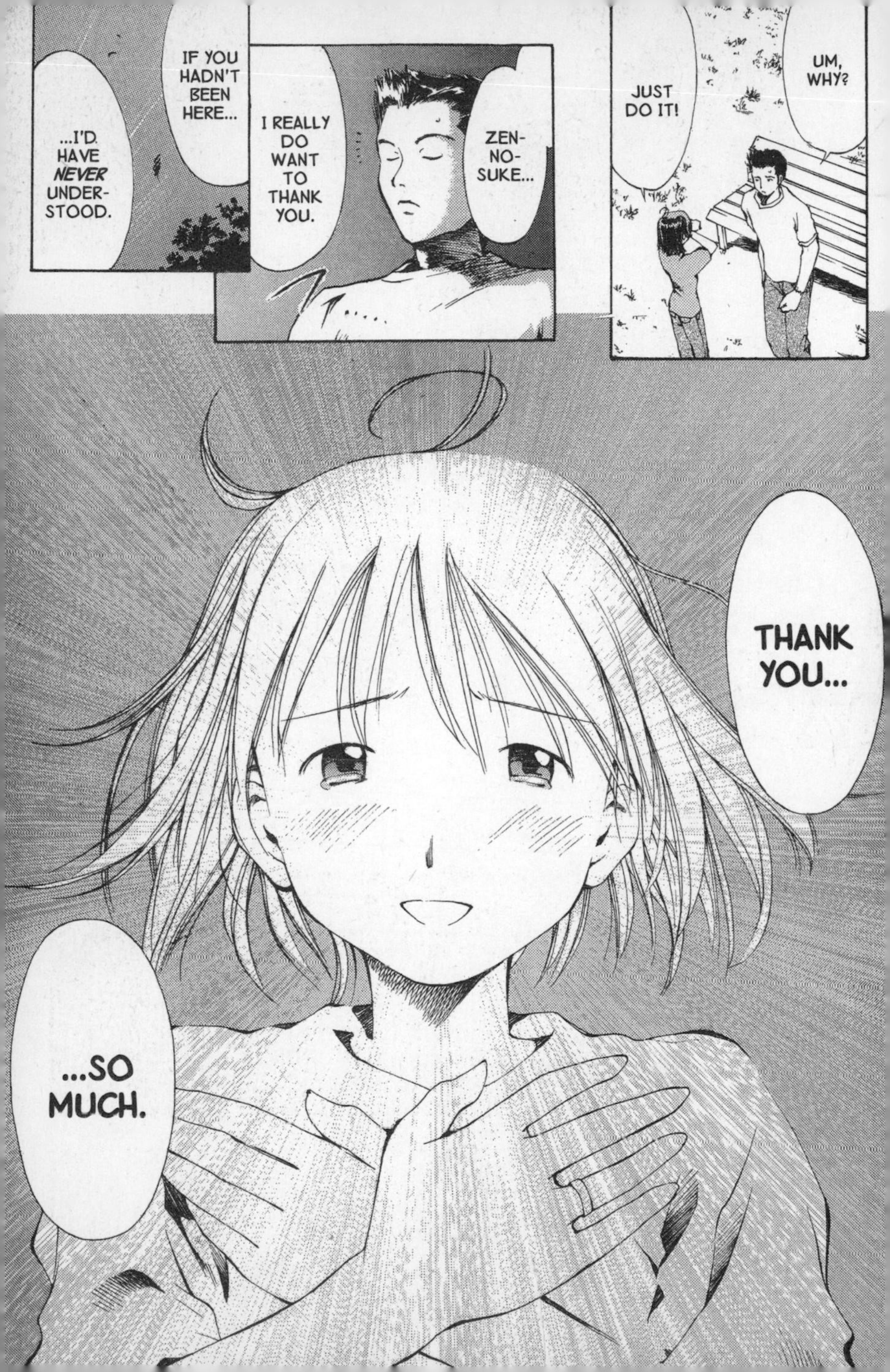
UM, WHY?
JUST DO IT!
ZEN-NO-SUKE...
I REALLY DO WANT TO THANK YOU.
IF YOU HADN'T BEEN HERE...
...I'D HAVE *NEVER* UNDER-STOOD.
THANK YOU...
...SO MUCH.

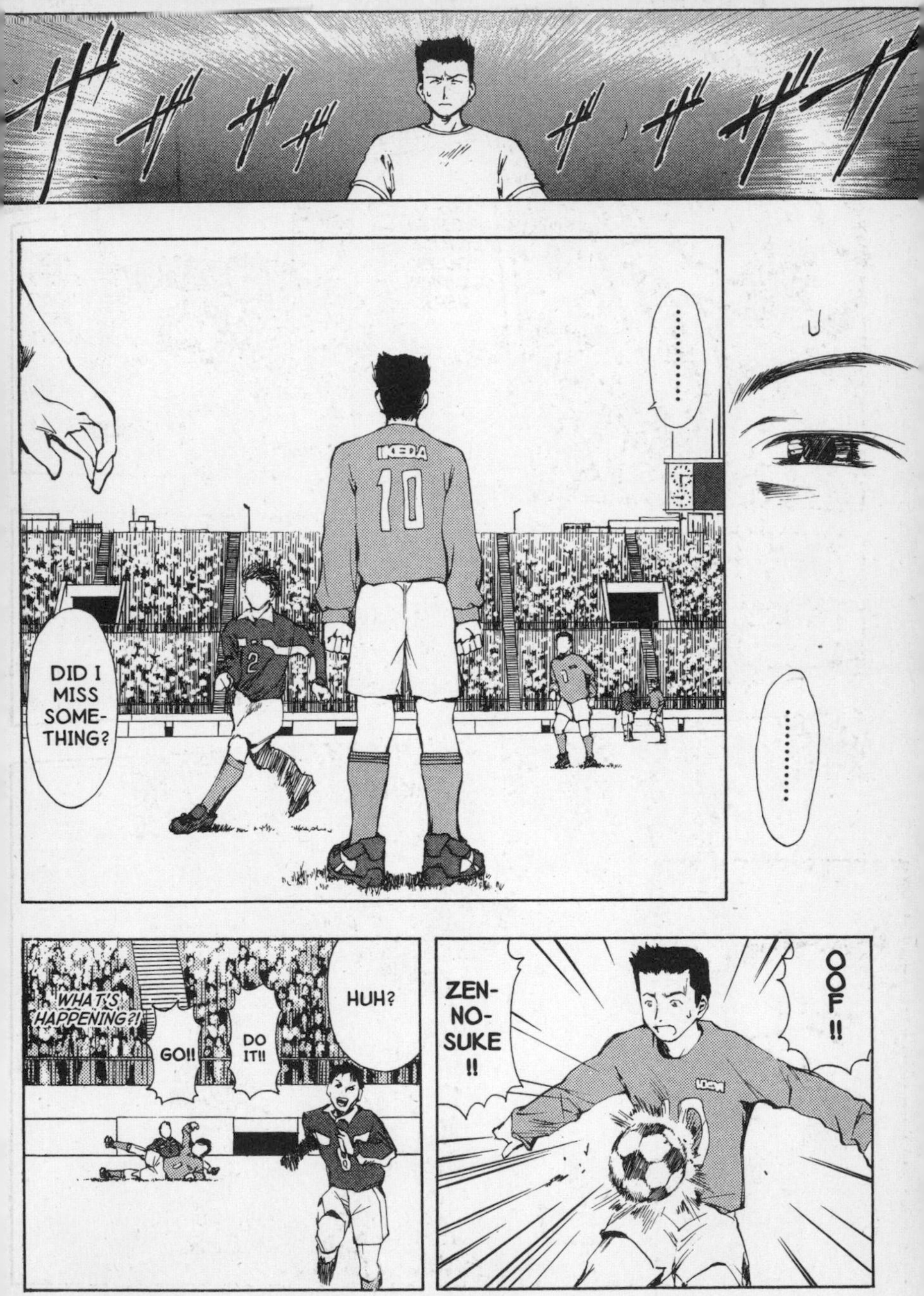

....
....
DID I MISS SOMETHING?
OOF!!
ZEN-NO-SUKE!!
HUH?
DO IT!!
GO!!
WHAT'S HAPPENING?!

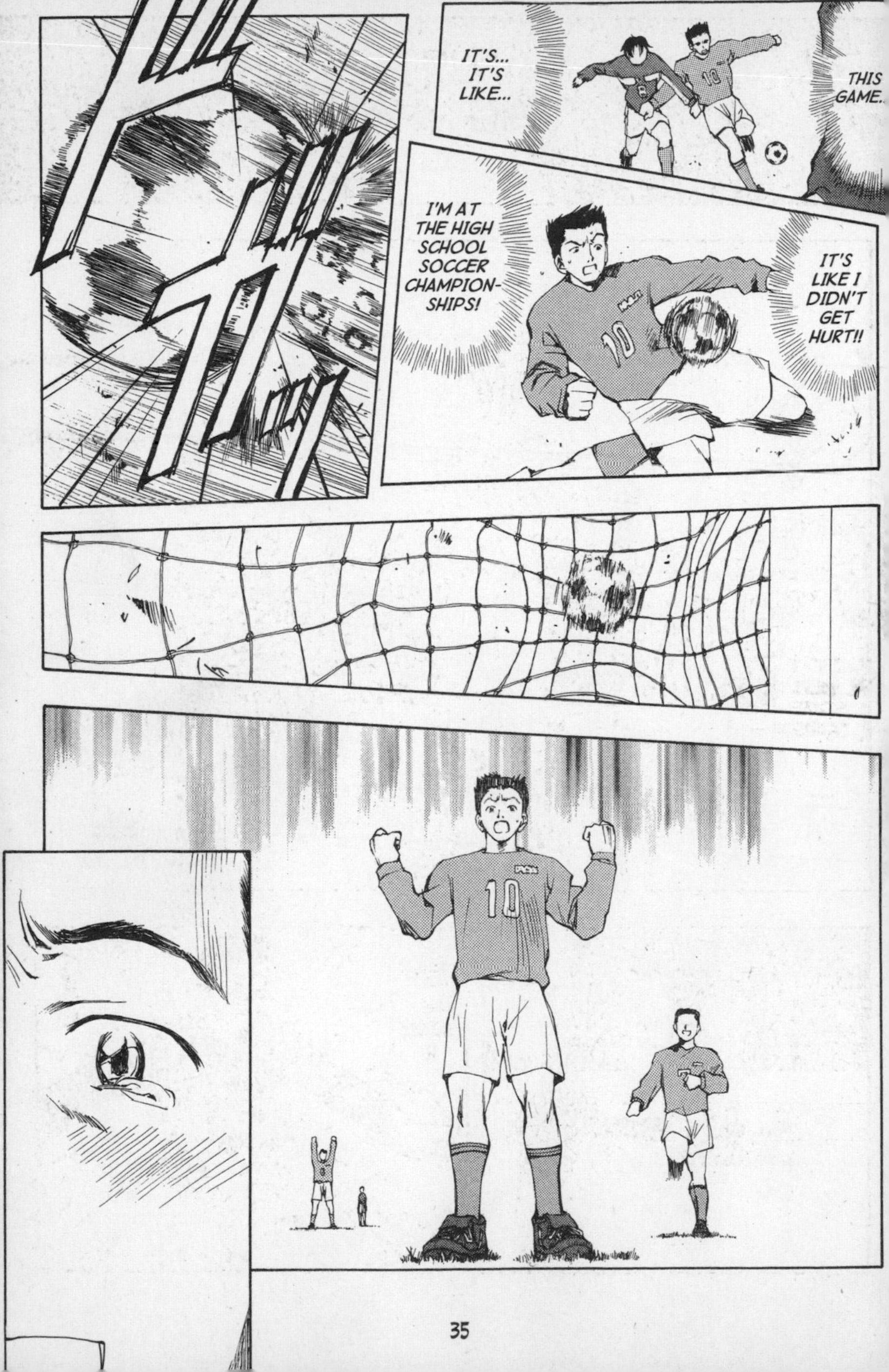
THIS GAME...
IT'S... IT'S LIKE...
IT'S LIKE I DIDN'T GET HURT!!
I'M AT THE HIGH SCHOOL SOCCER CHAMPION-SHIPS!

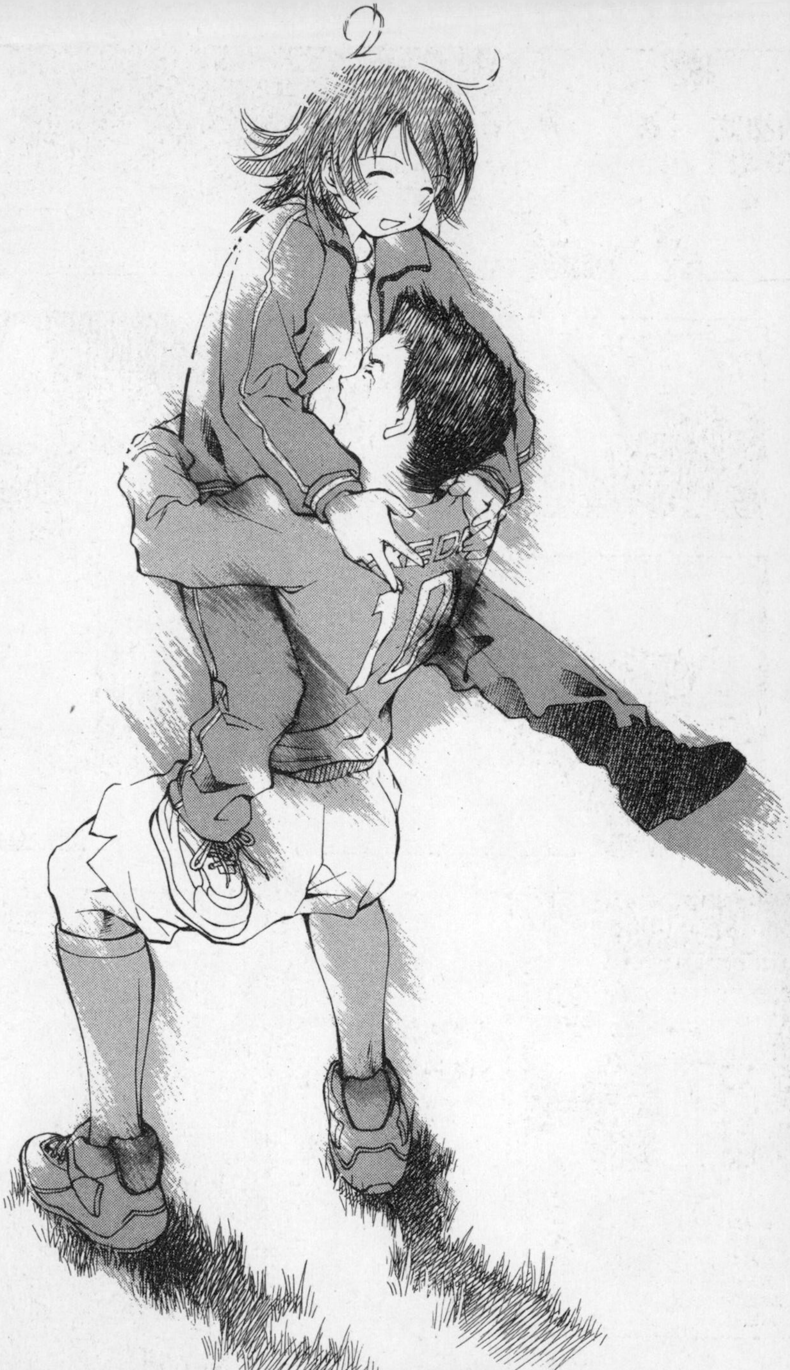

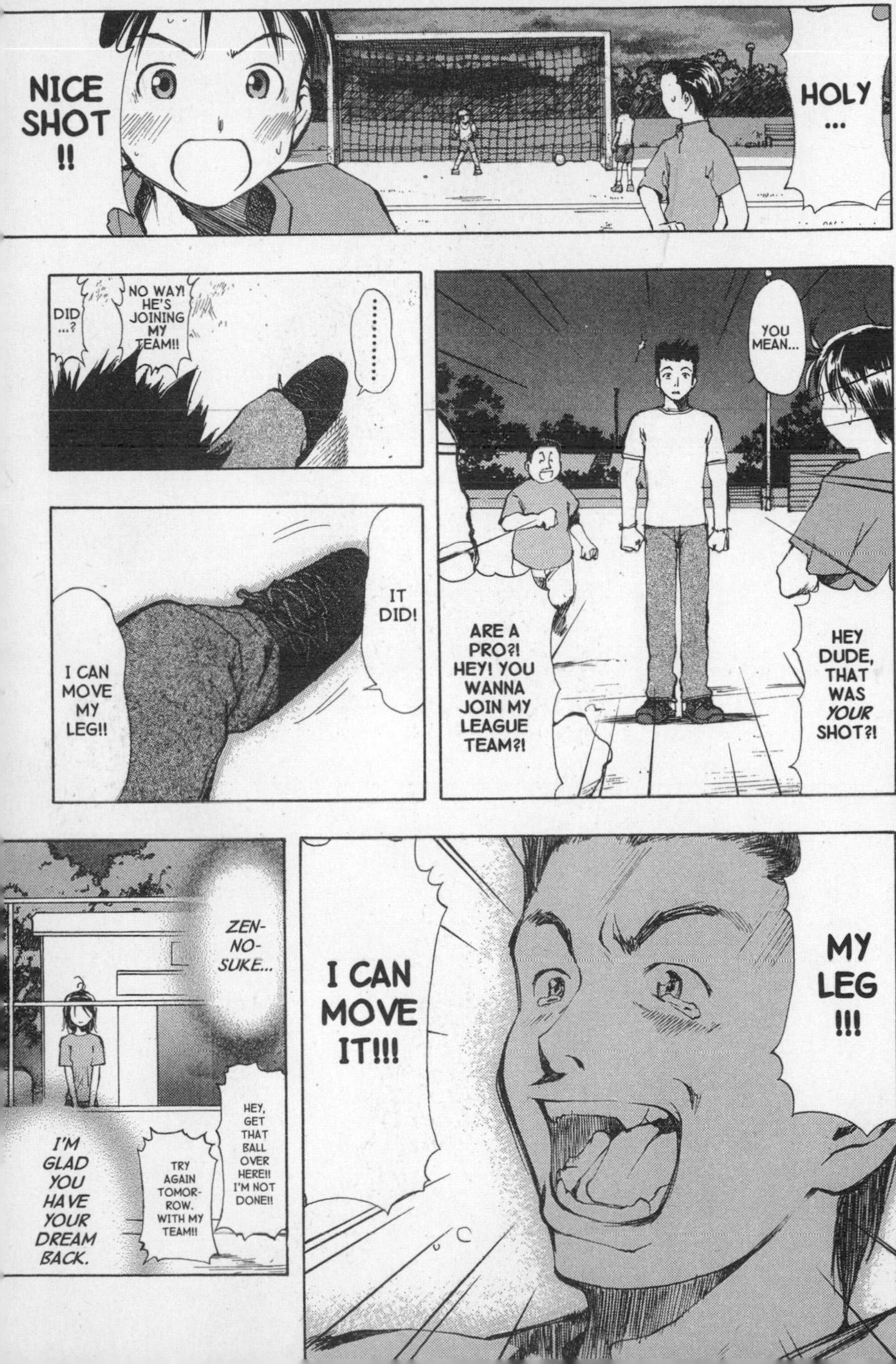
HOLY ...
NICE SHOT !!
YOU MEAN...
HEY DUDE, THAT WAS *YOUR* SHOT?!
ARE A PRO?! HEY! YOU WANNA JOIN MY LEAGUE TEAM?!
....
NO WAY! HE'S JOINING MY TEAM!!
DID ...?
IT DID!
I CAN MOVE MY LEG!!
MY LEG !!!
I CAN MOVE IT!!!
ZEN-NO-SUKE...
HEY, GET THAT BALL OVER HERE!! I'M NOT DONE!!
TRY AGAIN TOMOR-ROW. WITH MY TEAM!!
I'M GLAD YOU HAVE YOUR DREAM BACK.

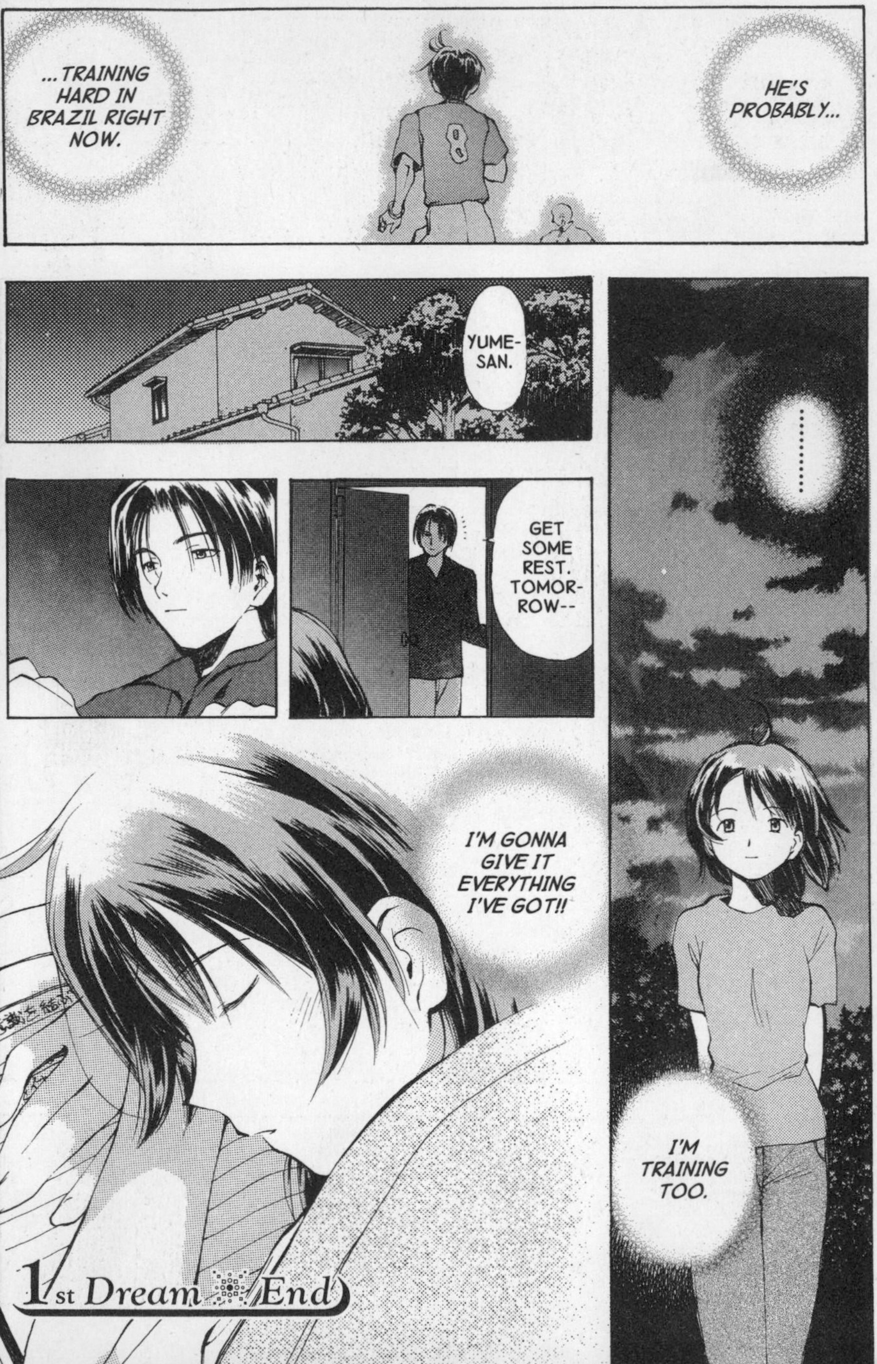
HE'S PROBABLY...
...TRAINING HARD IN BRAZIL RIGHT NOW.
......
I'M TRAINING TOO.
YUME-SAN.
GET SOME REST. TOMORROW--
I'M GONNA GIVE IT EVERYTHING I'VE GOT!!
1st Dream End

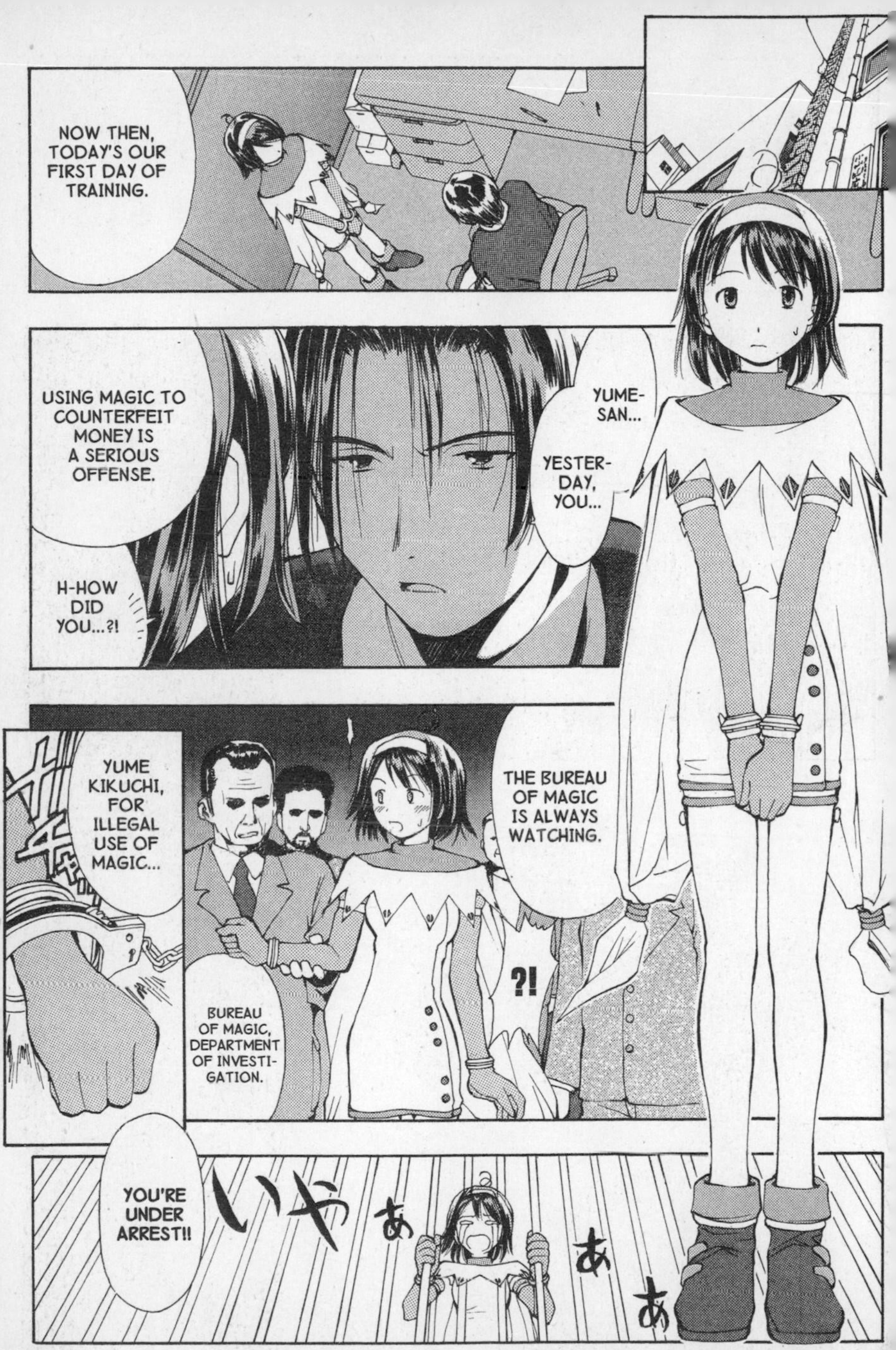
NOW THEN, TODAY'S OUR FIRST DAY OF TRAINING.
YUME-SAN...
YESTER-DAY, YOU...
USING MAGIC TO COUNTERFEIT MONEY IS A SERIOUS OFFENSE.
H-HOW DID YOU...?!
THE BUREAU OF MAGIC IS ALWAYS WATCHING.
YUME KIKUCHI, FOR ILLEGAL USE OF MAGIC...
?!
BUREAU OF MAGIC, DEPARTMENT OF INVESTI-GATION.
YOU'RE UNDER ARREST!!
いやあああ

2nd Dream
The Love Letter Within The Wall
(The Letter of No Return)

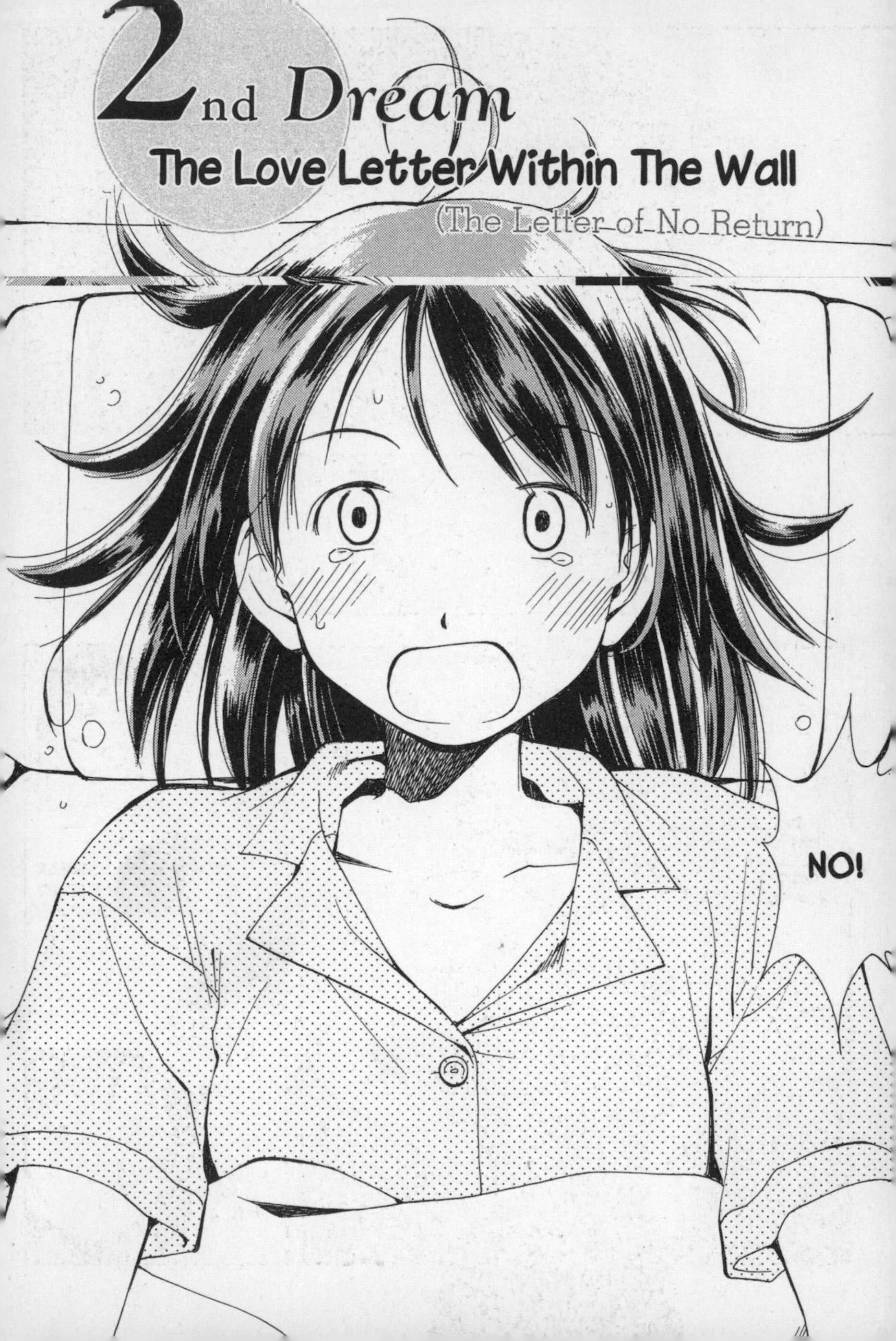
NO!

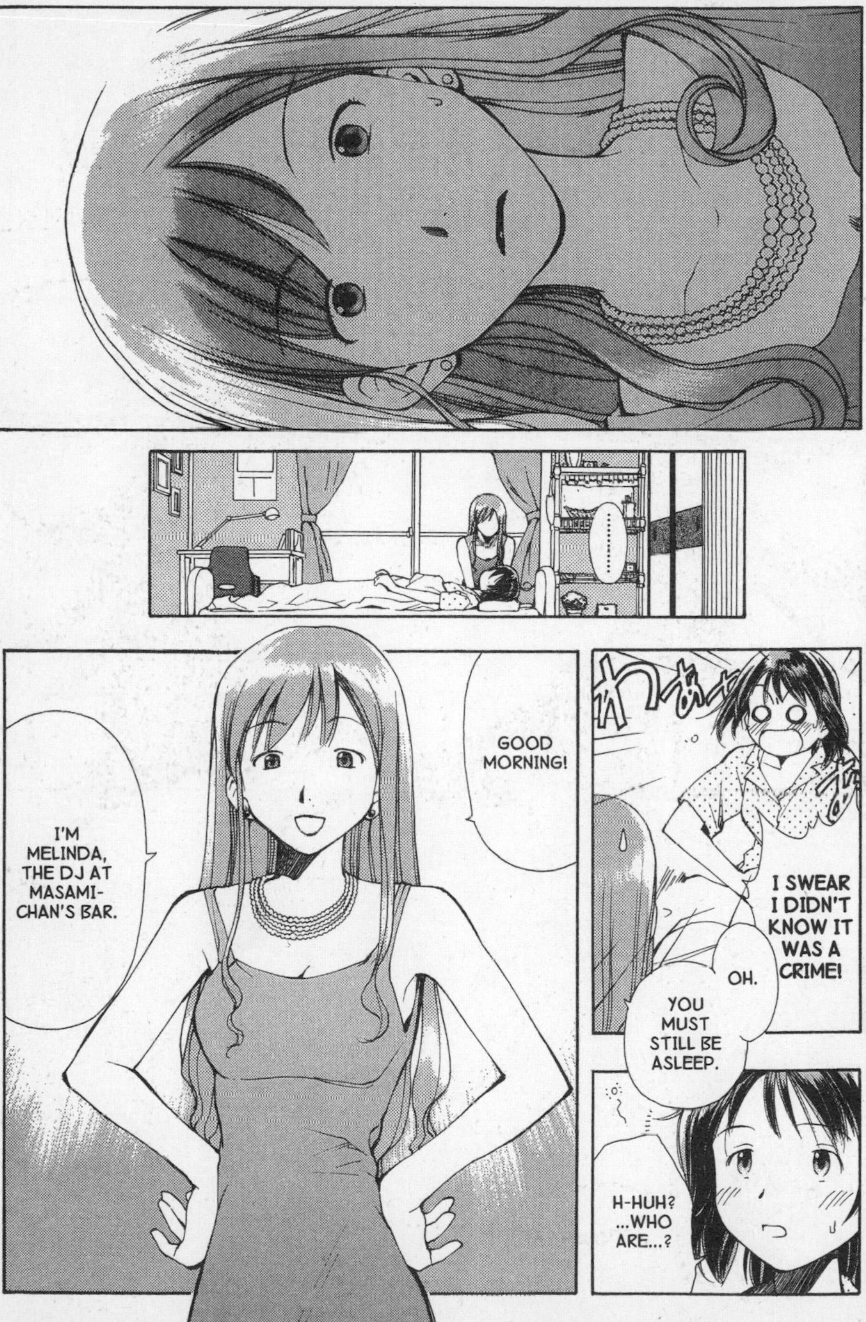
……
I SWEAR I DIDN'T KNOW IT WAS A CRIME!
OH. YOU MUST STILL BE ASLEEP.
H-HUH? ...WHO ARE...?
GOOD MORNING!
I'M MELINDA, THE DJ AT MASAMI-CHAN'S BAR.

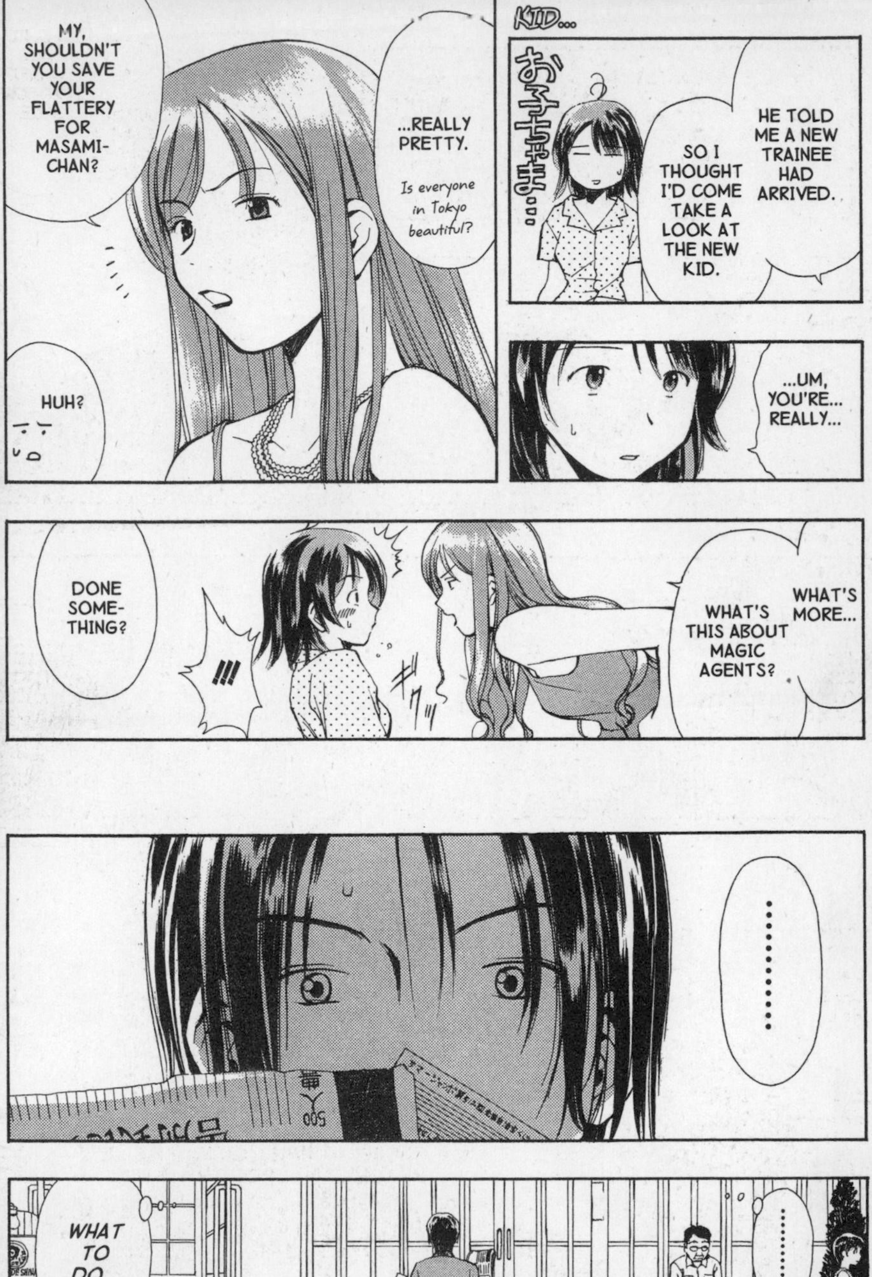

KID...
HE TOLD ME A NEW TRAINEE HAD ARRIVED.
SO I THOUGHT I'D COME TAKE A LOOK AT THE NEW KID.
おこちゃま...
...UM, YOU'RE... REALLY...
...REALLY PRETTY.
Is everyone in Tokyo beautiful?
MY, SHOULDN'T YOU SAVE YOUR FLATTERY FOR MASAMI-CHAN?
HUH?
WHAT'S MORE...
WHAT'S THIS ABOUT MAGIC AGENTS?
!!!
DONE SOMETHING?
....
....
WHAT TO DO...

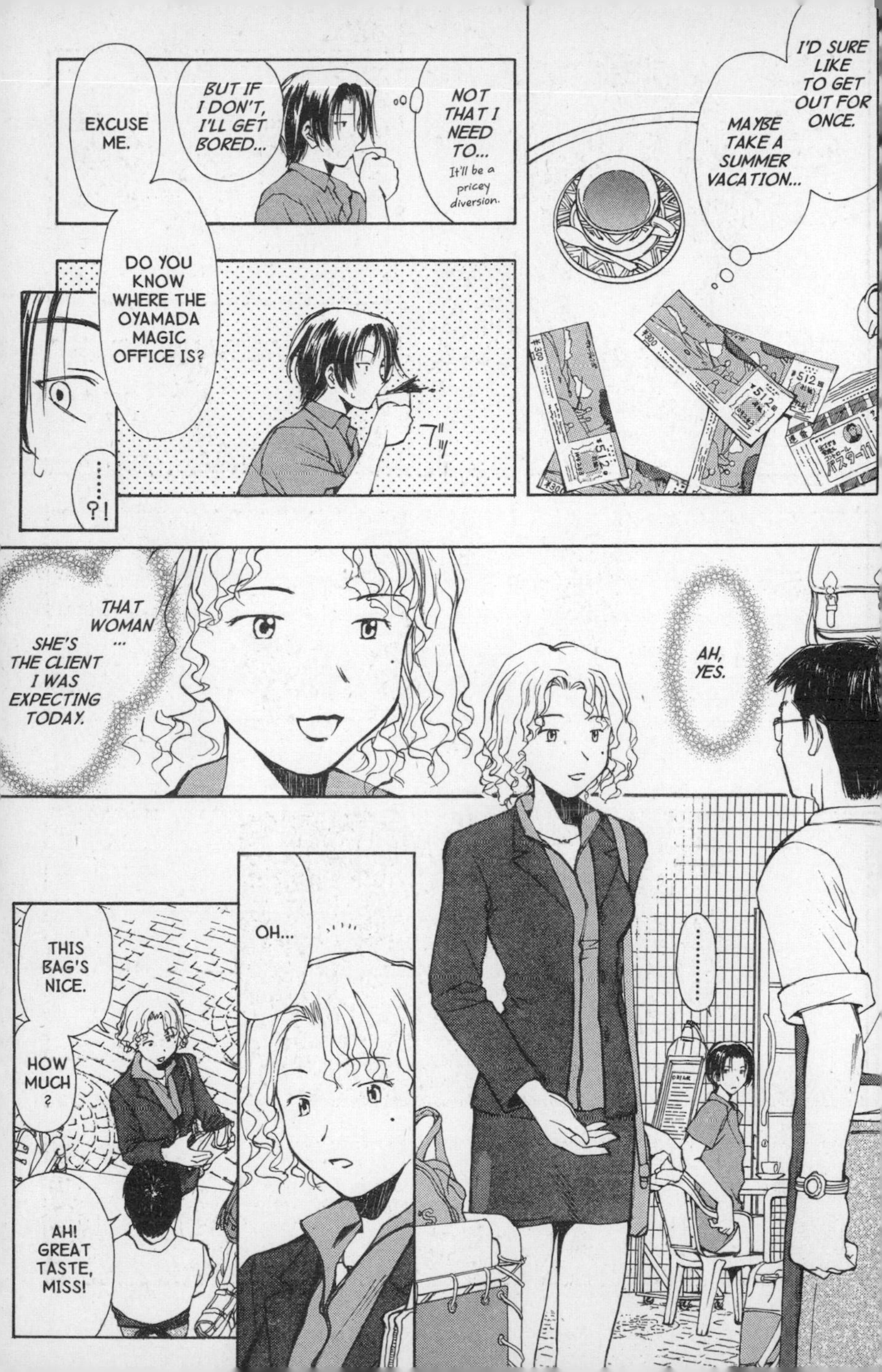
I'D SURE LIKE TO GET OUT FOR ONCE.
MAYBE TAKE A SUMMER VACATION...
NOT THAT I NEED TO...
It'll be a pricey diversion.
BUT IF I DON'T, I'LL GET BORED...
EXCUSE ME.
DO YOU KNOW WHERE THE OYAMADA MAGIC OFFICE IS?
......?!
AH, YES.
THAT WOMAN ...
SHE'S THE CLIENT I WAS EXPECTING TODAY.
....
OH...
THIS BAG'S NICE.
HOW MUCH?
AH! GREAT TASTE, MISS!

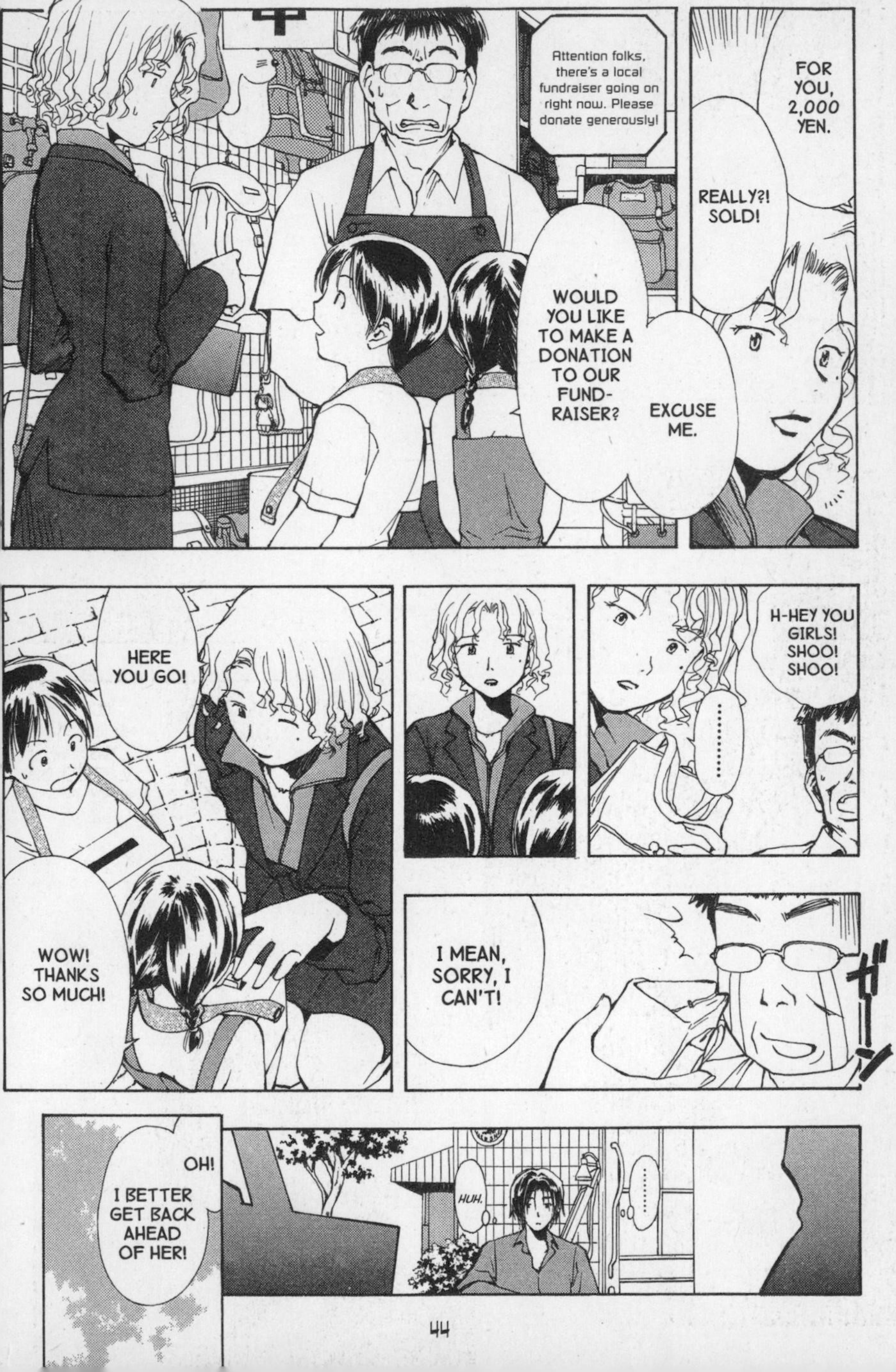

FOR YOU, 2,000 YEN.
REALLY?! SOLD!
Attention folks, there's a local fundraiser going on right now. Please donate generously!
EXCUSE ME.
WOULD YOU LIKE TO MAKE A DONATION TO OUR FUND-RAISER?
H-HEY YOU GIRLS! SHOO! SHOO!
......
I MEAN, SORRY, I CAN'T!
HERE YOU GO!
WOW! THANKS SO MUCH!
......
HUH.
OH! I BETTER GET BACK AHEAD OF HER!

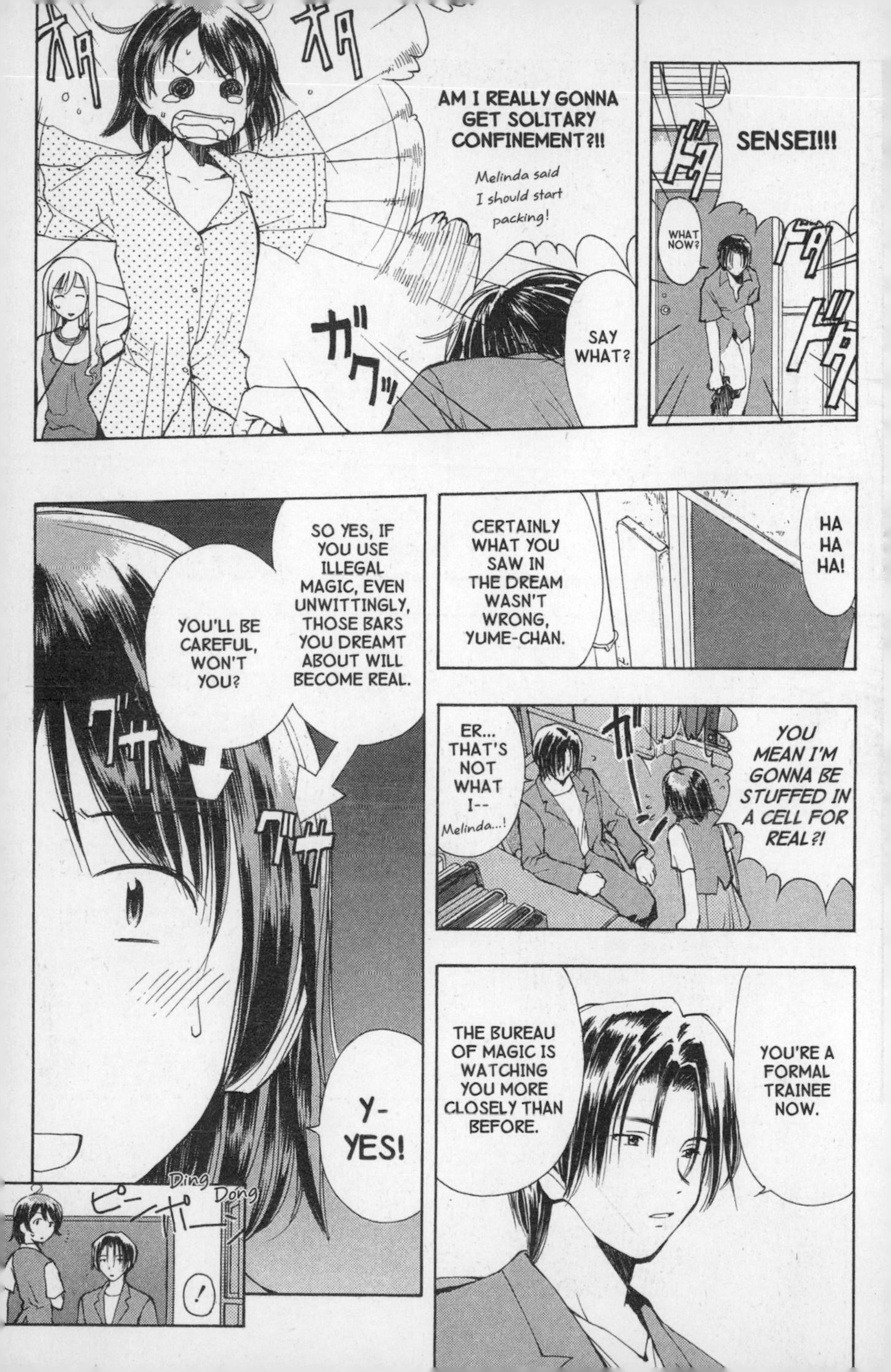
SENSEI!!!
WHAT NOW?
AM I REALLY GONNA GET SOLITARY CONFINEMENT?!!
Melinda said I should start packing!
SAY WHAT?
HA HA HA!
CERTAINLY WHAT YOU SAW IN THE DREAM WASN'T WRONG, YUME-CHAN.
YOU MEAN I'M GONNA BE STUFFED IN A CELL FOR REAL?!
ER... THAT'S NOT WHAT I--
Melinda...!
YOU'RE A FORMAL TRAINEE NOW.
THE BUREAU OF MAGIC IS WATCHING YOU MORE CLOSELY THAN BEFORE.
SO YES, IF YOU USE ILLEGAL MAGIC, EVEN UNWITTINGLY, THOSE BARS YOU DREAMT ABOUT WILL BECOME REAL.
YOU'LL BE CAREFUL, WON'T YOU?
Y-YES!
Ding Dong
!

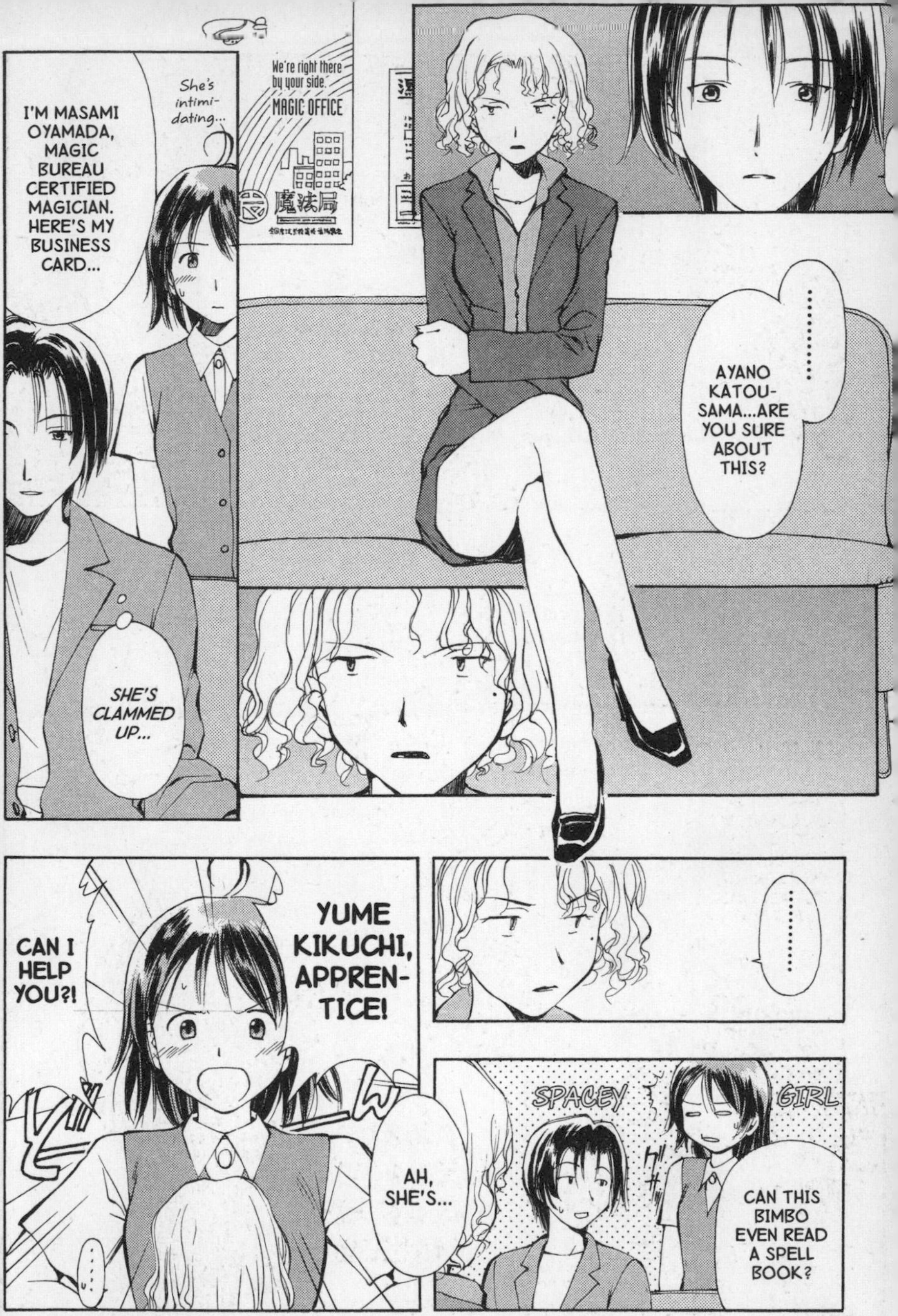

We're right there by your side.
MAGIC OFFICE
魔法局
......
AYANO KATOU-SAMA...ARE YOU SURE ABOUT THIS?
I'M MASAMI OYAMADA, MAGIC BUREAU CERTIFIED MAGICIAN. HERE'S MY BUSINESS CARD...
She's intimidating...
SHE'S CLAMMED UP...
......
SPACEY
GIRL
CAN THIS BIMBO EVEN READ A SPELL BOOK?
YUME KIKUCHI, APPRENTICE!
CAN I HELP YOU?!
AH, SHE'S...
...

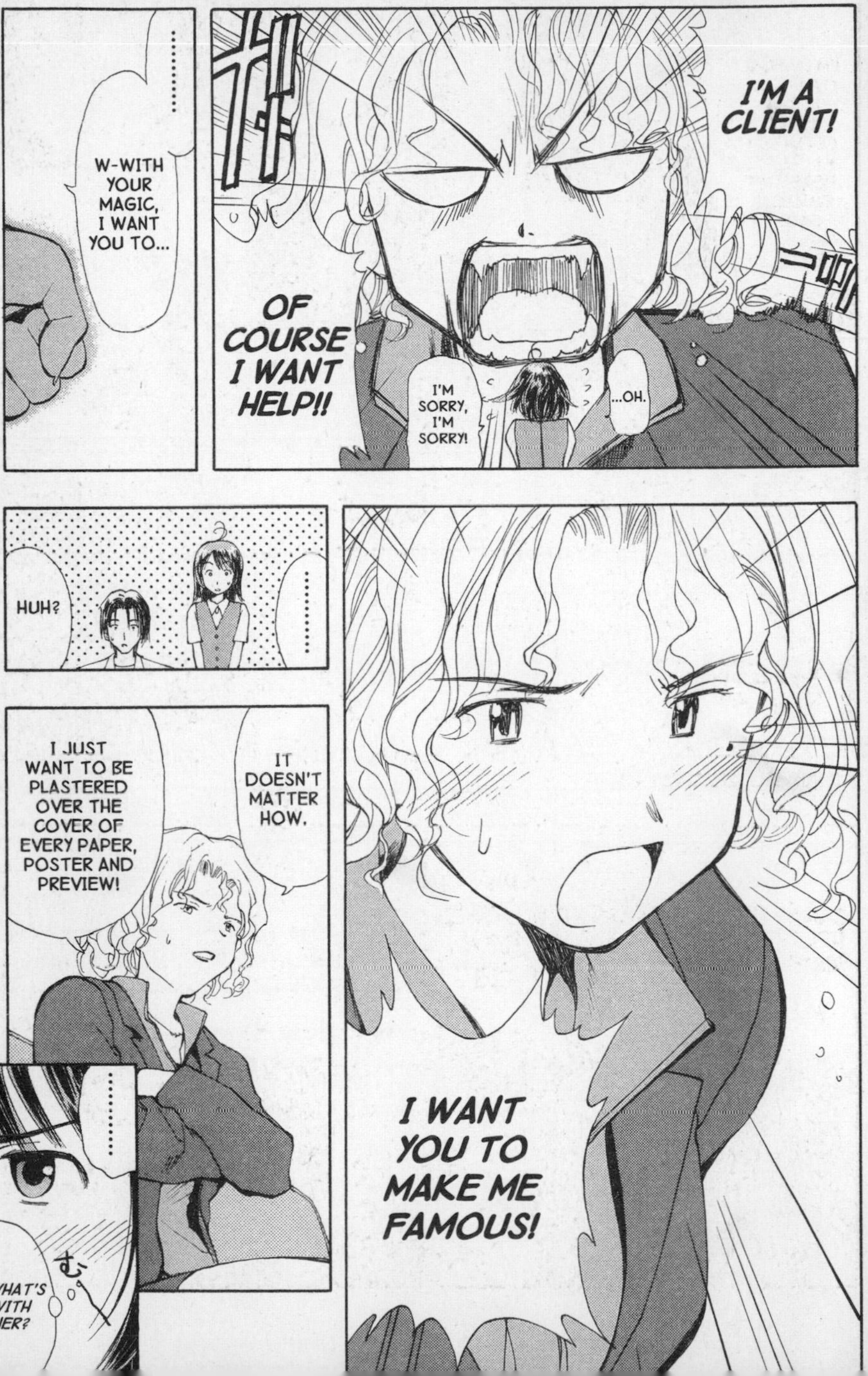

I'M A CLIENT!
...OH.
OF COURSE I WANT HELP!!
I'M SORRY, I'M SORRY!
......
W-WITH YOUR MAGIC, I WANT YOU TO...
I WANT YOU TO MAKE ME FAMOUS!
......
HUH?
IT DOESN'T MATTER HOW.
I JUST WANT TO BE PLASTERED OVER THE COVER OF EVERY PAPER, POSTER AND PREVIEW!
......
...WHAT'S WITH HER?

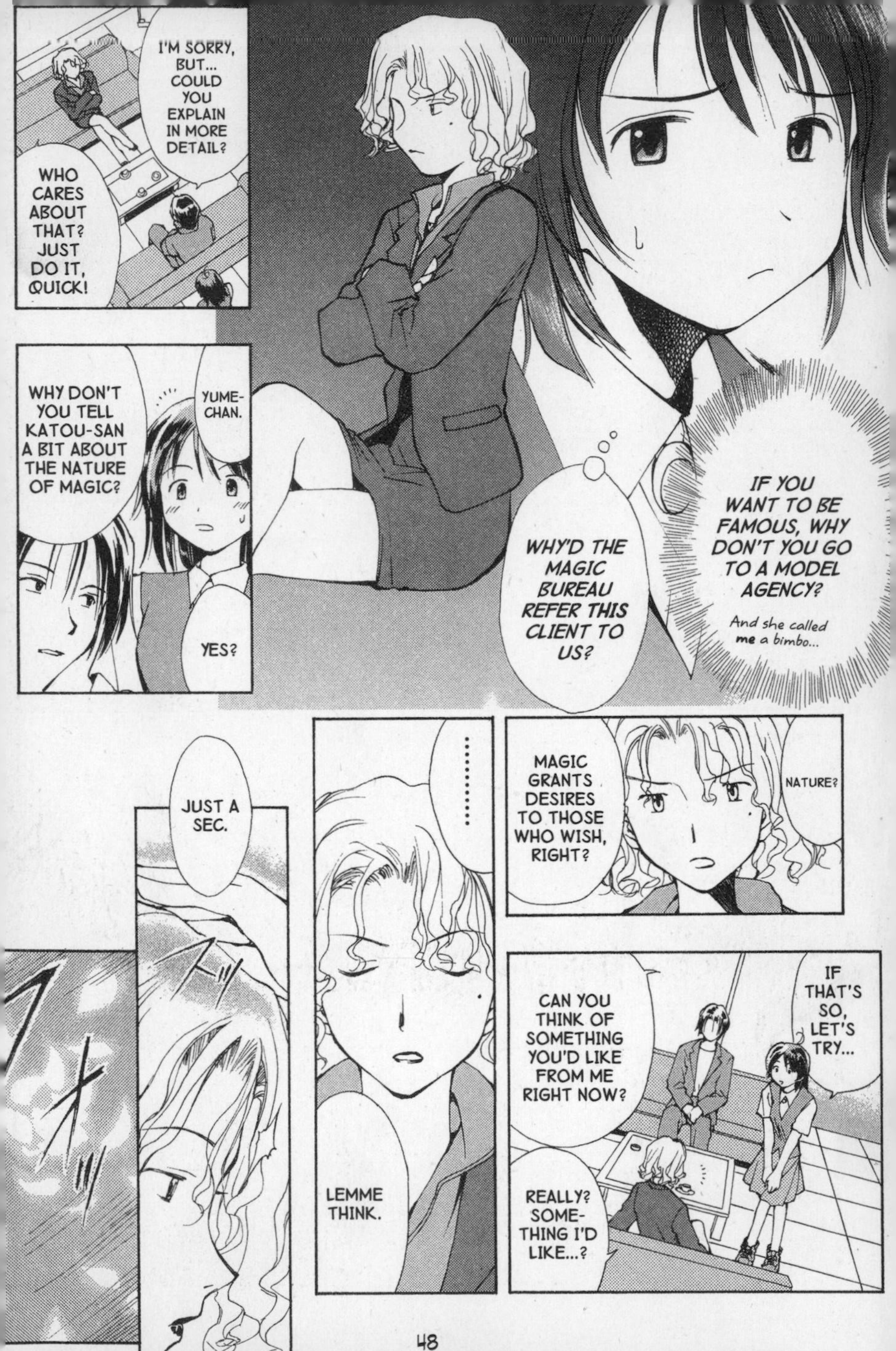
IF YOU WANT TO BE FAMOUS, WHY DON'T YOU GO TO A MODEL AGENCY?
And she called me a bimbo...
WHY'D THE MAGIC BUREAU REFER THIS CLIENT TO US?
I'M SORRY, BUT... COULD YOU EXPLAIN IN MORE DETAIL?
WHO CARES ABOUT THAT? JUST DO IT, QUICK!
YUME-CHAN.
WHY DON'T YOU TELL KATOU-SAN A BIT ABOUT THE NATURE OF MAGIC?
YES?
NATURE?
MAGIC GRANTS DESIRES TO THOSE WHO WISH, RIGHT?
IF THAT'S SO, LET'S TRY...
CAN YOU THINK OF SOMETHING YOU'D LIKE FROM ME RIGHT NOW?
REALLY? SOME-THING I'D LIKE...?
......
LEMME THINK.
JUST A SEC.

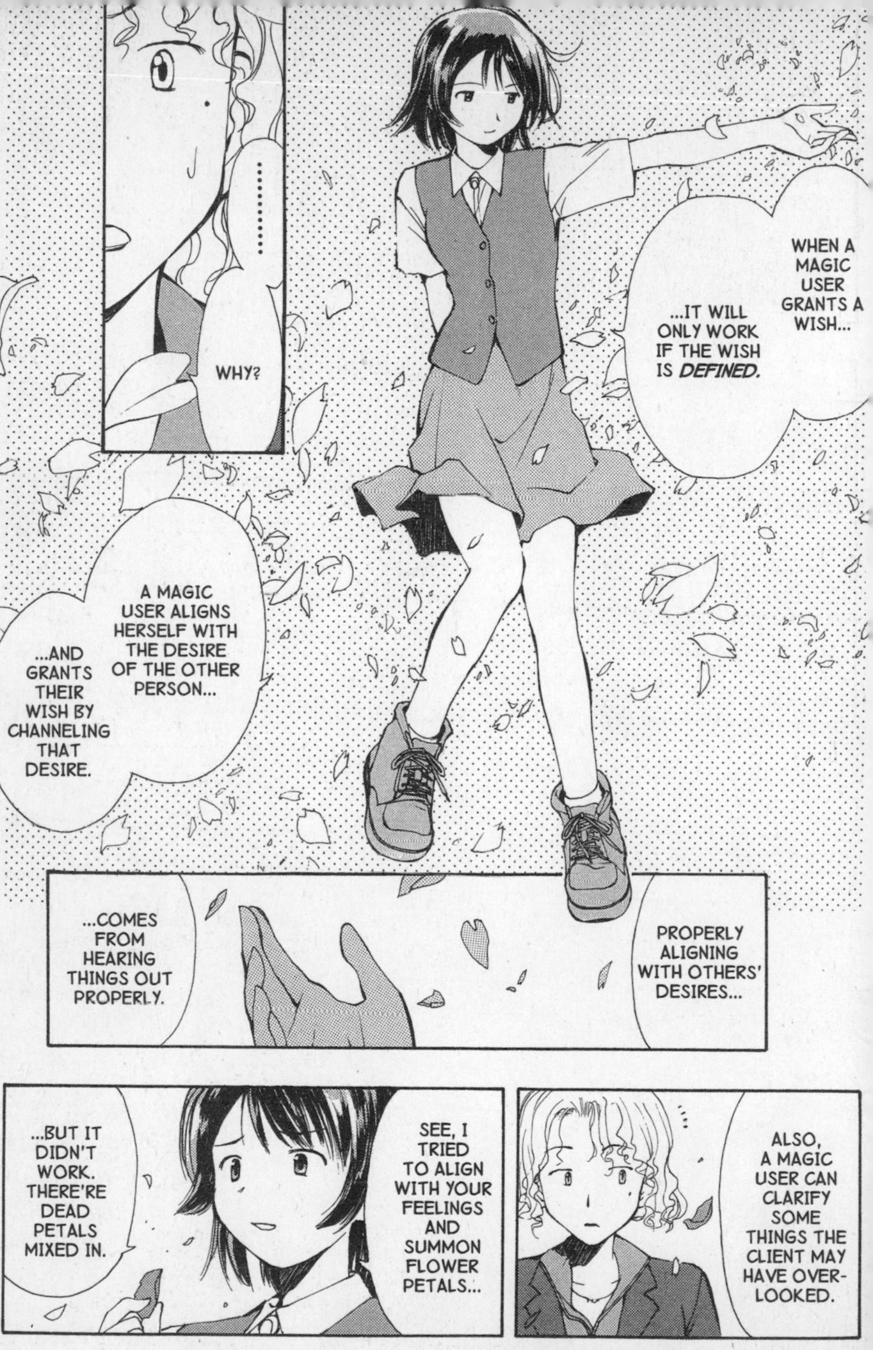
WHEN A MAGIC USER GRANTS A WISH...
...IT WILL ONLY WORK IF THE WISH IS *DEFINED.*
......
WHY?
A MAGIC USER ALIGNS HERSELF WITH THE DESIRE OF THE OTHER PERSON...
...AND GRANTS THEIR WISH BY CHANNELING THAT DESIRE.
PROPERLY ALIGNING WITH OTHERS' DESIRES...
...COMES FROM HEARING THINGS OUT PROPERLY.
ALSO, A MAGIC USER CAN CLARIFY SOME THINGS THE CLIENT MAY HAVE OVER-LOOKED.
SEE, I TRIED TO ALIGN WITH YOUR FEELINGS AND SUMMON FLOWER PETALS...
...BUT IT DIDN'T WORK. THERE'RE DEAD PETALS MIXED IN.

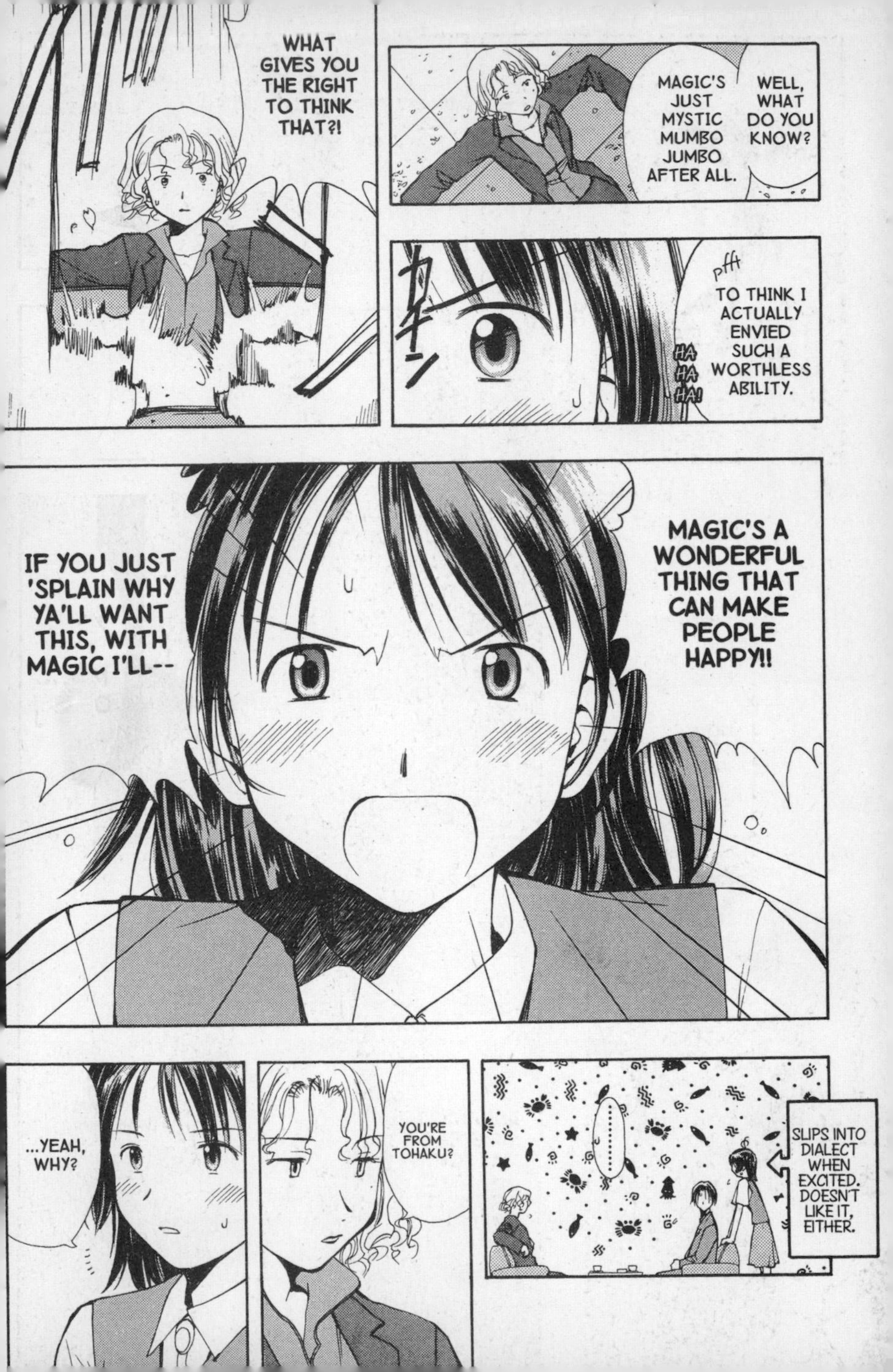
WELL, WHAT DO YOU KNOW?
MAGIC'S JUST MYSTIC MUMBO JUMBO AFTER ALL.
pfft
TO THINK I ACTUALLY ENVIED SUCH A WORTHLESS ABILITY.
HA HA HA!
WHAT GIVES YOU THE RIGHT TO THINK THAT?!
MAGIC'S A WONDERFUL THING THAT CAN MAKE PEOPLE HAPPY!!
IF YOU JUST 'SPLAIN WHY YA'LL WANT THIS, WITH MAGIC I'LL--
......
SLIPS INTO DIALECT WHEN EXCITED. DOESN'T LIKE IT, EITHER.
YOU'RE FROM TOHAKU?
...YEAH, WHY?

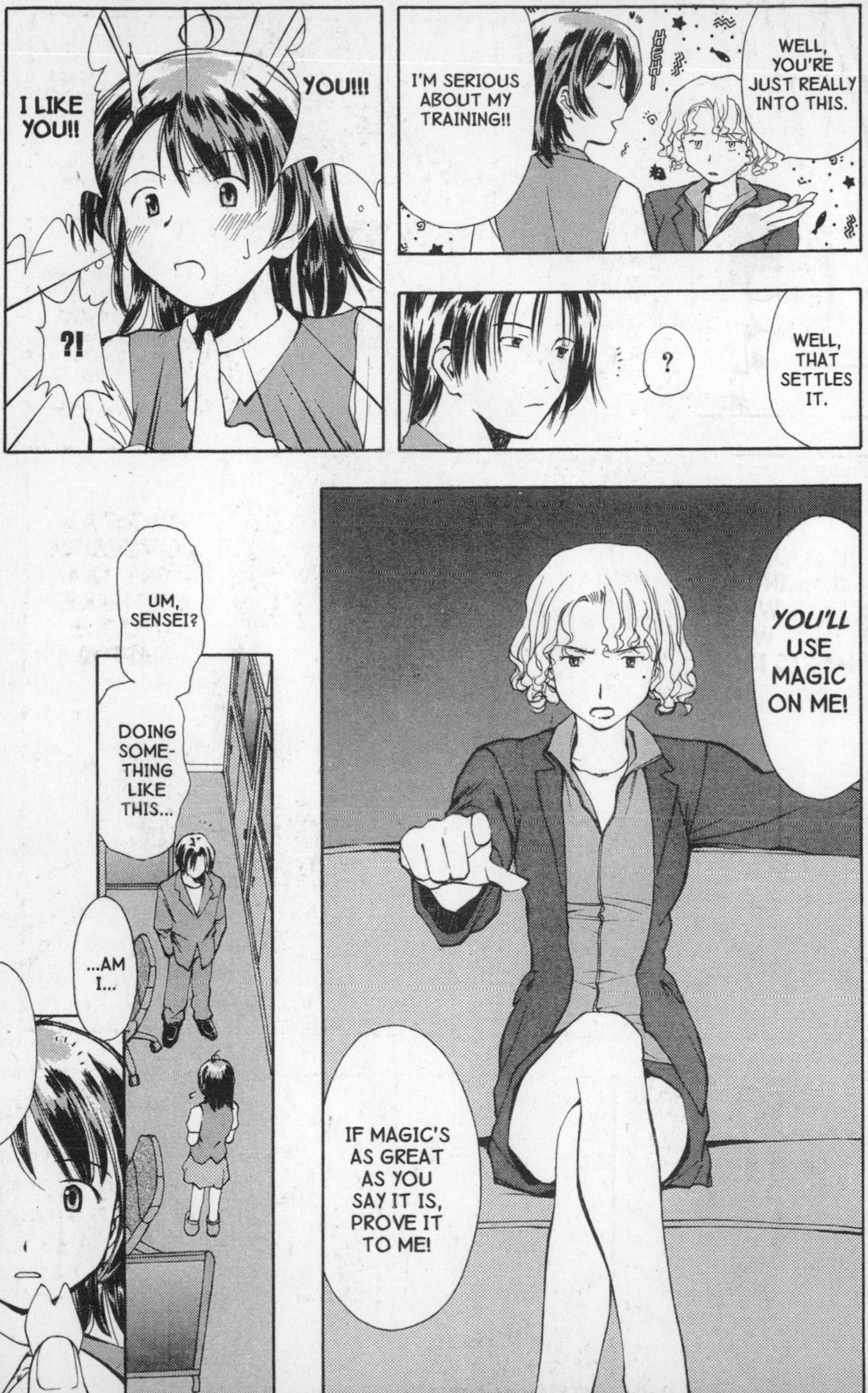
WELL, YOU'RE JUST REALLY INTO THIS.
I'M SERIOUS ABOUT MY TRAINING!!
WELL, THAT SETTLES IT.
?
YOU!!!
I LIKE YOU!!
?!
YOU'LL USE MAGIC ON ME!
IF MAGIC'S AS GREAT AS YOU SAY IT IS, PROVE IT TO ME!
UM, SENSEI?
DOING SOME-THING LIKE THIS...
...AM I...
...PREPARED?

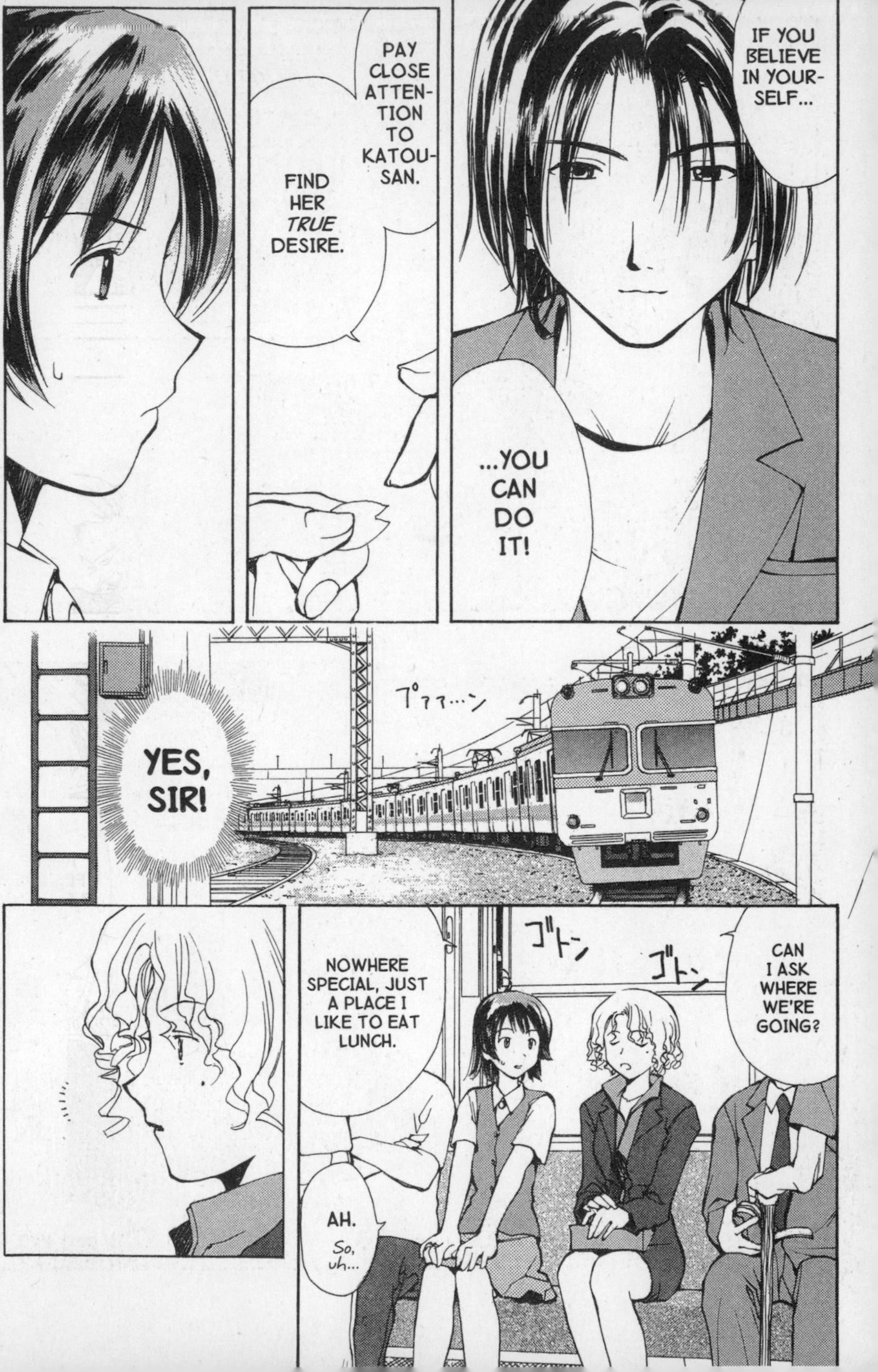
IF YOU BELIEVE IN YOUR-SELF...
...YOU CAN DO IT!
PAY CLOSE ATTEN-TION TO KATOU-SAN.
FIND HER *TRUE* DESIRE.
プァァ…ン
YES, SIR!
CAN I ASK WHERE WE'RE GOING?
ゴトン
ゴトン
NOWHERE SPECIAL, JUST A PLACE I LIKE TO EAT LUNCH.
AH.
So, uh...

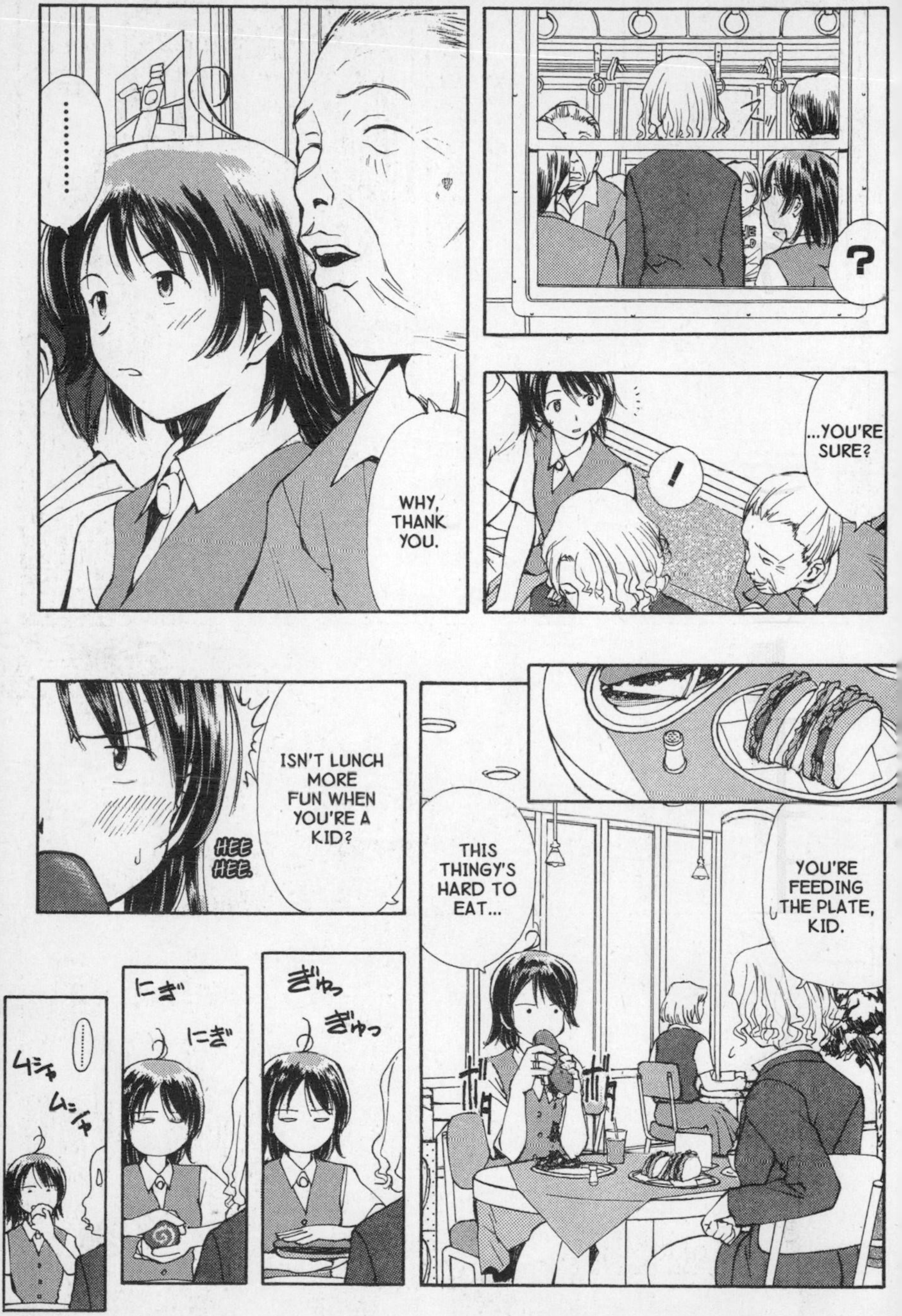

?
...YOU'RE SURE?
!
......
WHY, THANK YOU.
ISN'T LUNCH MORE FUN WHEN YOU'RE A KID?
HEE HEE
YOU'RE FEEDING THE PLATE, KID.
THIS THINGY'S HARD TO EAT...
ぎゅっ ぎゅっ
にぎ にぎ
......
ムシャ ムシャ

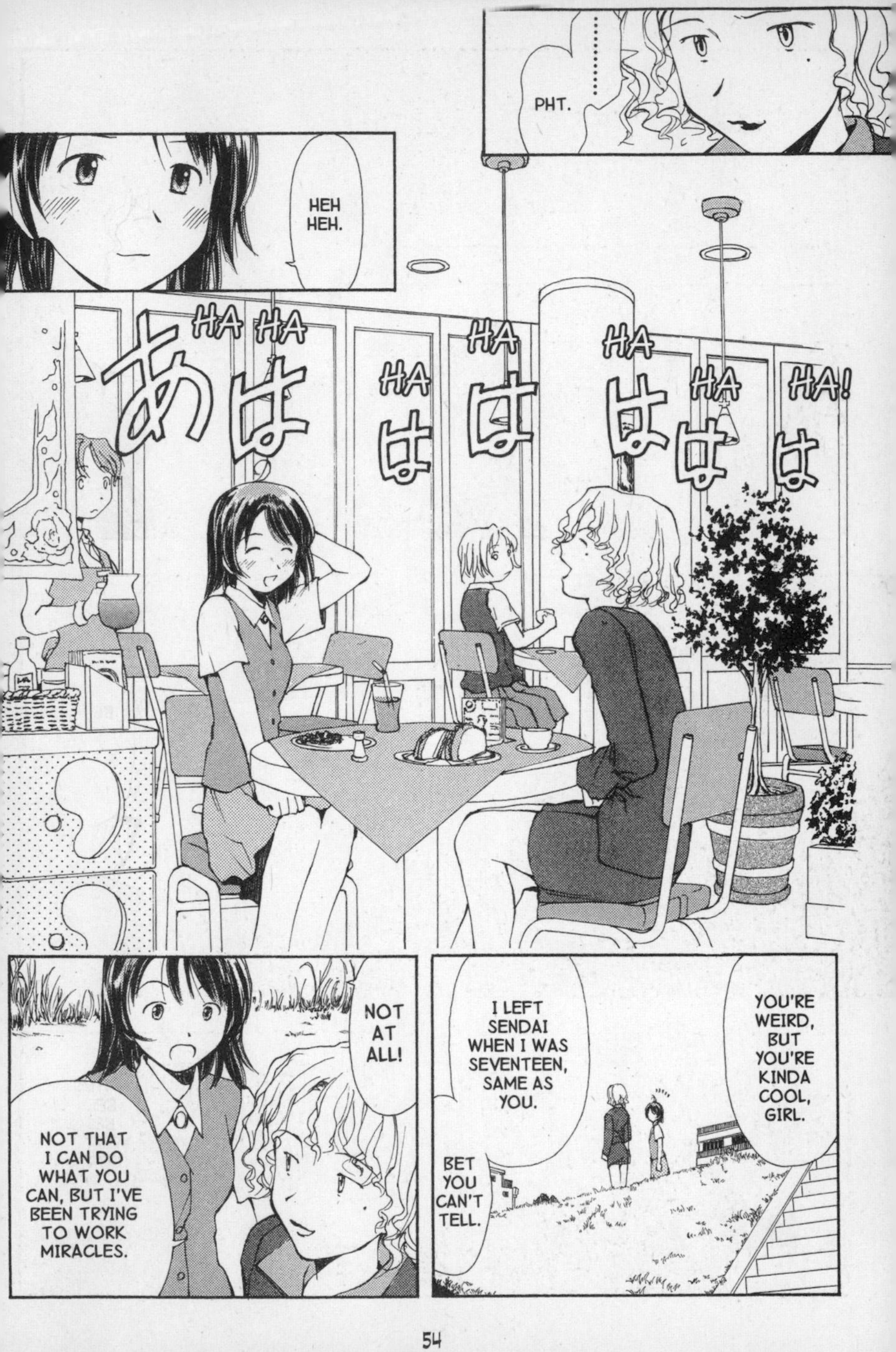
PHT.
HEH HEH.
HA HA HA HA HA HA HA!
あはははははは
YOU'RE WEIRD, BUT YOU'RE KINDA COOL, GIRL.
I LEFT SENDAI WHEN I WAS SEVENTEEN, SAME AS YOU.
BET YOU CAN'T TELL.
NOT AT ALL!
NOT THAT I CAN DO WHAT YOU CAN, BUT I'VE BEEN TRYING TO WORK MIRACLES.

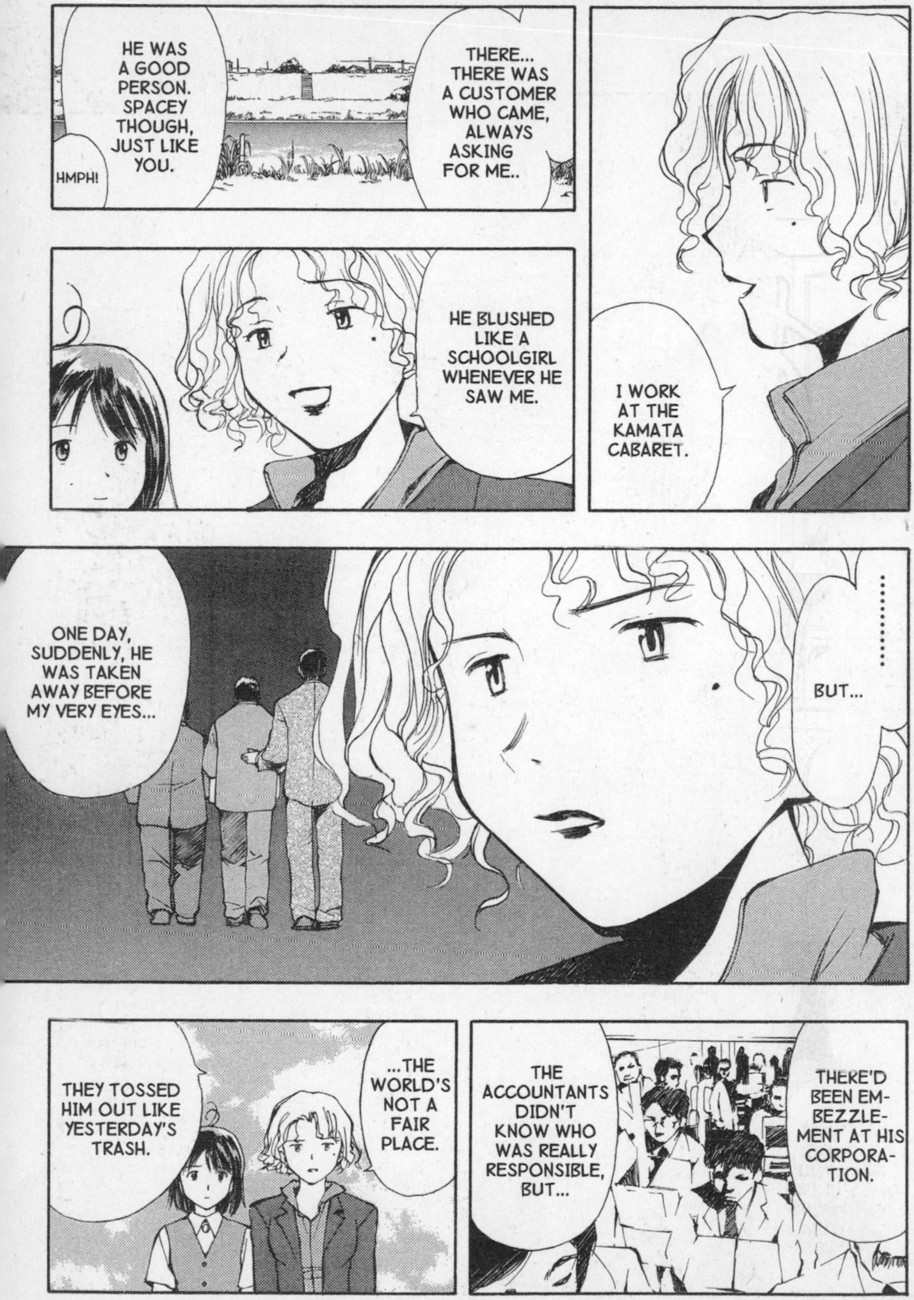
I WORK AT THE KAMATA CABARET.
THERE... THERE WAS A CUSTOMER WHO CAME, ALWAYS ASKING FOR ME..
HE WAS A GOOD PERSON. SPACEY THOUGH, JUST LIKE YOU.
HMPH!
HE BLUSHED LIKE A SCHOOLGIRL WHENEVER HE SAW ME.
....
BUT...
ONE DAY, SUDDENLY, HE WAS TAKEN AWAY BEFORE MY VERY EYES...
THERE'D BEEN EMBEZZLEMENT AT HIS CORPORATION.
THE ACCOUNTANTS DIDN'T KNOW WHO WAS REALLY RESPONSIBLE, BUT...
...THE WORLD'S NOT A FAIR PLACE.
THEY TOSSED HIM OUT LIKE YESTERDAY'S TRASH.

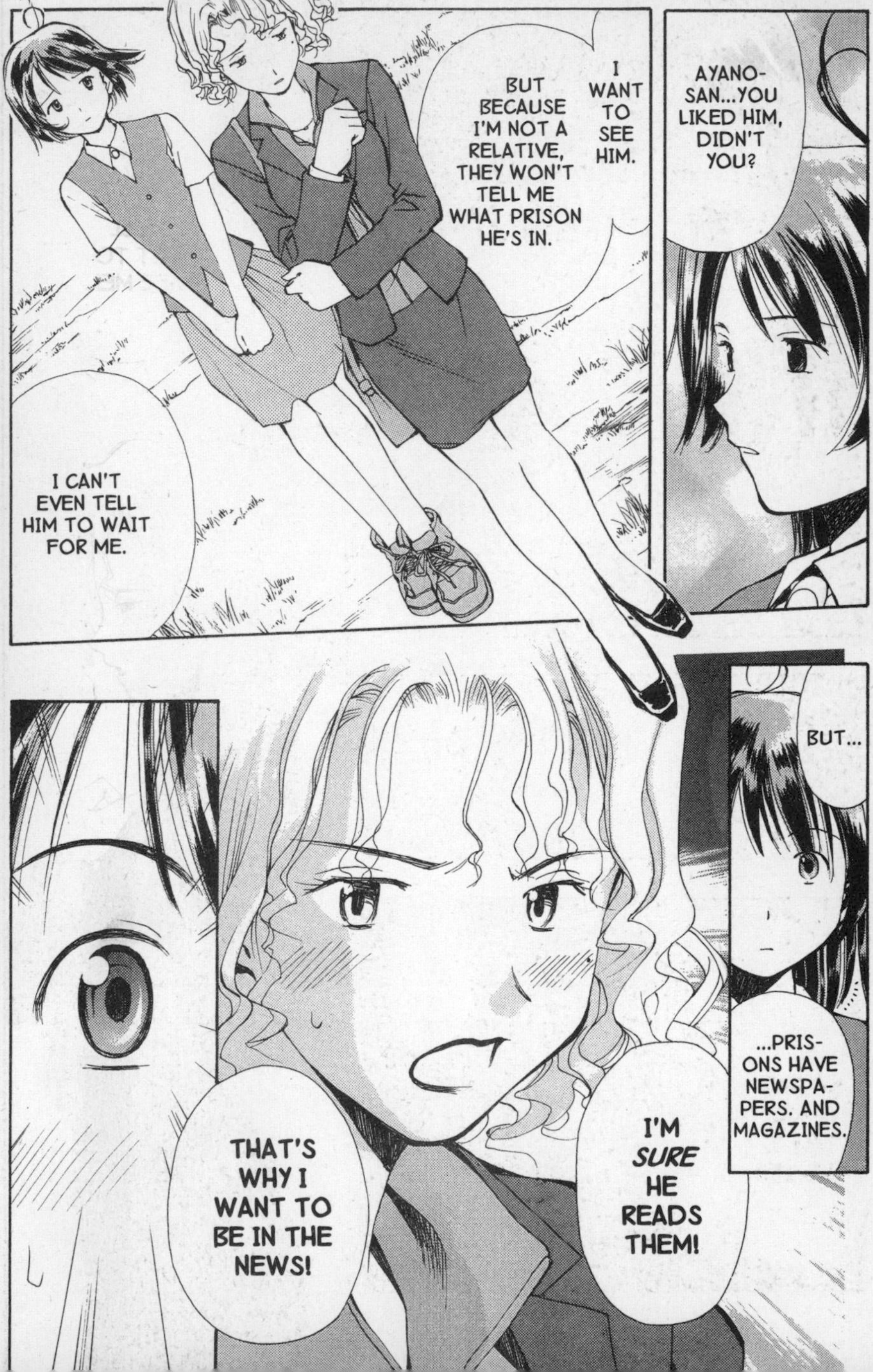
AYANO-SAN...YOU LIKED HIM, DIDN'T YOU?
I WANT TO SEE HIM.
BUT BECAUSE I'M NOT A RELATIVE, THEY WON'T TELL ME WHAT PRISON HE'S IN.
I CAN'T EVEN TELL HIM TO WAIT FOR ME.
BUT...
...PRISONS HAVE NEWSPAPERS. AND MAGAZINES.
I'M *SURE* HE READS THEM!
THAT'S WHY I WANT TO BE IN THE NEWS!

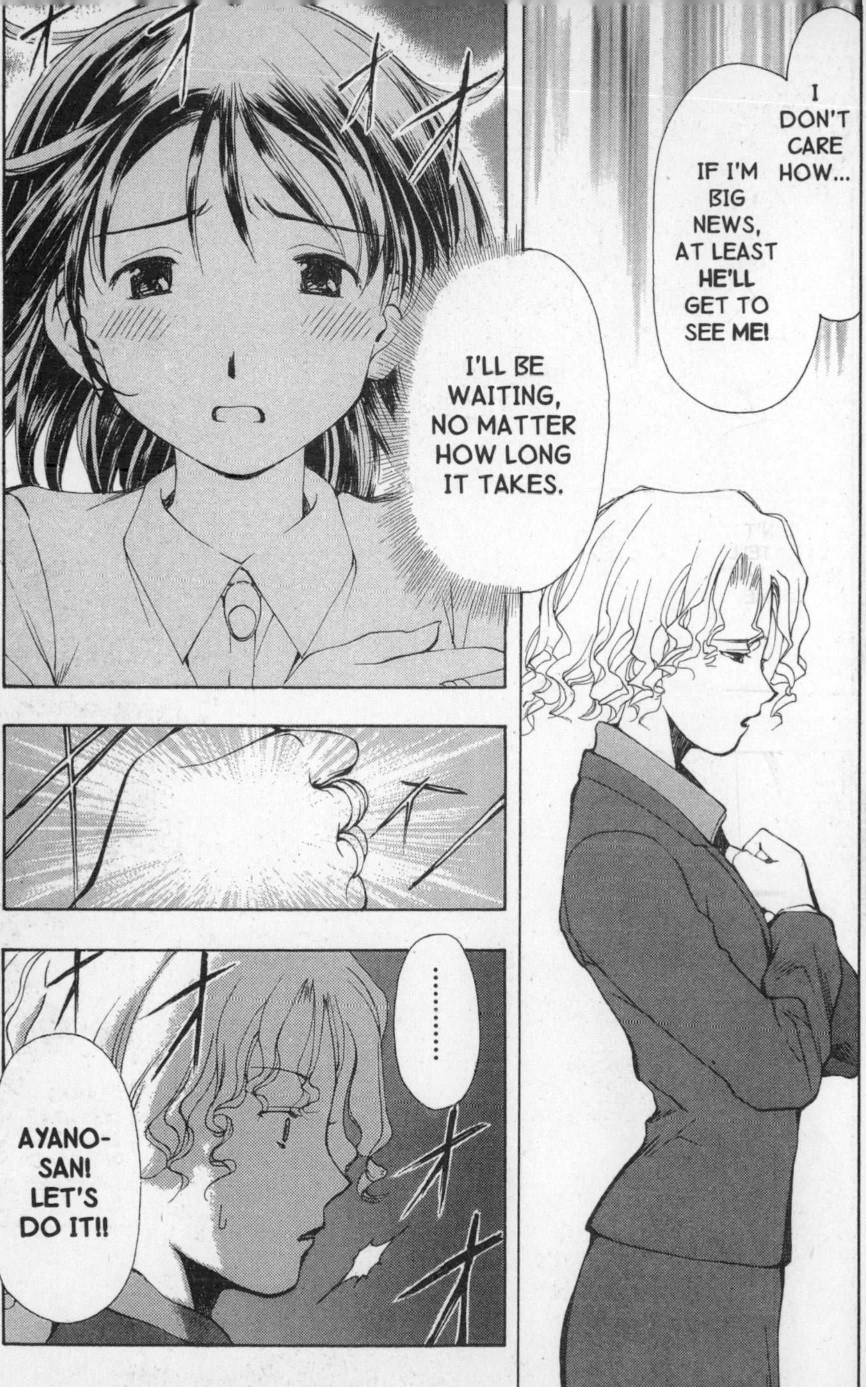
I DON'T CARE HOW...
IF I'M BIG NEWS, AT LEAST HE'LL GET TO SEE ME!
I'LL BE WAITING, NO MATTER HOW LONG IT TAKES.
......
AYANO-SAN! LET'S DO IT!!

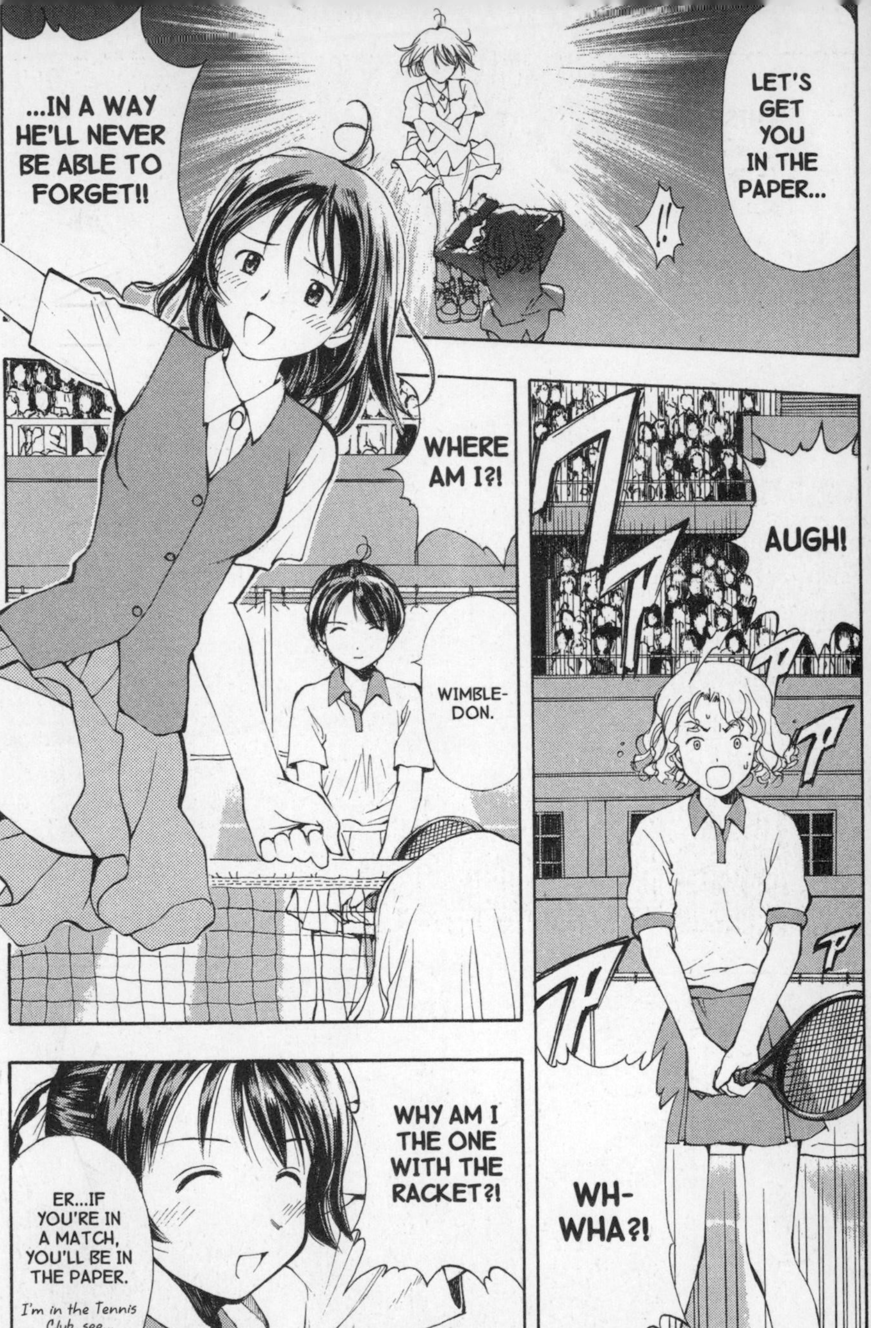
LET'S GET YOU IN THE PAPER...
!!
...IN A WAY HE'LL NEVER BE ABLE TO FORGET!!
AUGH!
WH-WHA?!
WHERE AM I?!
WIMBLE-DON.
WHY AM I THE ONE WITH THE RACKET?!
ER...IF YOU'RE IN A MATCH, YOU'LL BE IN THE PAPER.
I'm in the Tennis Club, see...

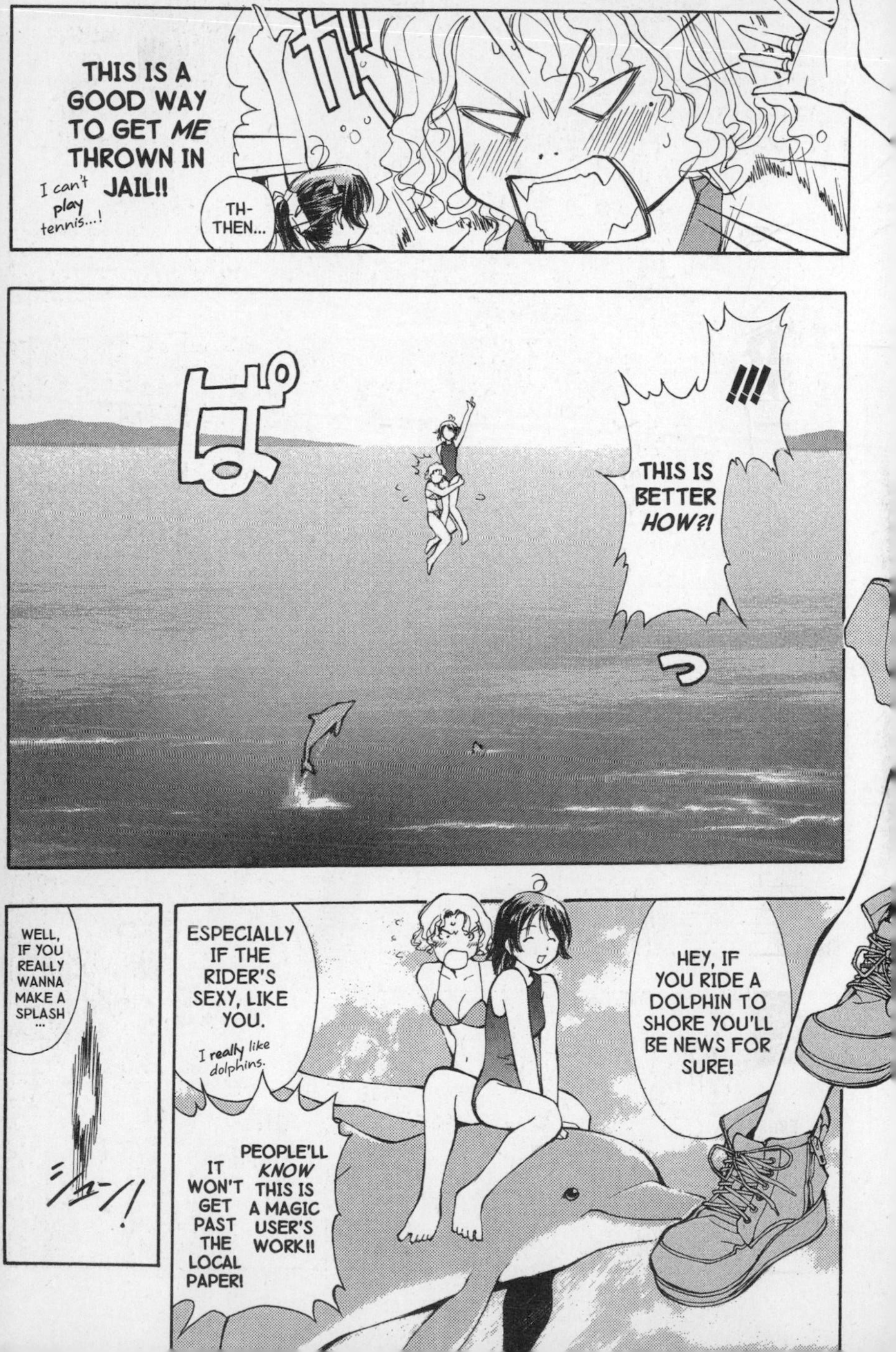
THIS IS A GOOD WAY TO GET *ME* THROWN IN JAIL!!
I can't play tennis...!
TH- THEN...
ぱ
!!!
THIS IS BETTER *HOW*?!
つ
HEY, IF YOU RIDE A DOLPHIN TO SHORE YOU'LL BE NEWS FOR SURE!
ESPECIALLY IF THE RIDER'S SEXY, LIKE YOU.
I really like dolphins.
PEOPLE'LL *KNOW* THIS IS A MAGIC USER'S WORK!!
IT WON'T GET PAST THE LOCAL PAPER!
WELL, IF YOU REALLY WANNA MAKE A SPLASH ...

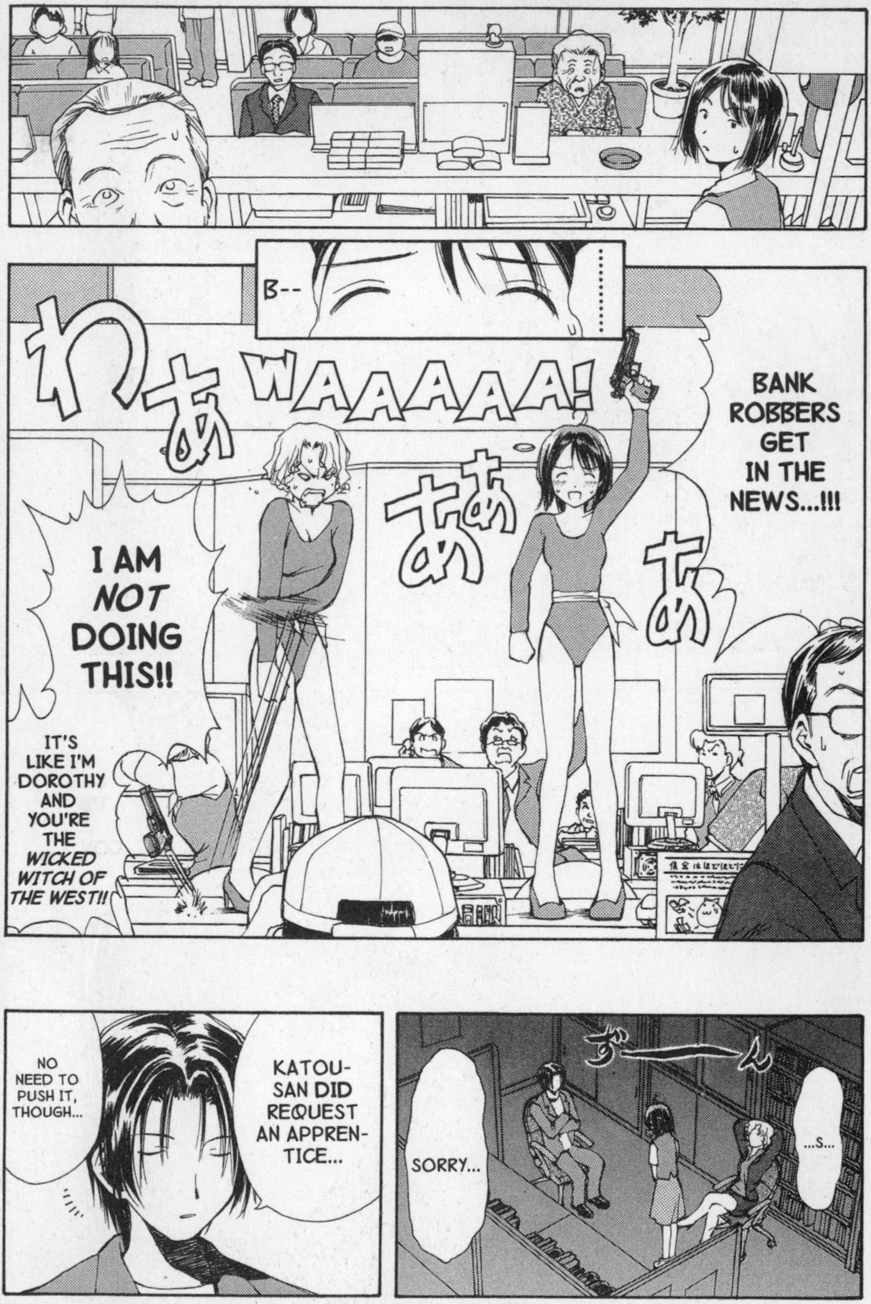

......
B--
BANK ROBBERS GET IN THE NEWS...!!!
WAAAAA!
わあああああ
I AM *NOT* DOING THIS!!
IT'S LIKE I'M DOROTHY AND YOU'RE THE *WICKED WITCH OF THE WEST*!!
...S...
ずーーん
SORRY...
KATOU-SAN DID REQUEST AN APPRENTICE...
NO NEED TO PUSH IT, THOUGH...

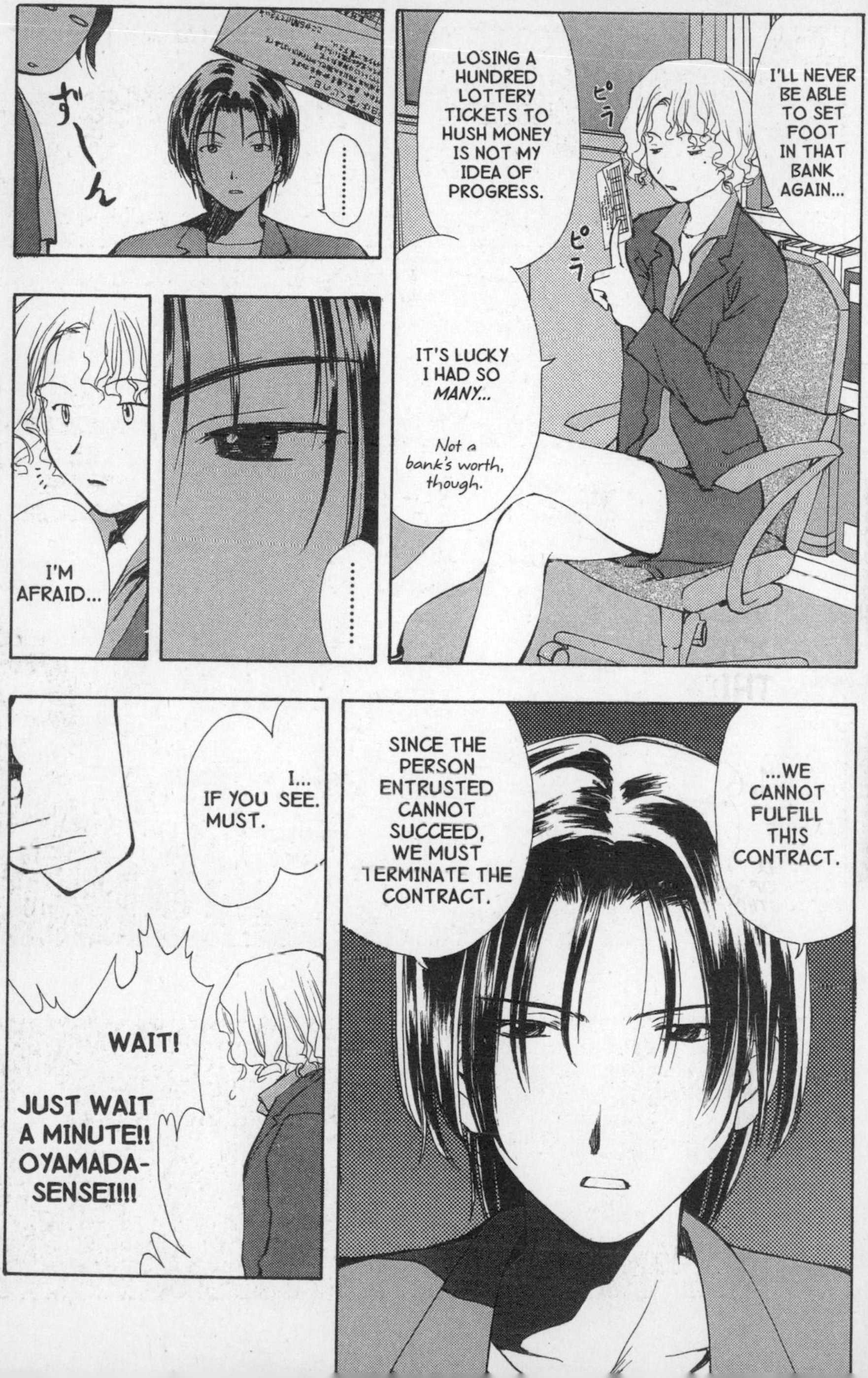
I'LL NEVER BE ABLE TO SET FOOT IN THAT BANK AGAIN...
LOSING A HUNDRED LOTTERY TICKETS TO HUSH MONEY IS NOT MY IDEA OF PROGRESS.
ピラ
ピラ
IT'S LUCKY I HAD SO *MANY*...
Not a bank's worth, though.
ずーん
......
......
I'M AFRAID...
...WE CANNOT FULFILL THIS CONTRACT.
SINCE THE PERSON ENTRUSTED CANNOT SUCCEED, WE MUST TERMINATE THE CONTRACT.
I... SEE. IF YOU MUST.
WAIT!
JUST WAIT A MINUTE!! OYAMADA-SENSEI!!!

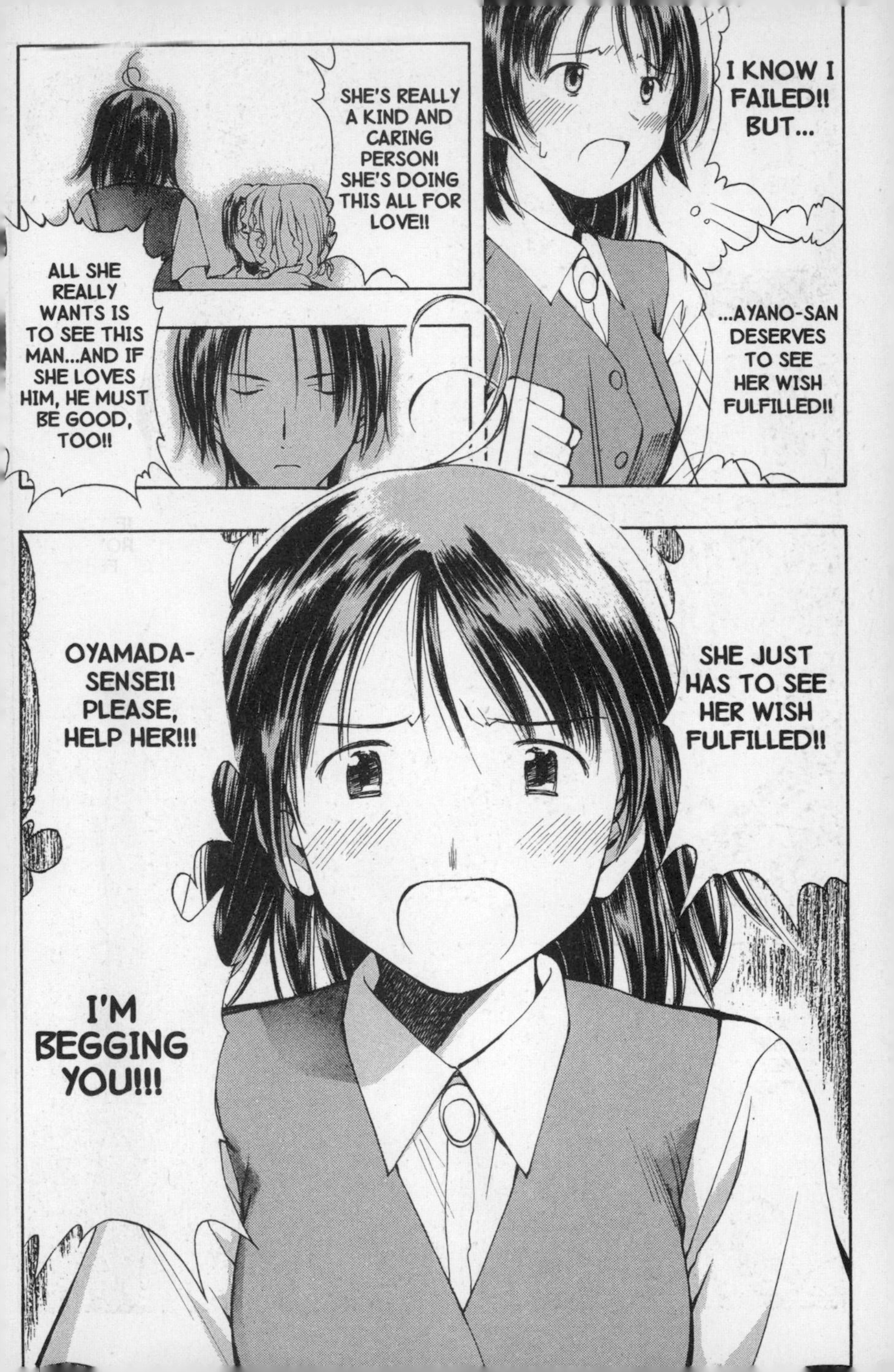
I KNOW I FAILED!! BUT...
...AYANO-SAN DESERVES TO SEE HER WISH FULFILLED!!
SHE'S REALLY A KIND AND CARING PERSON! SHE'S DOING THIS ALL FOR LOVE!!
ALL SHE REALLY WANTS IS TO SEE THIS MAN...AND IF SHE LOVES HIM, HE MUST BE GOOD, TOO!!
SHE JUST HAS TO SEE HER WISH FULFILLED!!
OYAMADA-SENSEI! PLEASE, HELP HER!!!
I'M BEGGING YOU!!!

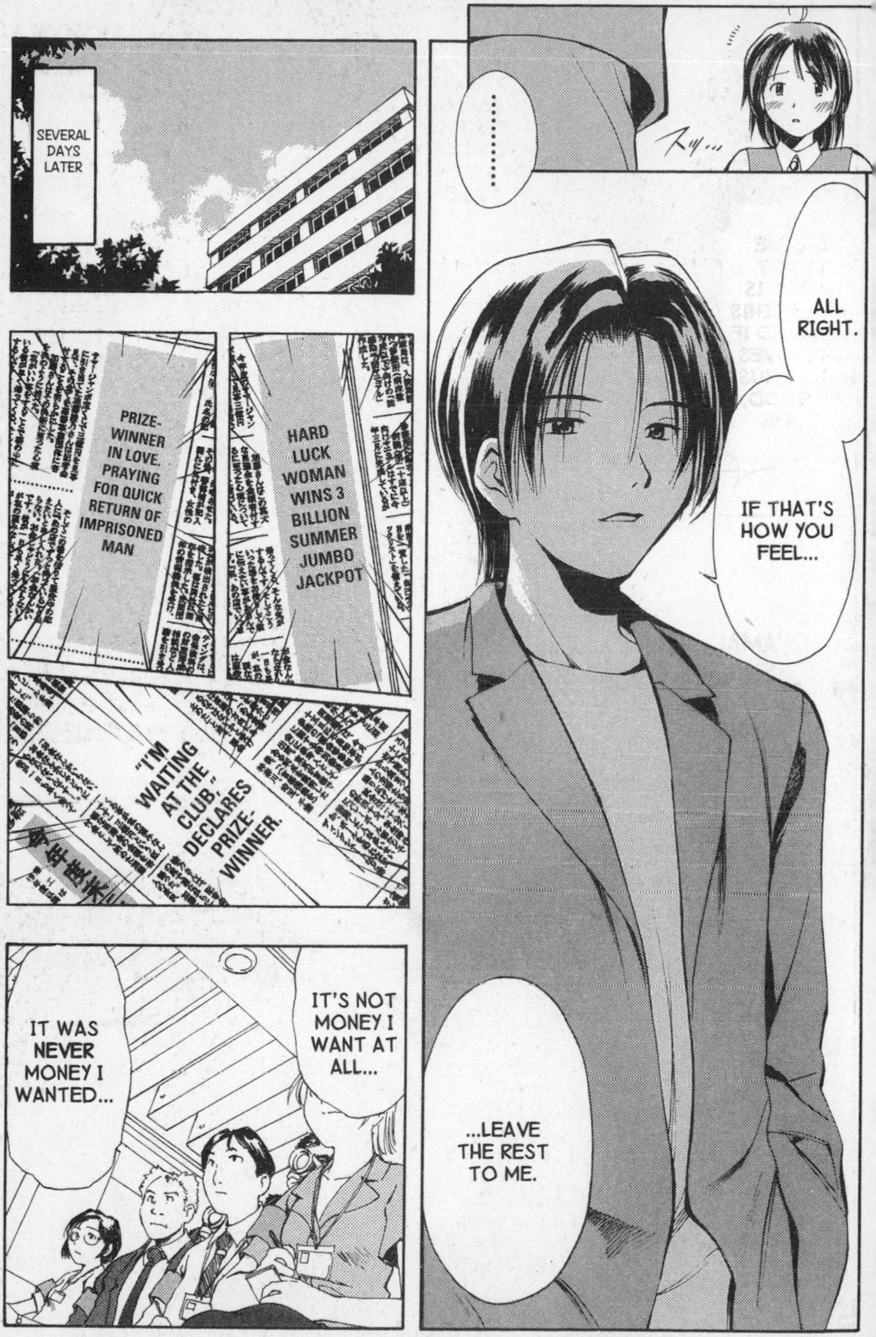

......
スッ…
ALL RIGHT.
IF THAT'S HOW YOU FEEL...
...LEAVE THE REST TO ME.
SEVERAL DAYS LATER
HARD LUCK WOMAN WINS 3 BILLION SUMMER JUMBO JACKPOT
PRIZE-WINNER IN LOVE. PRAYING FOR QUICK RETURN OF IMPRISONED MAN
"I'M WAITING AT THE CLUB," DECLARES PRIZE-WINNER.
IT'S NOT MONEY I WANT AT ALL...
IT WAS NEVER MONEY I WANTED...

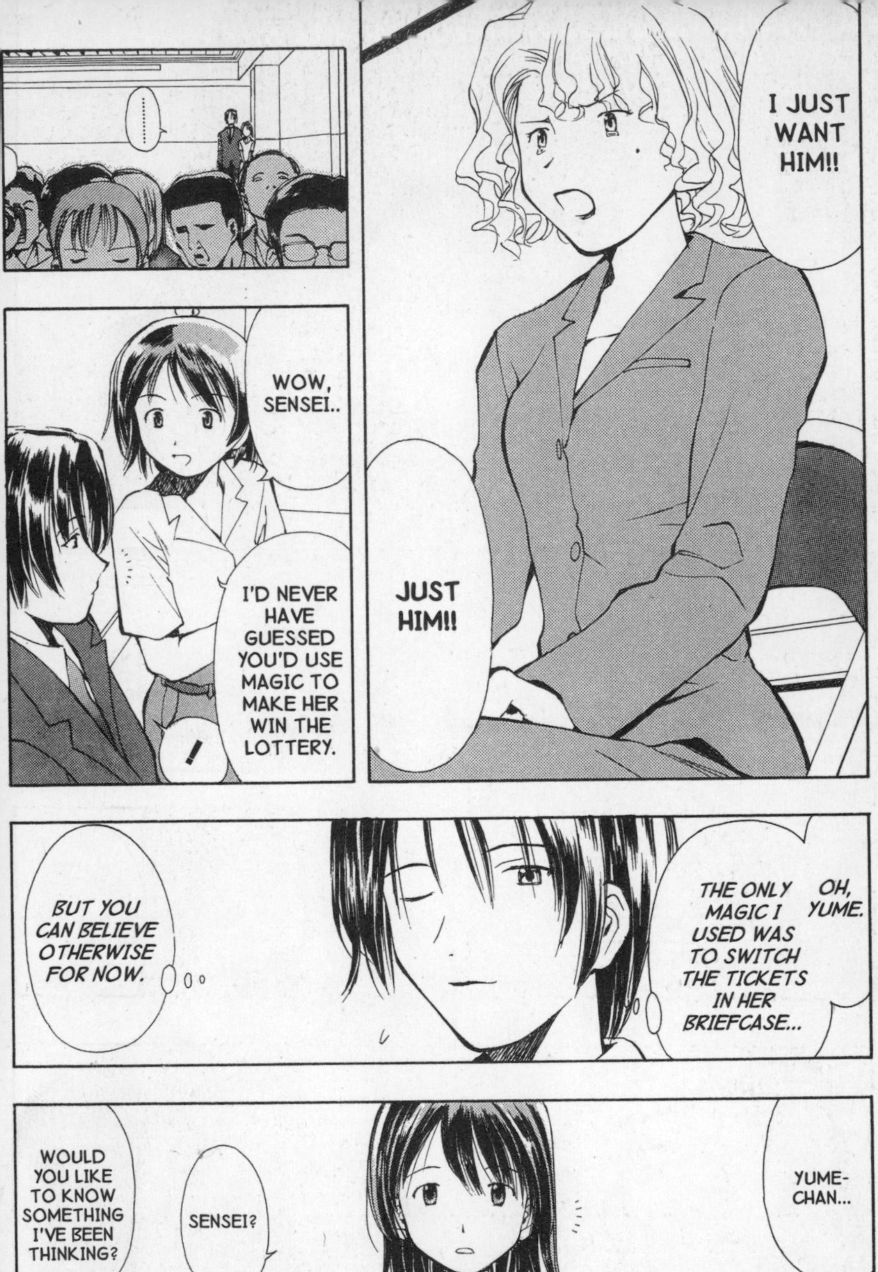
I JUST WANT HIM!!
JUST HIM!!
......
WOW, SENSEI..
I'D NEVER HAVE GUESSED YOU'D USE MAGIC TO MAKE HER WIN THE LOTTERY.
!
OH, YUME.
THE ONLY MAGIC I USED WAS TO SWITCH THE TICKETS IN HER BRIEFCASE...
BUT YOU CAN BELIEVE OTHERWISE FOR NOW.
YUME-CHAN...
SENSEI?
WOULD YOU LIKE TO KNOW SOMETHING I'VE BEEN THINKING?

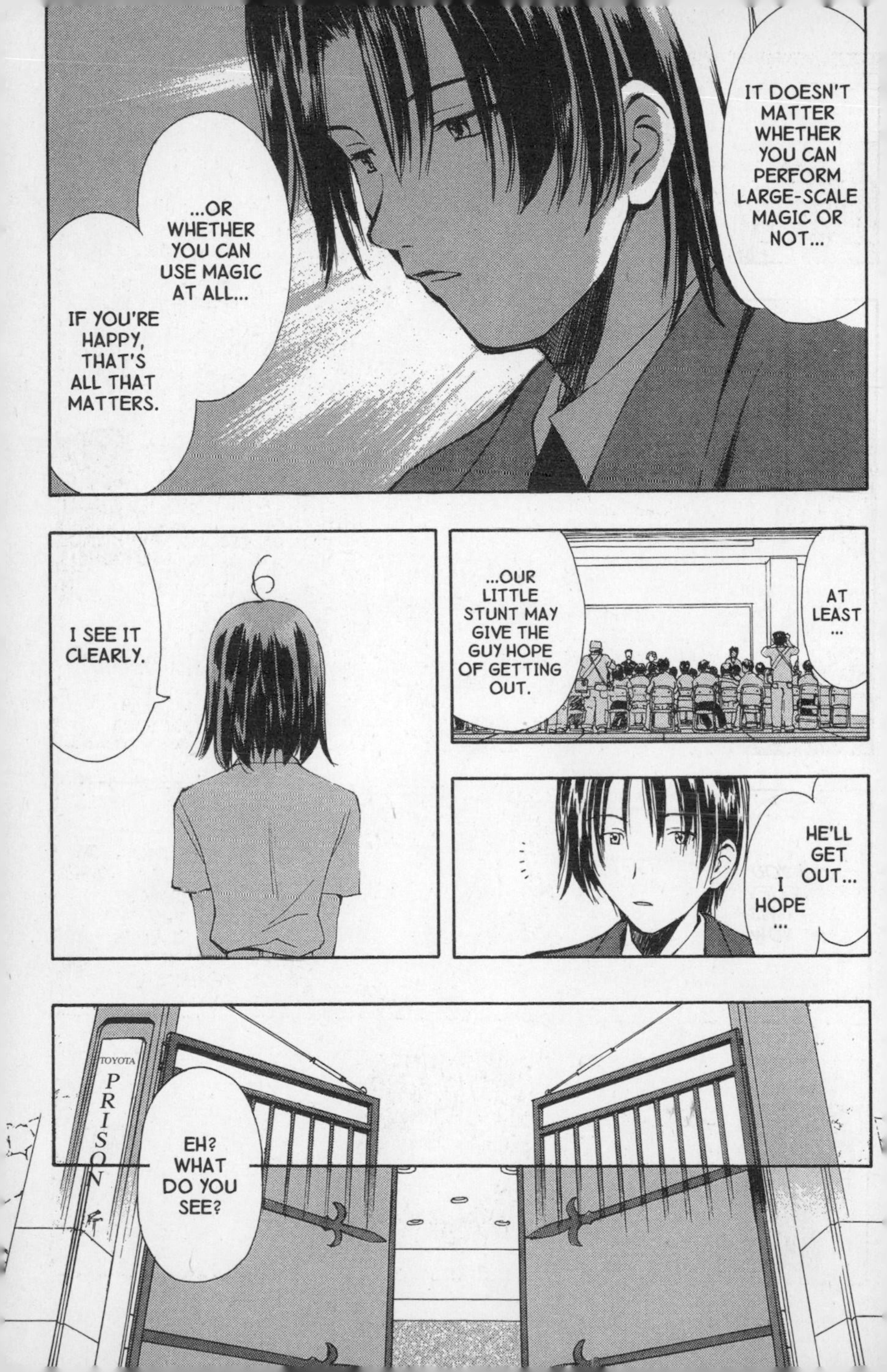
IT DOESN'T MATTER WHETHER YOU CAN PERFORM LARGE-SCALE MAGIC OR NOT...
...OR WHETHER YOU CAN USE MAGIC AT ALL...
IF YOU'RE HAPPY, THAT'S ALL THAT MATTERS.
AT LEAST ...
...OUR LITTLE STUNT MAY GIVE THE GUY HOPE OF GETTING OUT.
HE'LL GET OUT...
I HOPE ...
I SEE IT CLEARLY.
TOYOTA PRISON
EH? WHAT DO YOU SEE?

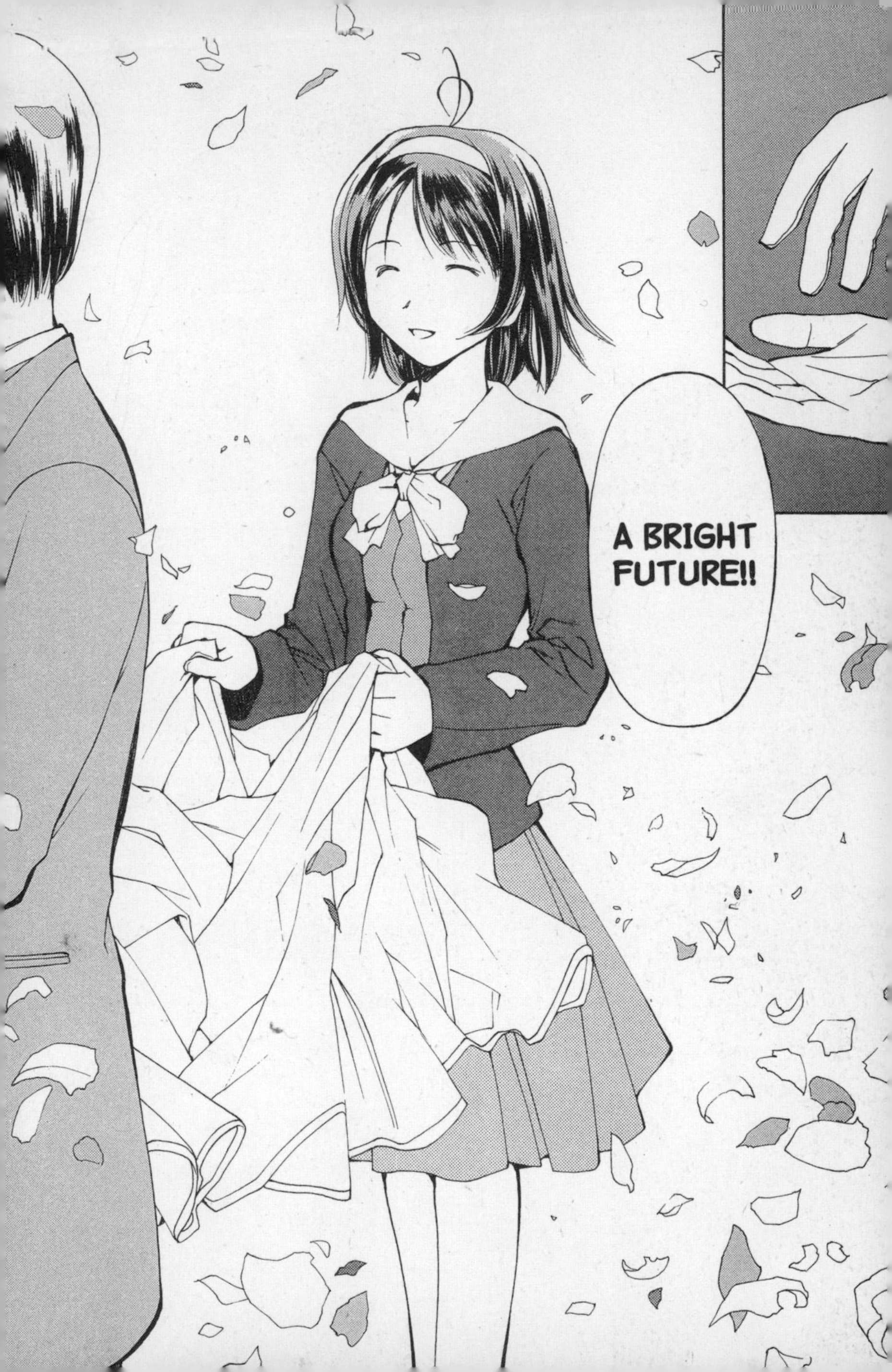
A BRIGHT FUTURE!!

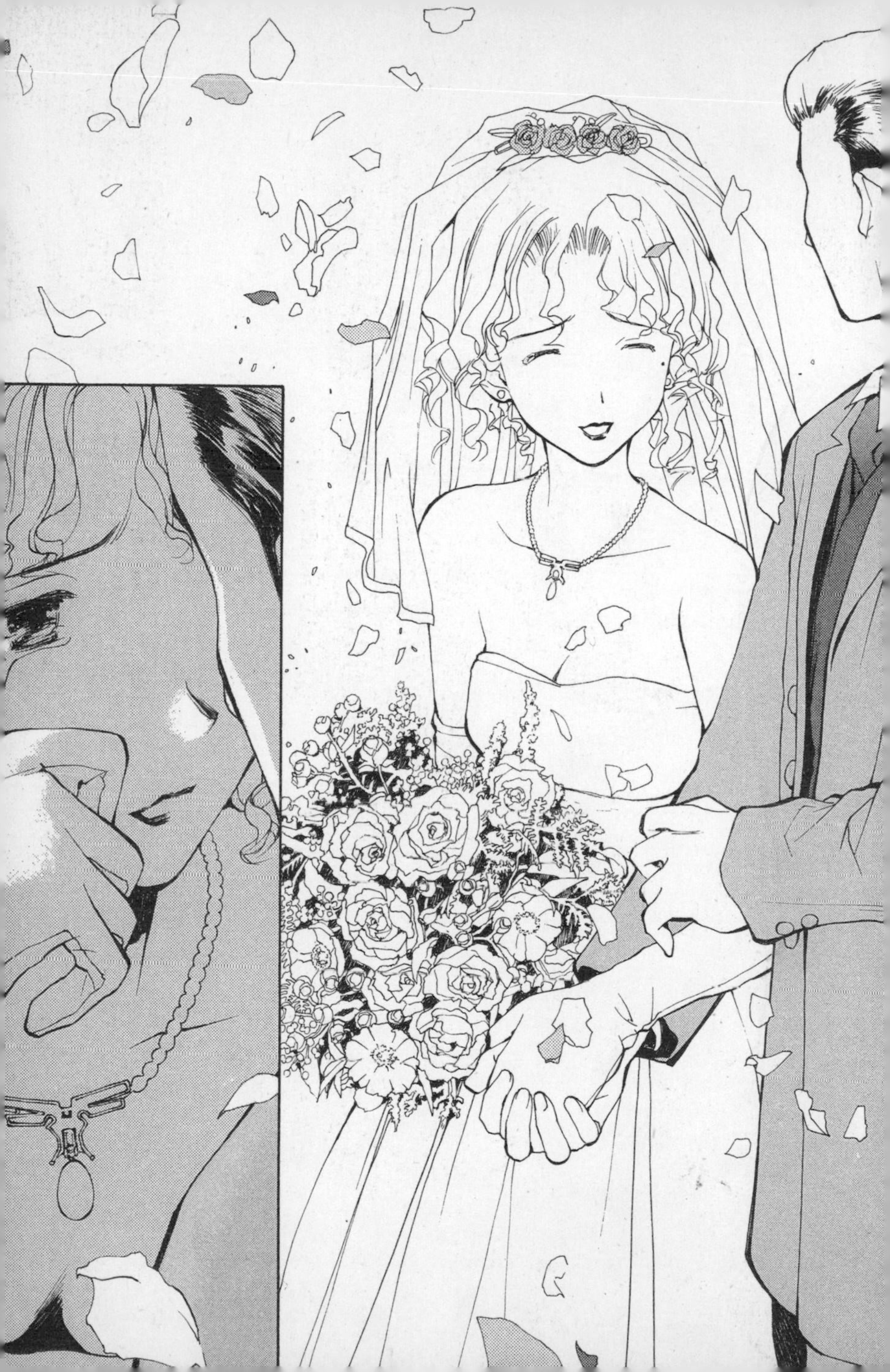

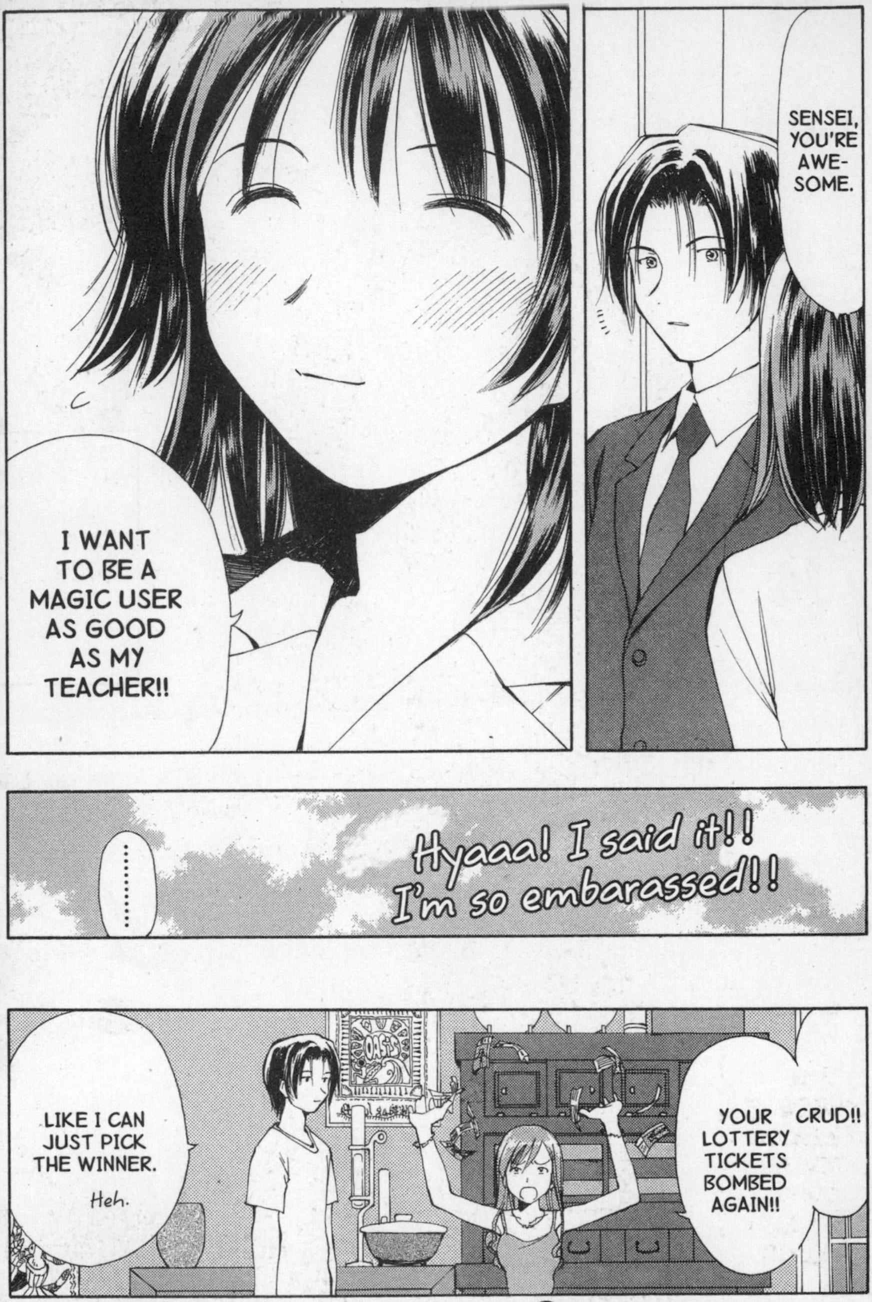

SENSEI, YOU'RE AWE-SOME.
I WANT TO BE A MAGIC USER AS GOOD AS MY TEACHER!!
Hyaaa! I said it!! I'm so embarassed!!
......
CRUD!!
YOUR LOTTERY TICKETS BOMBED AGAIN!!
LIKE I CAN JUST PICK THE WINNER.
Heh.

2nd Dream ⁘ End

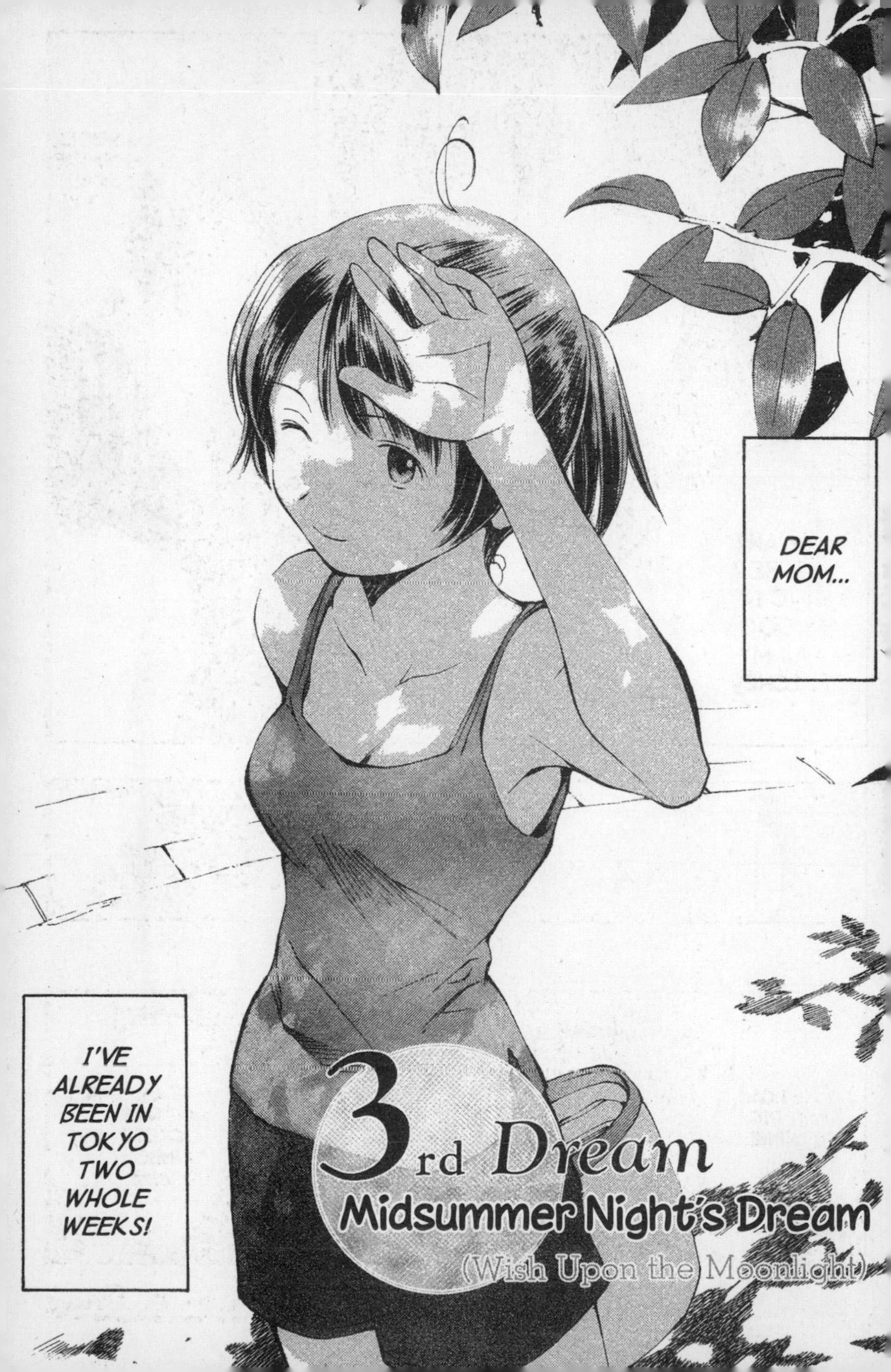
DEAR MOM...
I'VE ALREADY BEEN IN TOKYO TWO WHOLE WEEKS!
3rd Dream
Midsummer Night's Dream
(Wish Upon the Moonlight)

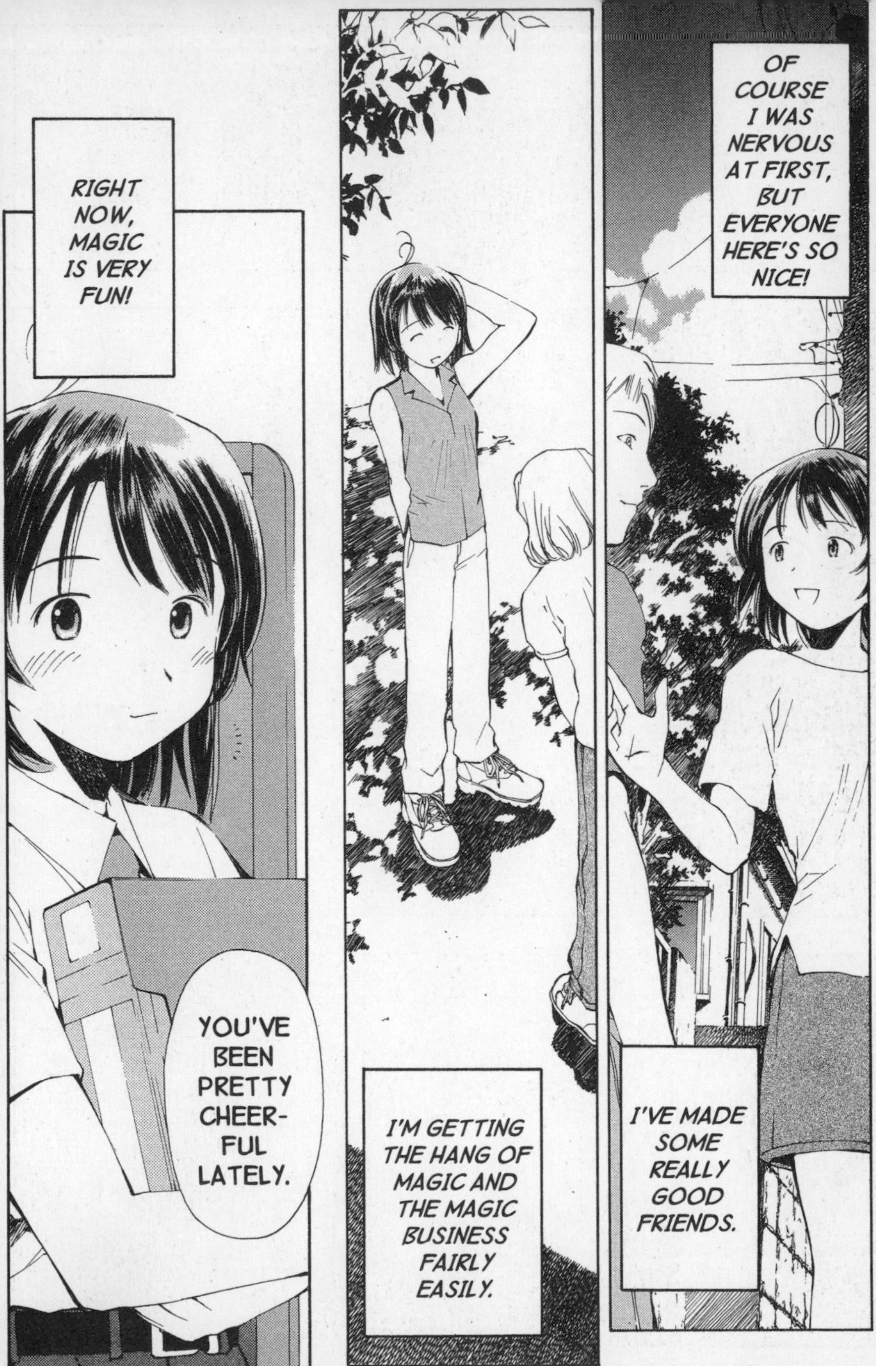
OF COURSE I WAS NERVOUS AT FIRST, BUT EVERYONE HERE'S SO NICE!
I'VE MADE SOME REALLY GOOD FRIENDS.
I'M GETTING THE HANG OF MAGIC AND THE MAGIC BUSINESS FAIRLY EASILY.
RIGHT NOW, MAGIC IS VERY FUN!
YOU'VE BEEN PRETTY CHEER-FUL LATELY.

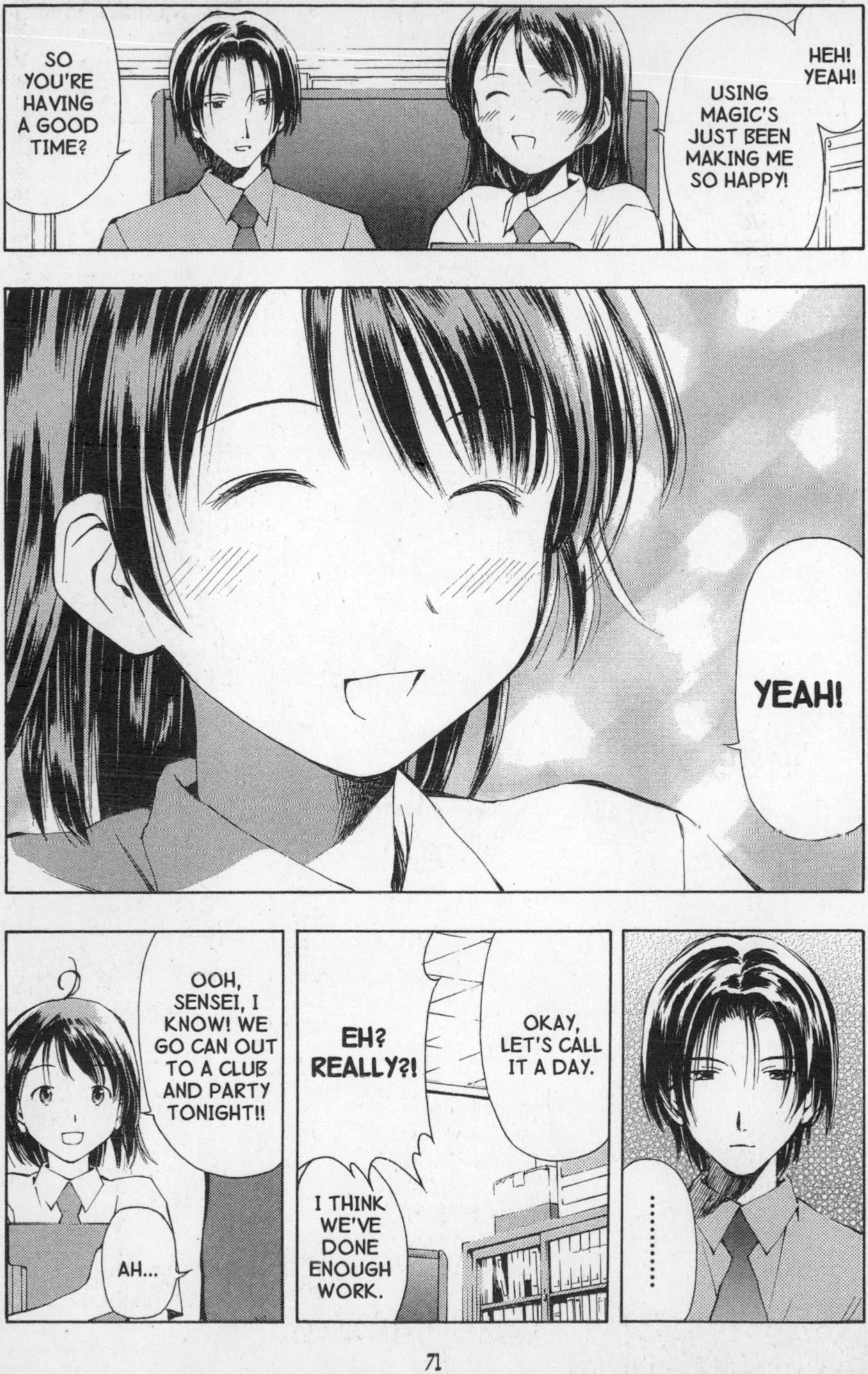

HEH! YEAH!
USING MAGIC'S JUST BEEN MAKING ME SO HAPPY!
SO YOU'RE HAVING A GOOD TIME?
YEAH!
....
OKAY, LET'S CALL IT A DAY.
EH? REALLY?!
I THINK WE'VE DONE ENOUGH WORK.
OOH, SENSEI, I KNOW! WE GO CAN OUT TO A CLUB AND PARTY TONIGHT!!
AH...

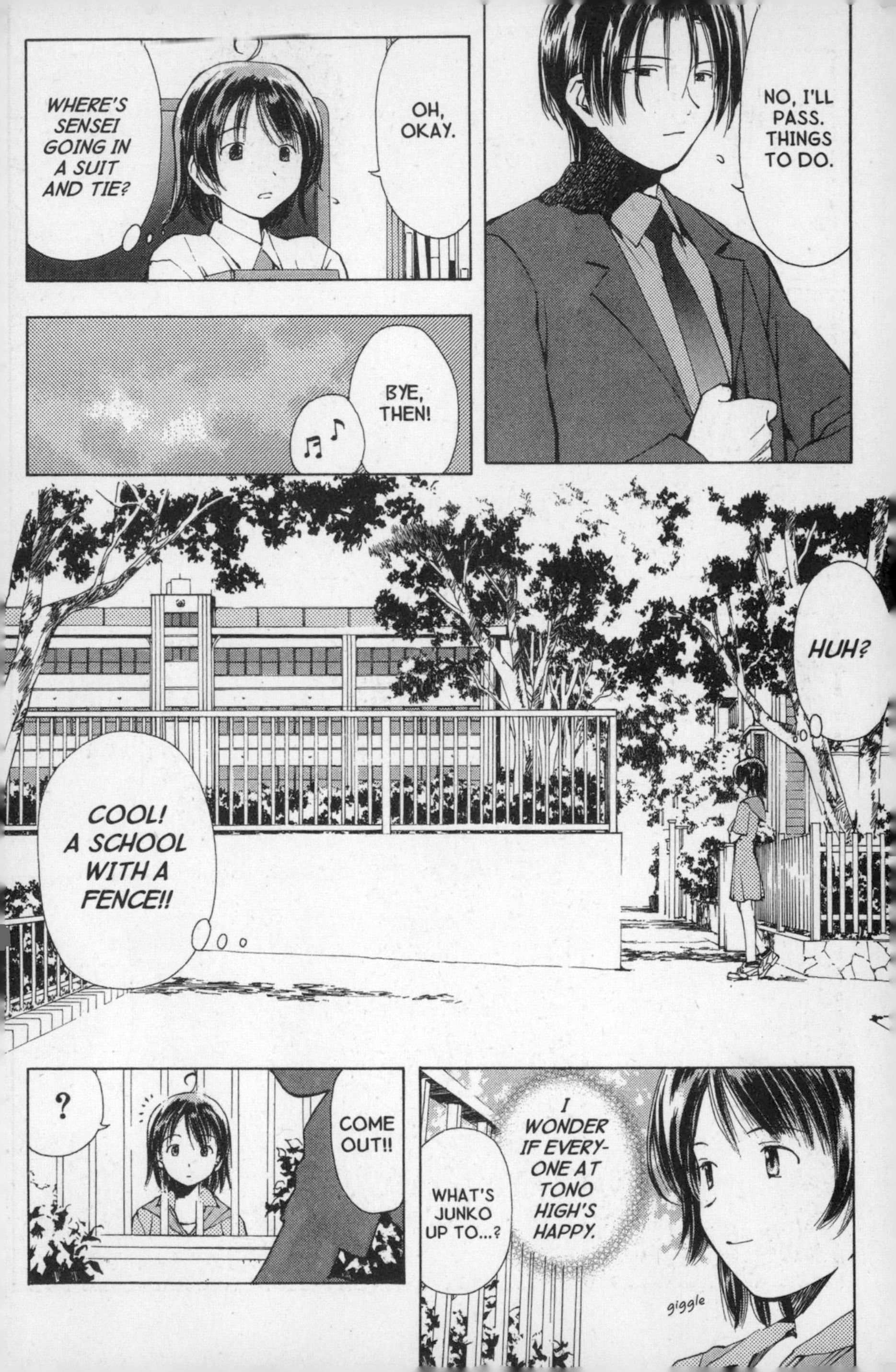
NO, I'LL PASS. THINGS TO DO.
OH, OKAY.
WHERE'S SENSEI GOING IN A SUIT AND TIE?
BYE, THEN!
♫ ♪
HUH?
COOL! A SCHOOL WITH A FENCE!!
I WONDER IF EVERY-ONE AT TONO HIGH'S HAPPY.
WHAT'S JUNKO UP TO...?
giggle
COME OUT!!
?

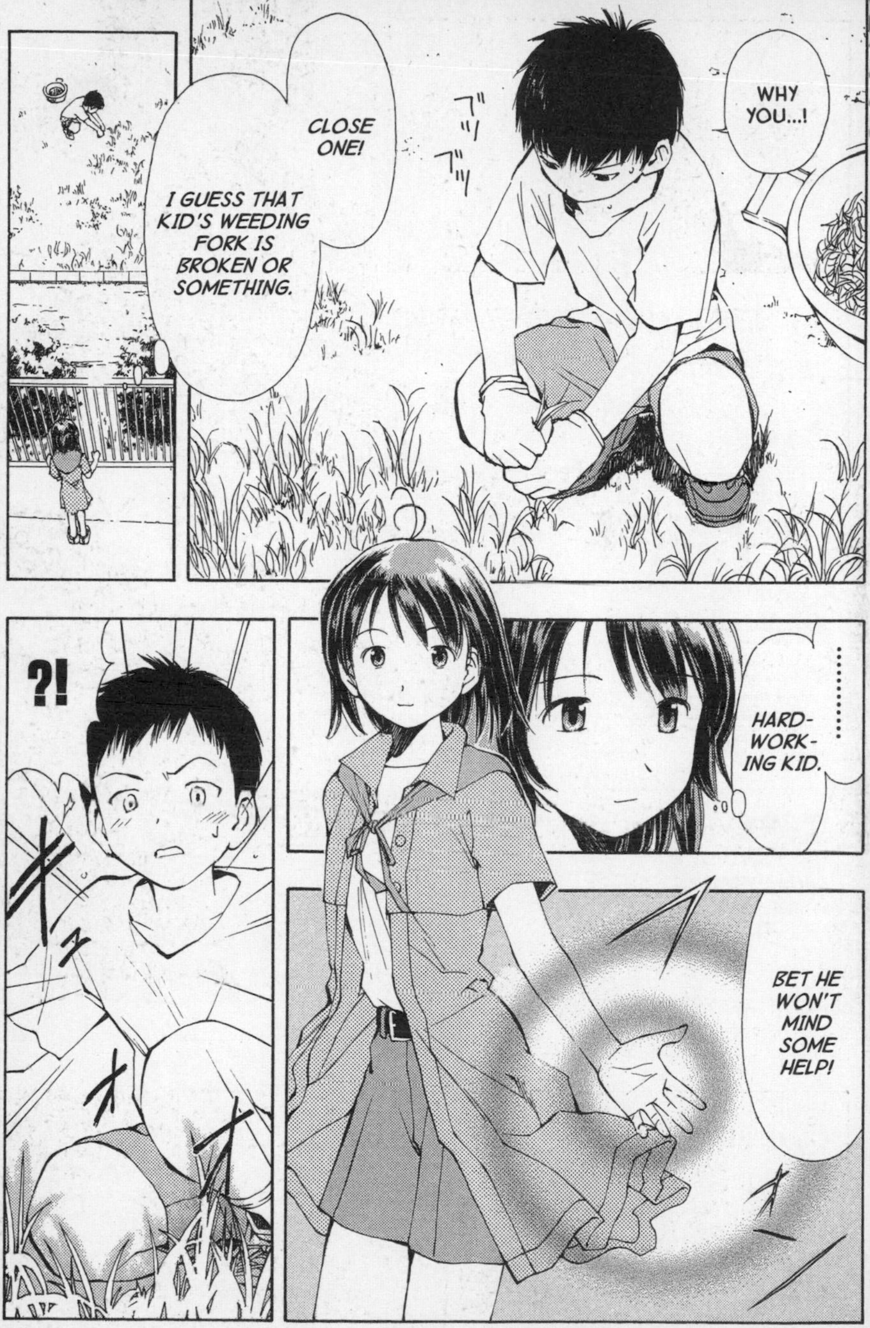

WHY YOU...!
ブツ
ブツ
CLOSE ONE!
I GUESS THAT KID'S WEEDING FORK IS BROKEN OR SOMETHING.
...... HARD-WORKING KID.
BET HE WON'T MIND SOME HELP!
?!

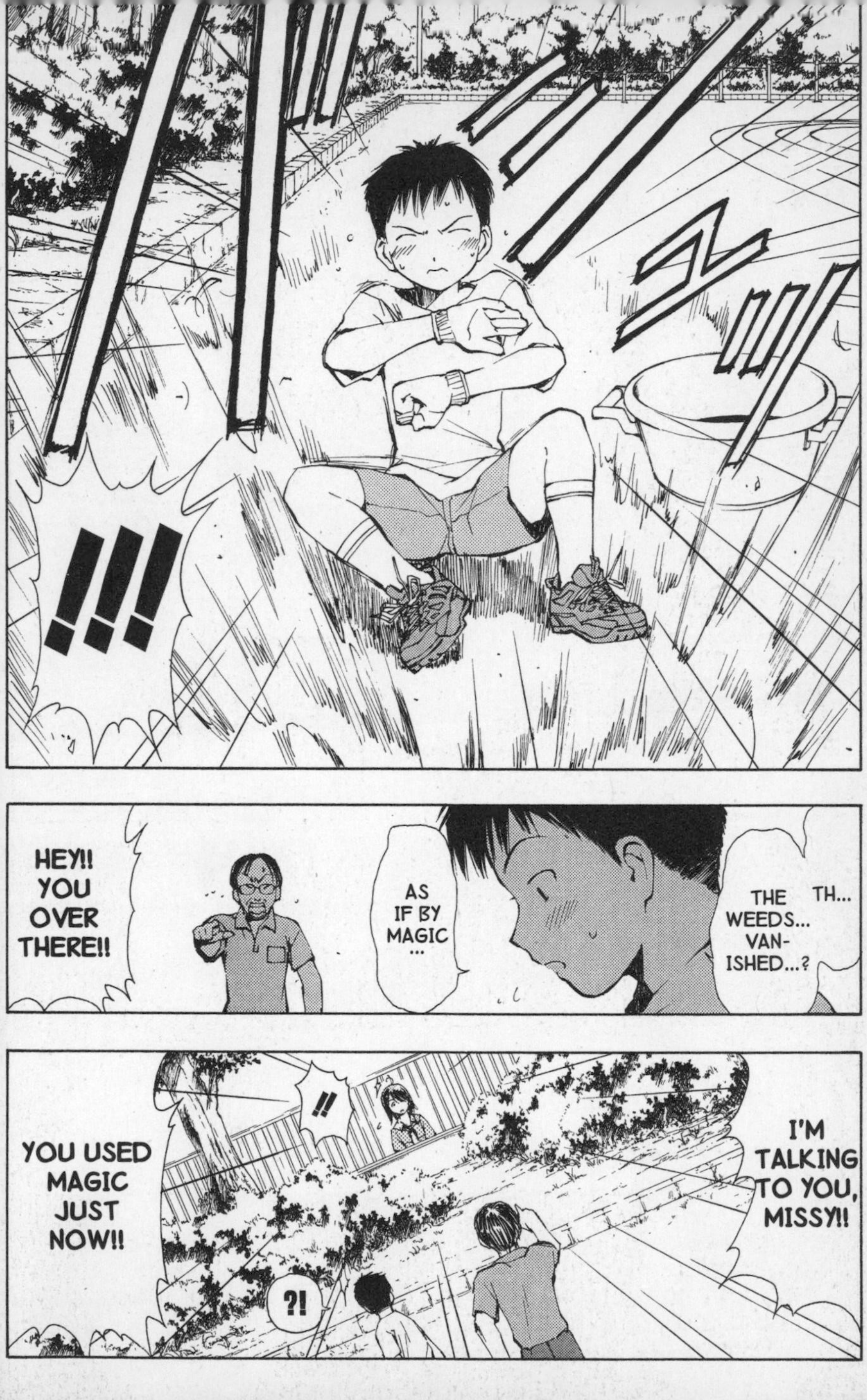
!!!
TH... THE WEEDS... VAN-ISHED...?
AS IF BY MAGIC ...
HEY!! YOU OVER THERE!!
I'M TALKING TO YOU, MISSY!!
!!
YOU USED MAGIC JUST NOW!!
?!

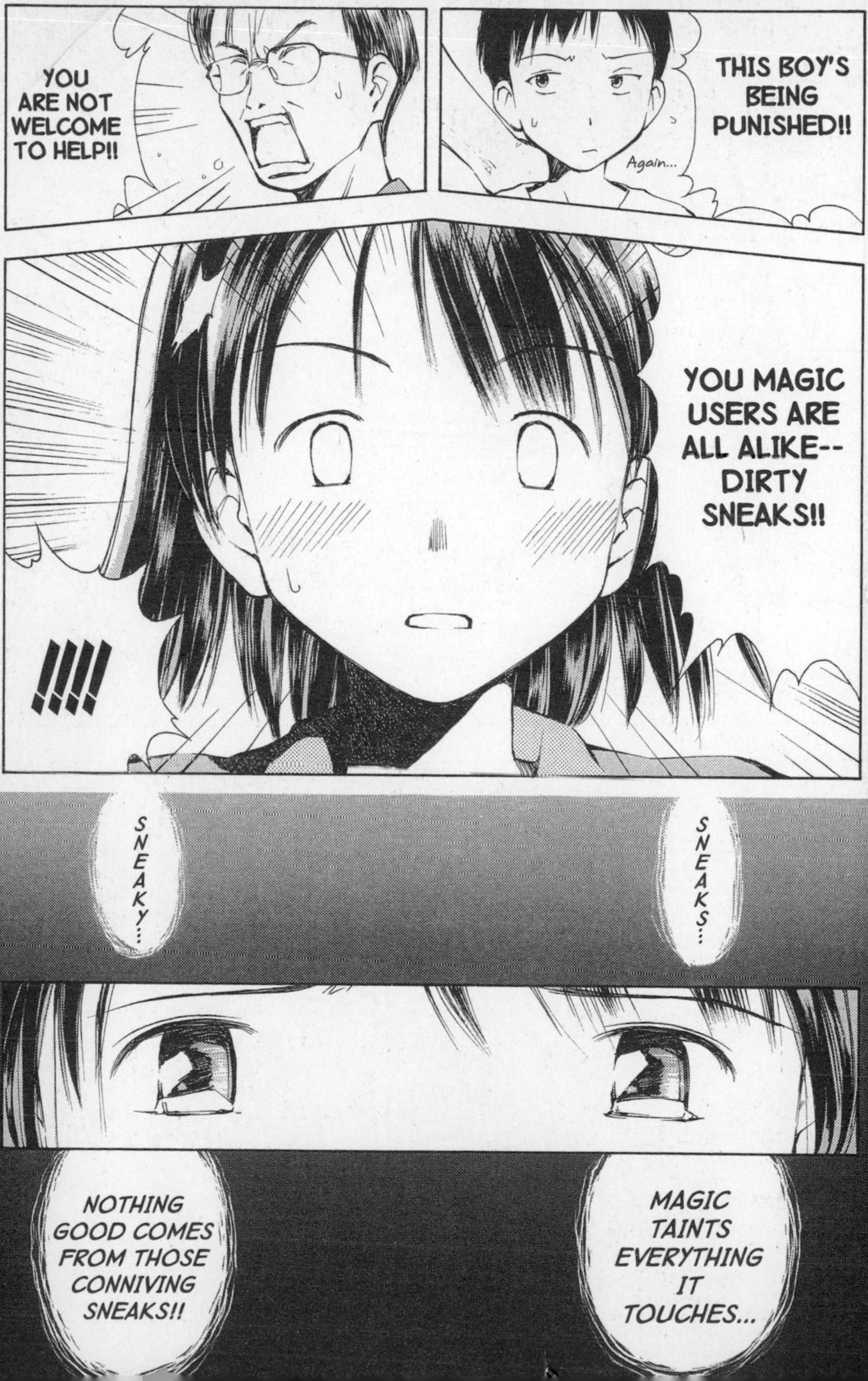
THIS BOY'S BEING PUNISHED!!
Again...
YOU ARE NOT WELCOME TO HELP!!
YOU MAGIC USERS ARE ALL ALIKE-- DIRTY SNEAKS!!
!!!!!
SNEAKS...
SNEAKY...
MAGIC TAINTS EVERYTHING IT TOUCHES...
NOTHING GOOD COMES FROM THOSE CONNIVING SNEAKS!!

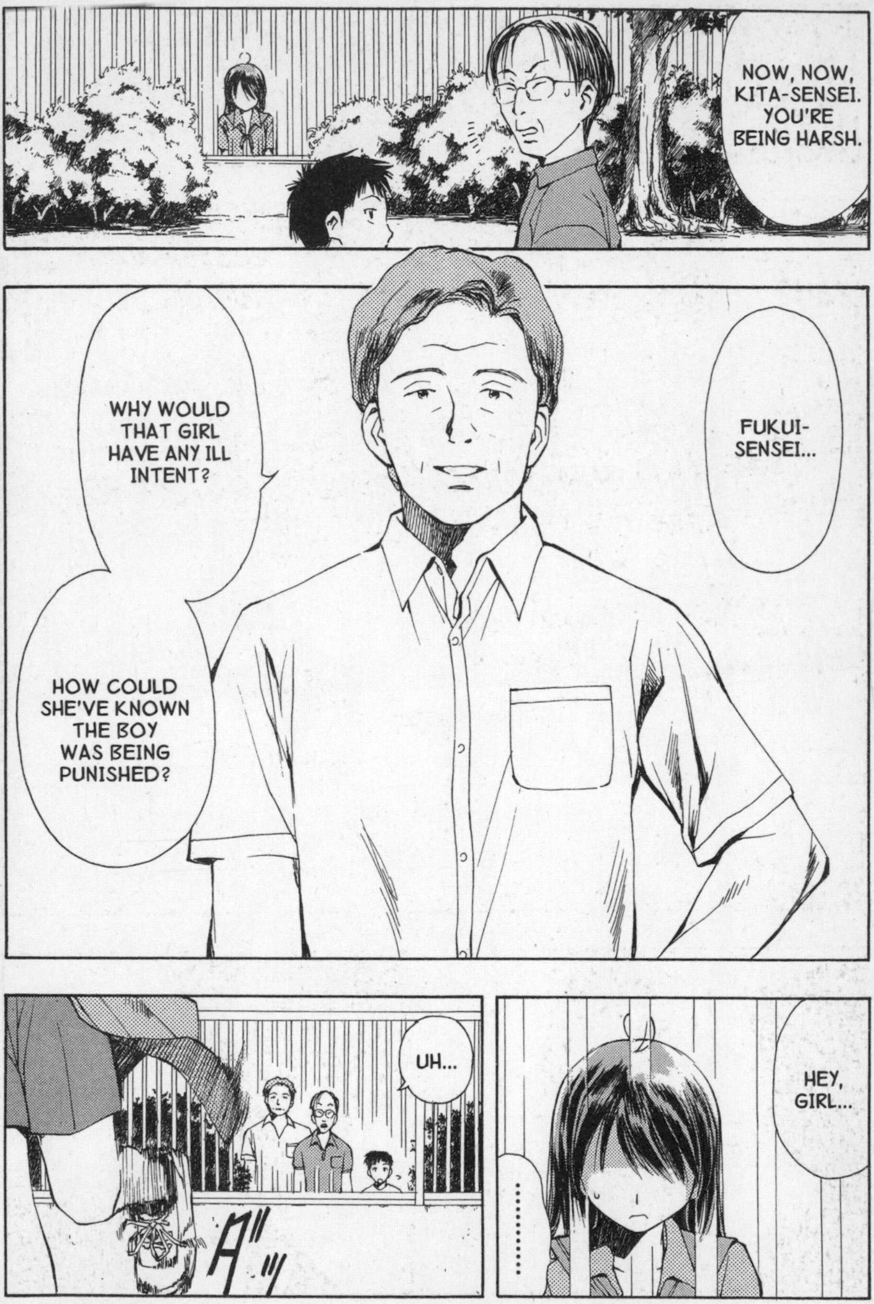
NOW, NOW, KITA-SENSEI. YOU'RE BEING HARSH.
FUKUI-SENSEI...
WHY WOULD THAT GIRL HAVE ANY ILL INTENT?
HOW COULD SHE'VE KNOWN THE BOY WAS BEING PUNISHED?
HEY, GIRL...
......
UH...
ダッ

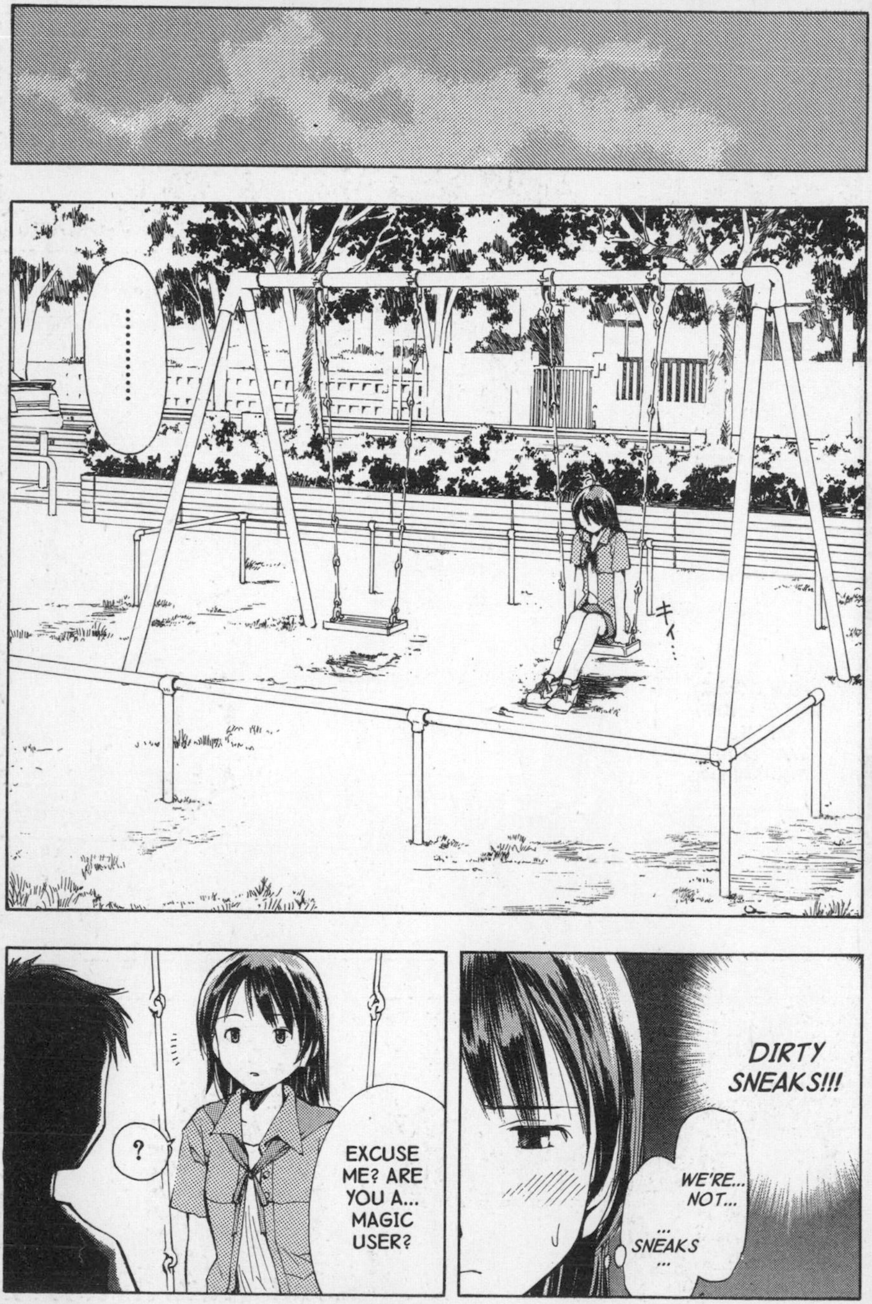
......
キィ…
DIRTY SNEAKS!!!
WE'RE... NOT...
... SNEAKS ...
?
EXCUSE ME? ARE YOU A... MAGIC USER?

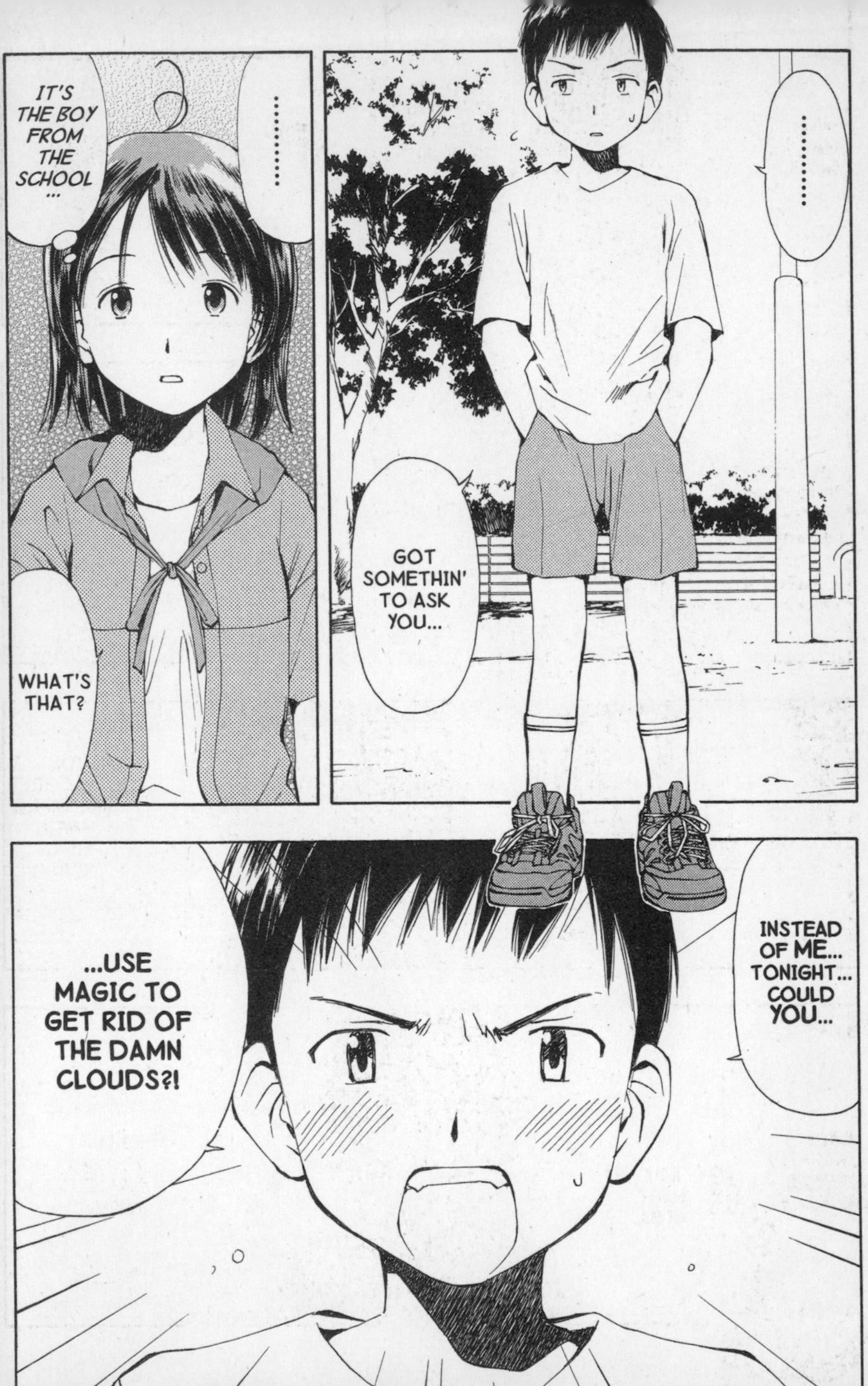
......
GOT SOMETHIN' TO ASK YOU...
IT'S THE BOY FROM THE SCHOOL...
......
WHAT'S THAT?
INSTEAD OF ME... TONIGHT... COULD YOU...
...USE MAGIC TO GET RID OF THE DAMN CLOUDS?!

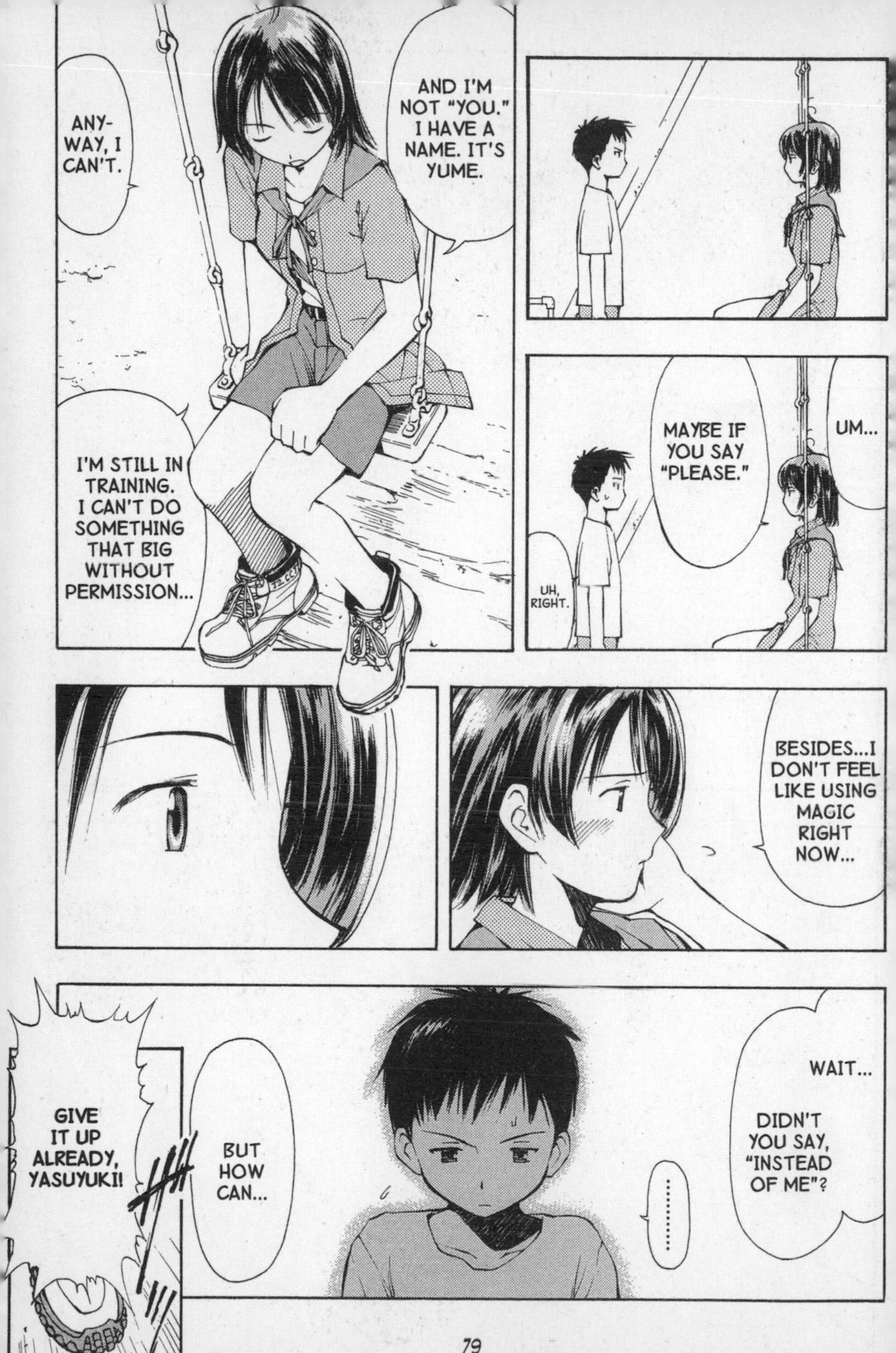
UM...
MAYBE IF YOU SAY "PLEASE."
UH, RIGHT.
AND I'M NOT "YOU." I HAVE A NAME. IT'S YUME.
ANY-WAY, I CAN'T.
I'M STILL IN TRAINING. I CAN'T DO SOMETHING THAT BIG WITHOUT PERMISSION...
BESIDES...I DON'T FEEL LIKE USING MAGIC RIGHT NOW...
WAIT...
DIDN'T YOU SAY, "INSTEAD OF ME"?
......
BUT HOW CAN...
GIVE IT UP ALREADY, YASUYUKI!

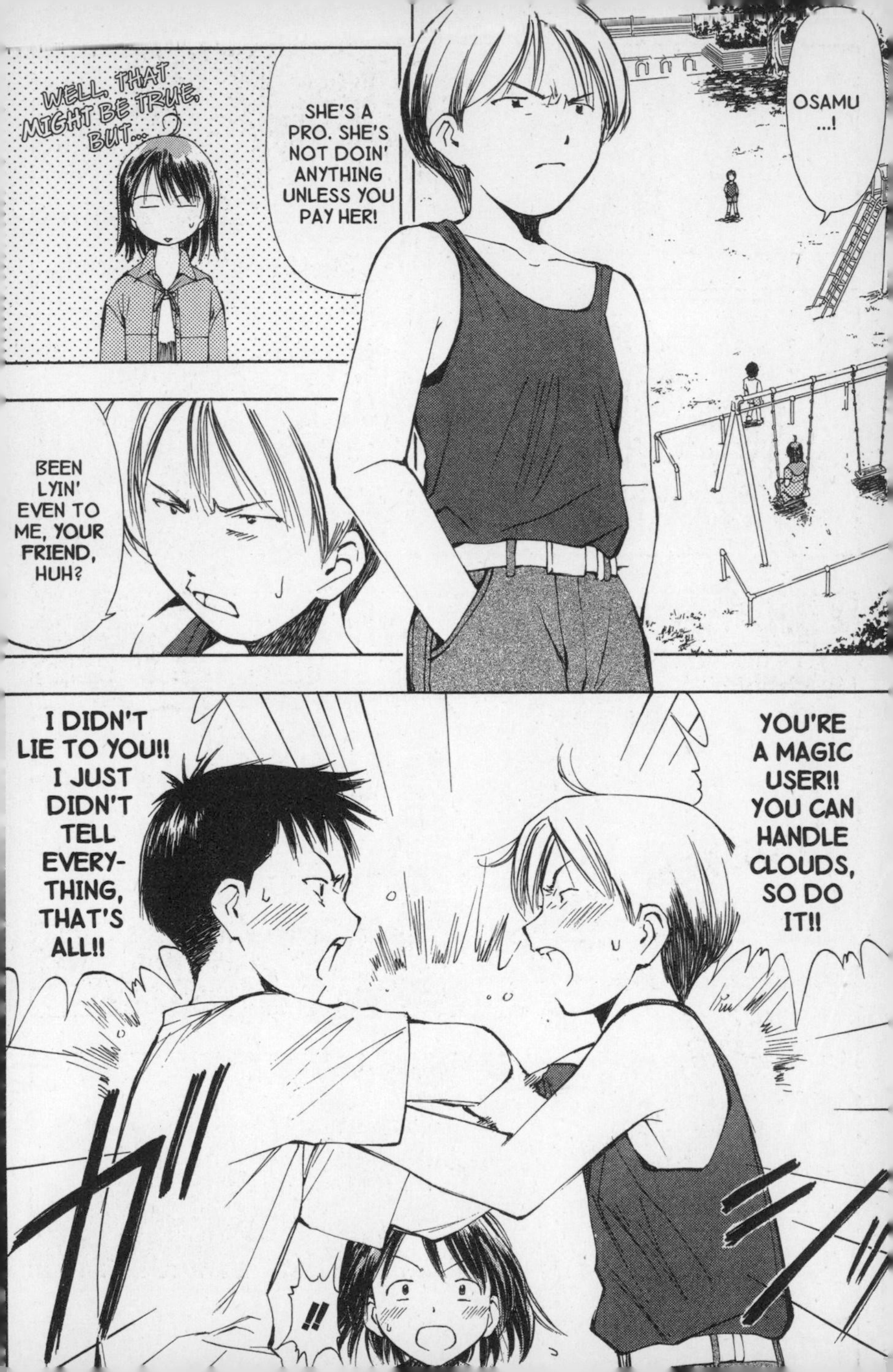
OSAMU ...!
SHE'S A PRO. SHE'S NOT DOIN' ANYTHING UNLESS YOU PAY HER!
WELL, THAT MIGHT BE TRUE, BUT...
BEEN LYIN' EVEN TO ME, YOUR FRIEND, HUH?
YOU'RE A MAGIC USER!! YOU CAN HANDLE CLOUDS, SO DO IT!!
I DIDN'T LIE TO YOU!! I JUST DIDN'T TELL EVERY-THING, THAT'S ALL!!
!!

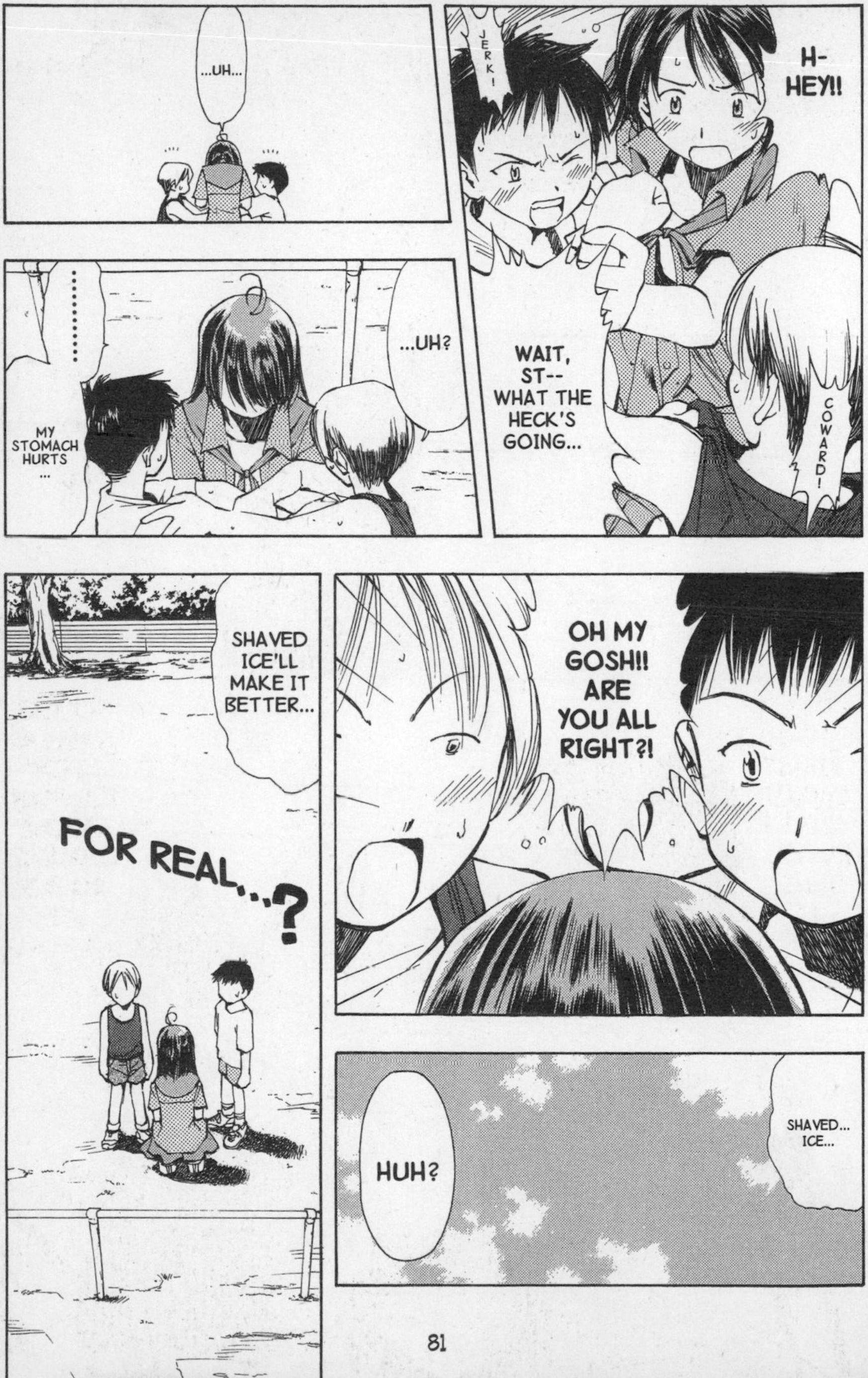
H-HEY!!
JERK!
COWARD!
WAIT, ST-- WHAT THE HECK'S GOING...
...UH...
...UH?
......
MY STOMACH HURTS ...
OH MY GOSH!! ARE YOU ALL RIGHT?!
SHAVED... ICE...
HUH?
SHAVED ICE'LL MAKE IT BETTER...
FOR REAL...?

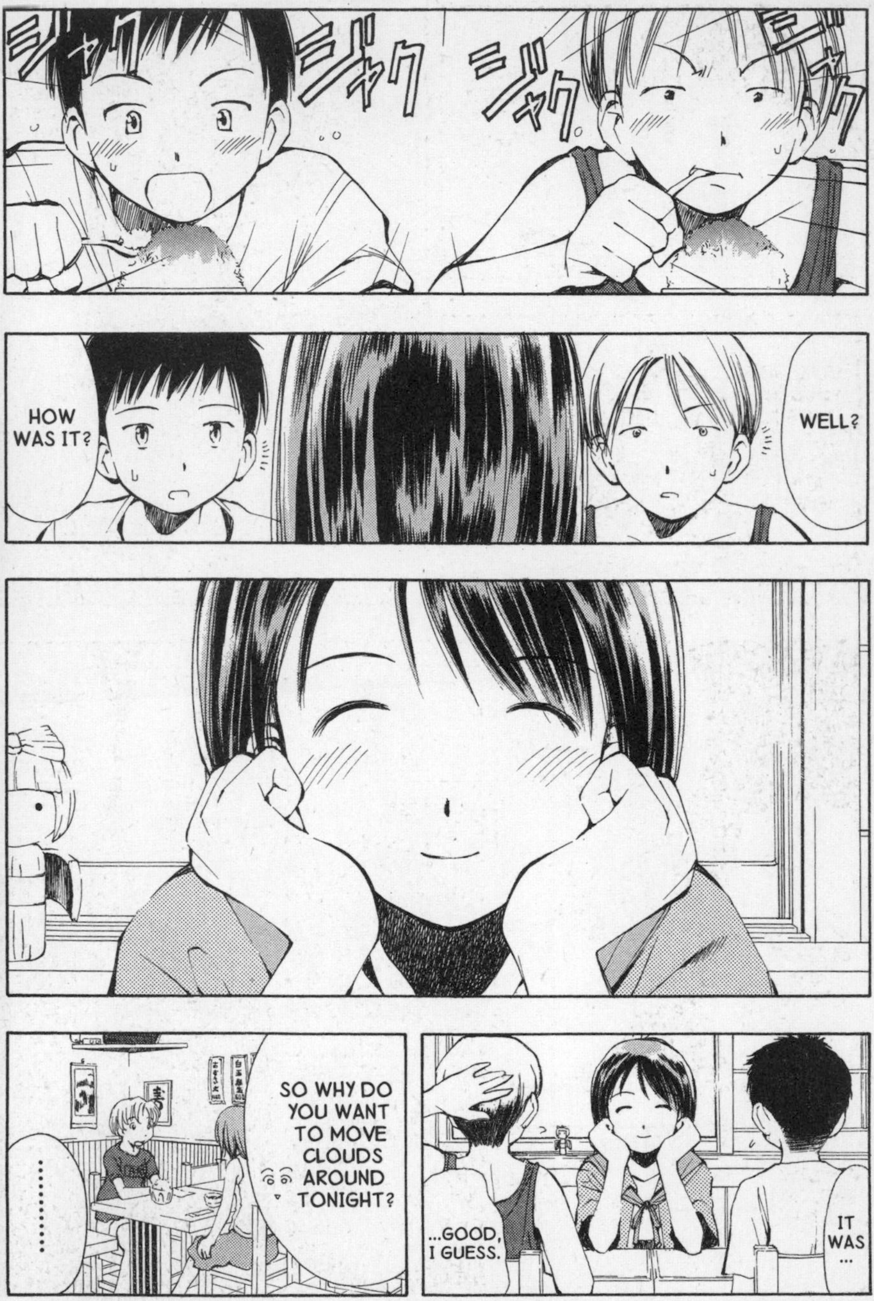
ジャク
ジャク
ジャク
ジャク
WELL?
HOW WAS IT?
IT WAS ...
...GOOD, I GUESS.
SO WHY DO YOU WANT TO MOVE CLOUDS AROUND TONIGHT?
....

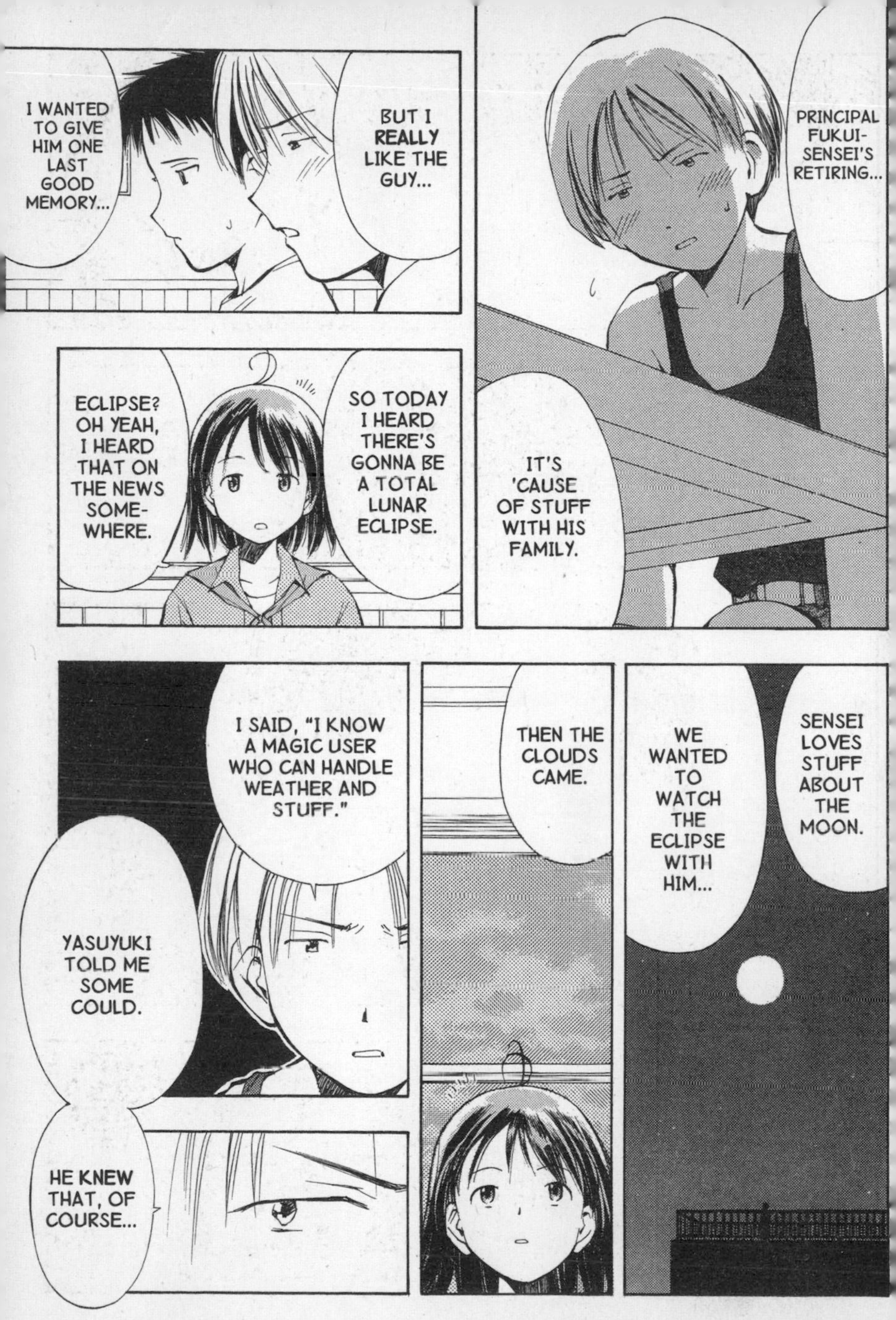
PRINCIPAL FUKUI-SENSEI'S RETIRING...
IT'S 'CAUSE OF STUFF WITH HIS FAMILY.
BUT I **REALLY** LIKE THE GUY...
I WANTED TO GIVE HIM ONE LAST GOOD MEMORY...
SO TODAY I HEARD THERE'S GONNA BE A TOTAL LUNAR ECLIPSE.
ECLIPSE? OH YEAH, I HEARD THAT ON THE NEWS SOMEWHERE.
SENSEI LOVES STUFF ABOUT THE MOON.
WE WANTED TO WATCH THE ECLIPSE WITH HIM...
THEN THE CLOUDS CAME.
I SAID, "I KNOW A MAGIC USER WHO CAN HANDLE WEATHER AND STUFF."
YASUYUKI TOLD ME SOME COULD.
HE KNEW THAT, OF COURSE...

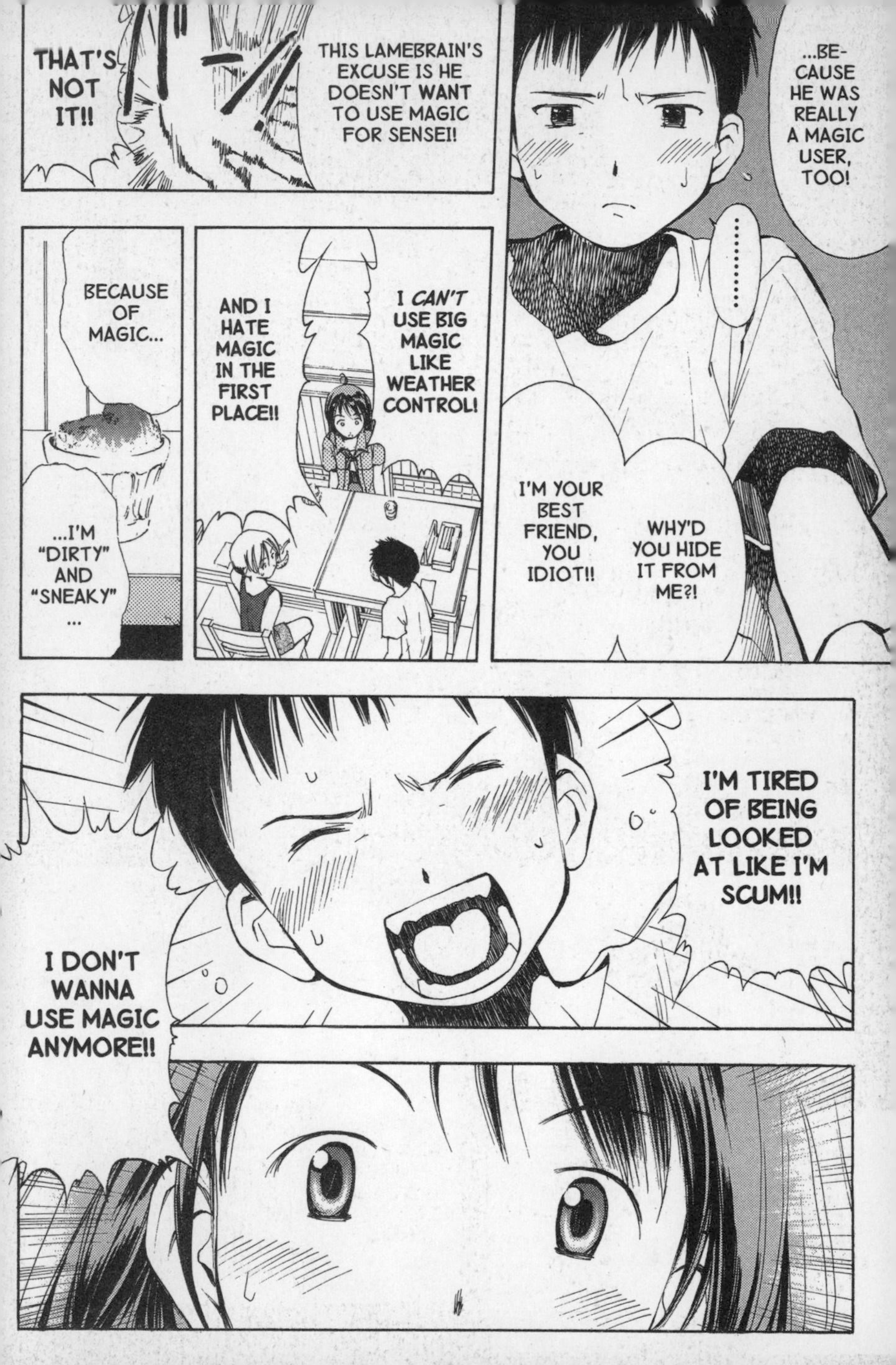
...BE-CAUSE HE WAS REALLY A MAGIC USER, TOO!
......
WHY'D YOU HIDE IT FROM ME?!
I'M YOUR BEST FRIEND, YOU IDIOT!!
THIS LAMEBRAIN'S EXCUSE IS HE DOESN'T WANT TO USE MAGIC FOR SENSEI!
THAT'S NOT IT!!
I *CAN'T* USE BIG MAGIC LIKE WEATHER CONTROL!
AND I HATE MAGIC IN THE FIRST PLACE!!
BECAUSE OF MAGIC...
...I'M "DIRTY" AND "SNEAKY" ...
I'M TIRED OF BEING LOOKED AT LIKE I'M SCUM!!
I DON'T WANNA USE MAGIC ANYMORE!!

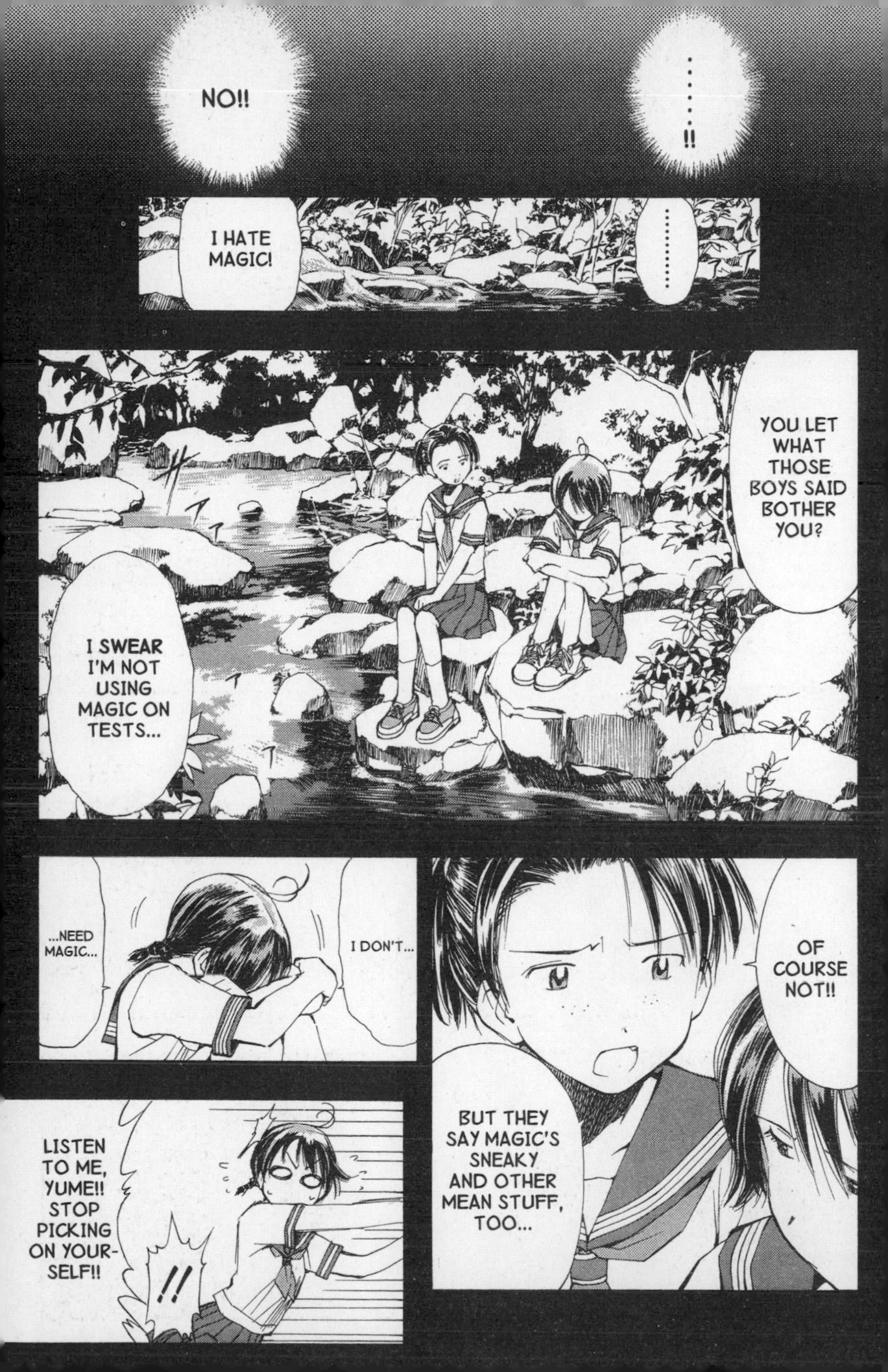
......!!
NO!!
......
I HATE MAGIC!
YOU LET WHAT THOSE BOYS SAID BOTHER YOU?
I SWEAR I'M NOT USING MAGIC ON TESTS...
OF COURSE NOT!!
BUT THEY SAY MAGIC'S SNEAKY AND OTHER MEAN STUFF, TOO...
I DON'T...
...NEED MAGIC...
LISTEN TO ME, YUME!! STOP PICKING ON YOURSELF!!
!!

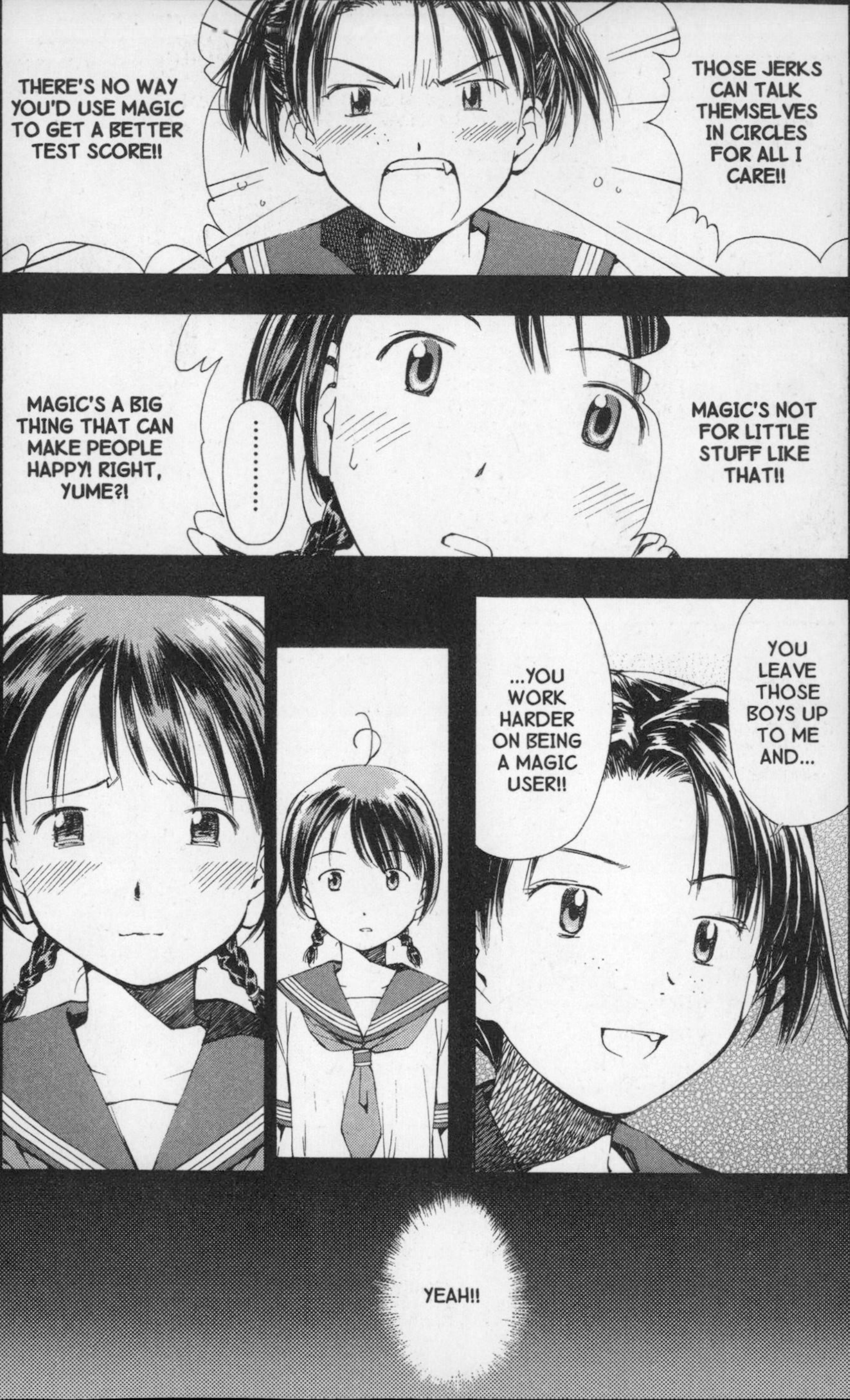
THOSE JERKS CAN TALK THEMSELVES IN CIRCLES FOR ALL I CARE!!
THERE'S NO WAY YOU'D USE MAGIC TO GET A BETTER TEST SCORE!!
MAGIC'S NOT FOR LITTLE STUFF LIKE THAT!!
MAGIC'S A BIG THING THAT CAN MAKE PEOPLE HAPPY! RIGHT, YUME?!
....
YOU LEAVE THOSE BOYS UP TO ME AND...
...YOU WORK HARDER ON BEING A MAGIC USER!!
YEAH!!

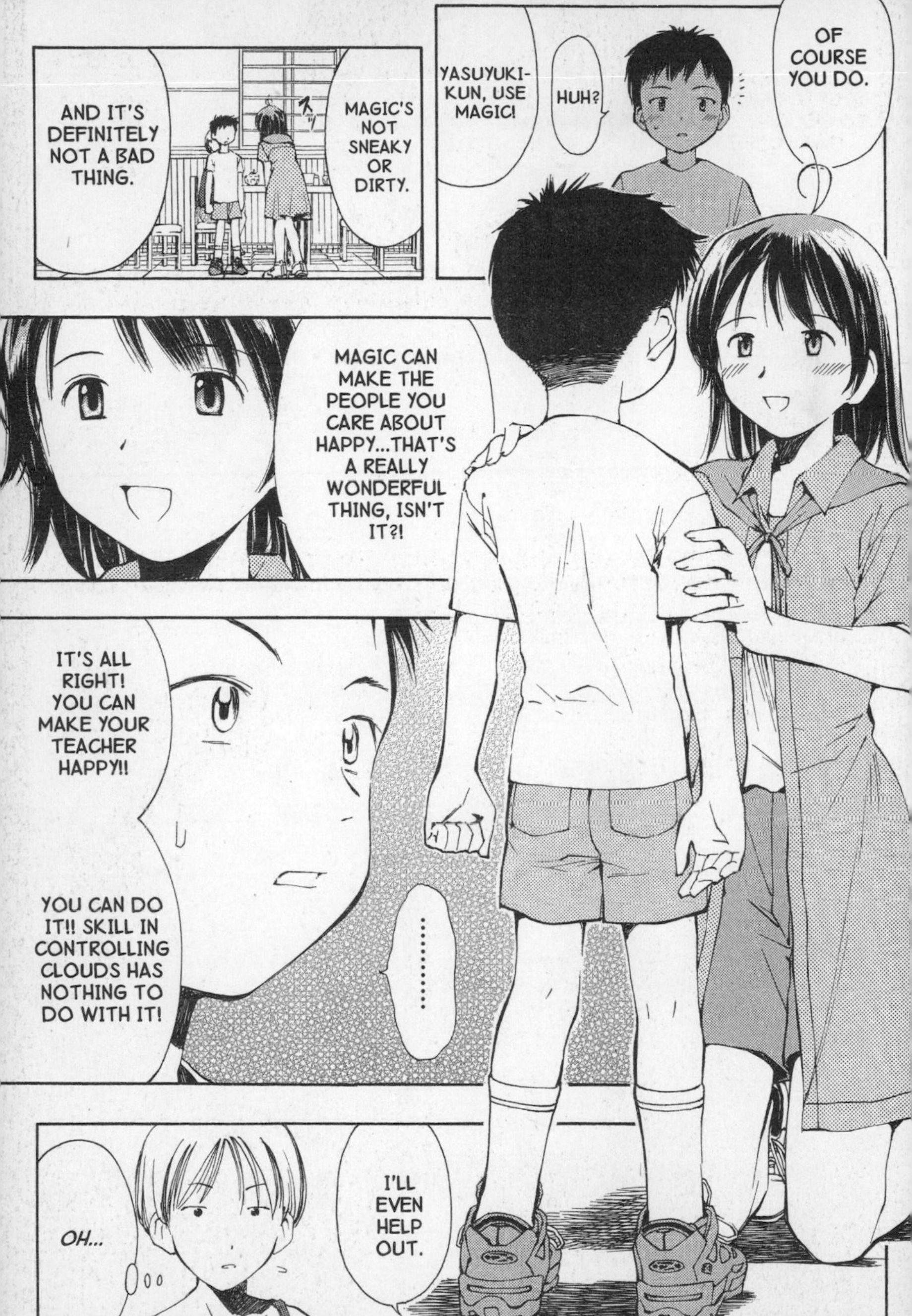
YASUYUKI-KUN, USE MAGIC!
HUH?
OF COURSE YOU DO.
MAGIC'S NOT SNEAKY OR DIRTY.
AND IT'S DEFINITELY NOT A BAD THING.
MAGIC CAN MAKE THE PEOPLE YOU CARE ABOUT HAPPY...THAT'S A REALLY WONDERFUL THING, ISN'T IT?!
IT'S ALL RIGHT! YOU CAN MAKE YOUR TEACHER HAPPY!!
YOU CAN DO IT!! SKILL IN CONTROLLING CLOUDS HAS NOTHING TO DO WITH IT!
......
I'LL EVEN HELP OUT.
OH...

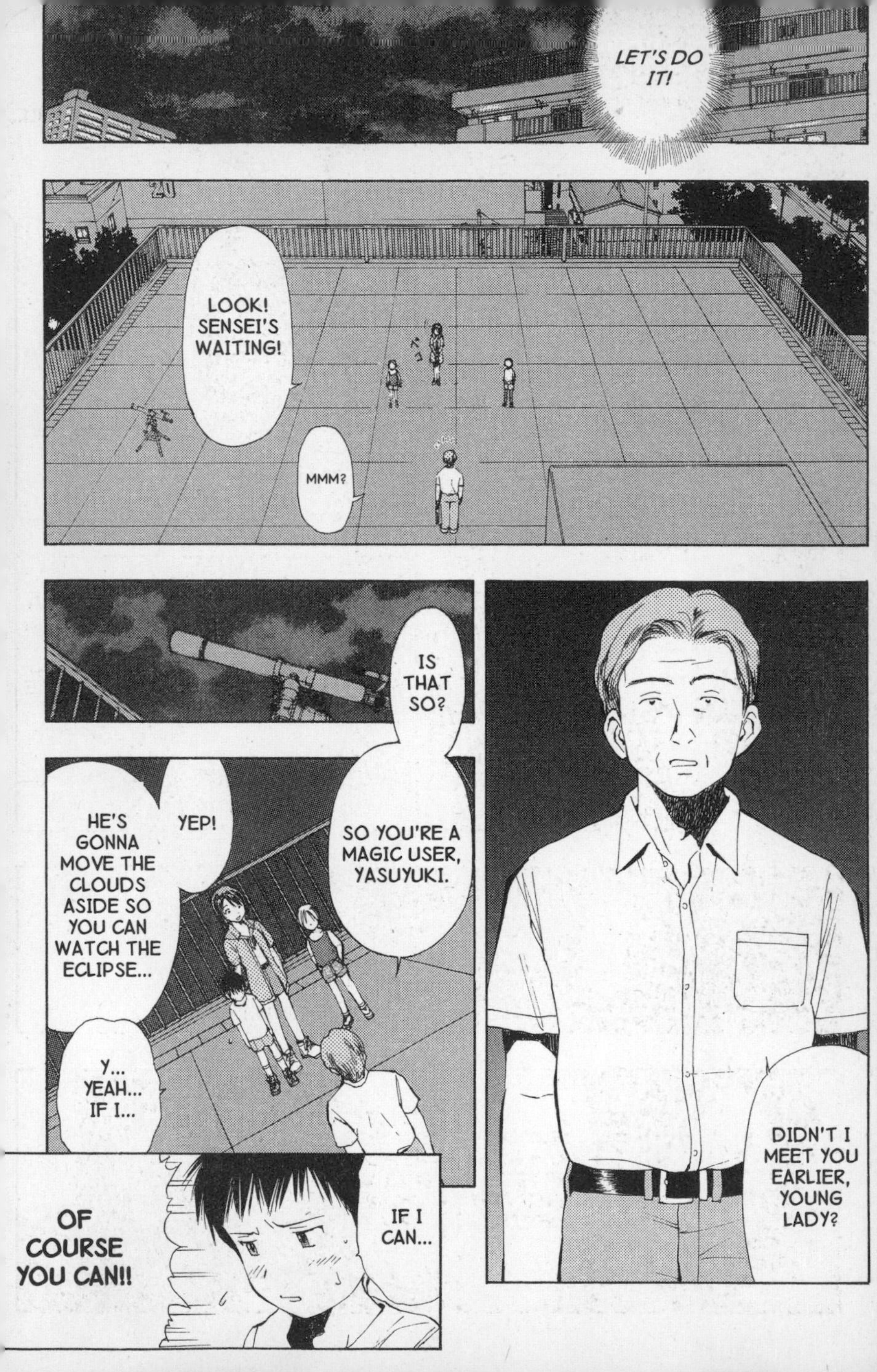
LET'S DO IT!
LOOK! SENSEI'S WAITING!
MMM?
DIDN'T I MEET YOU EARLIER, YOUNG LADY?
IS THAT SO?
SO YOU'RE A MAGIC USER, YASUYUKI.
YEP!
HE'S GONNA MOVE THE CLOUDS ASIDE SO YOU CAN WATCH THE ECLIPSE...
Y... YEAH... IF I...
IF I CAN...
OF COURSE YOU CAN!!

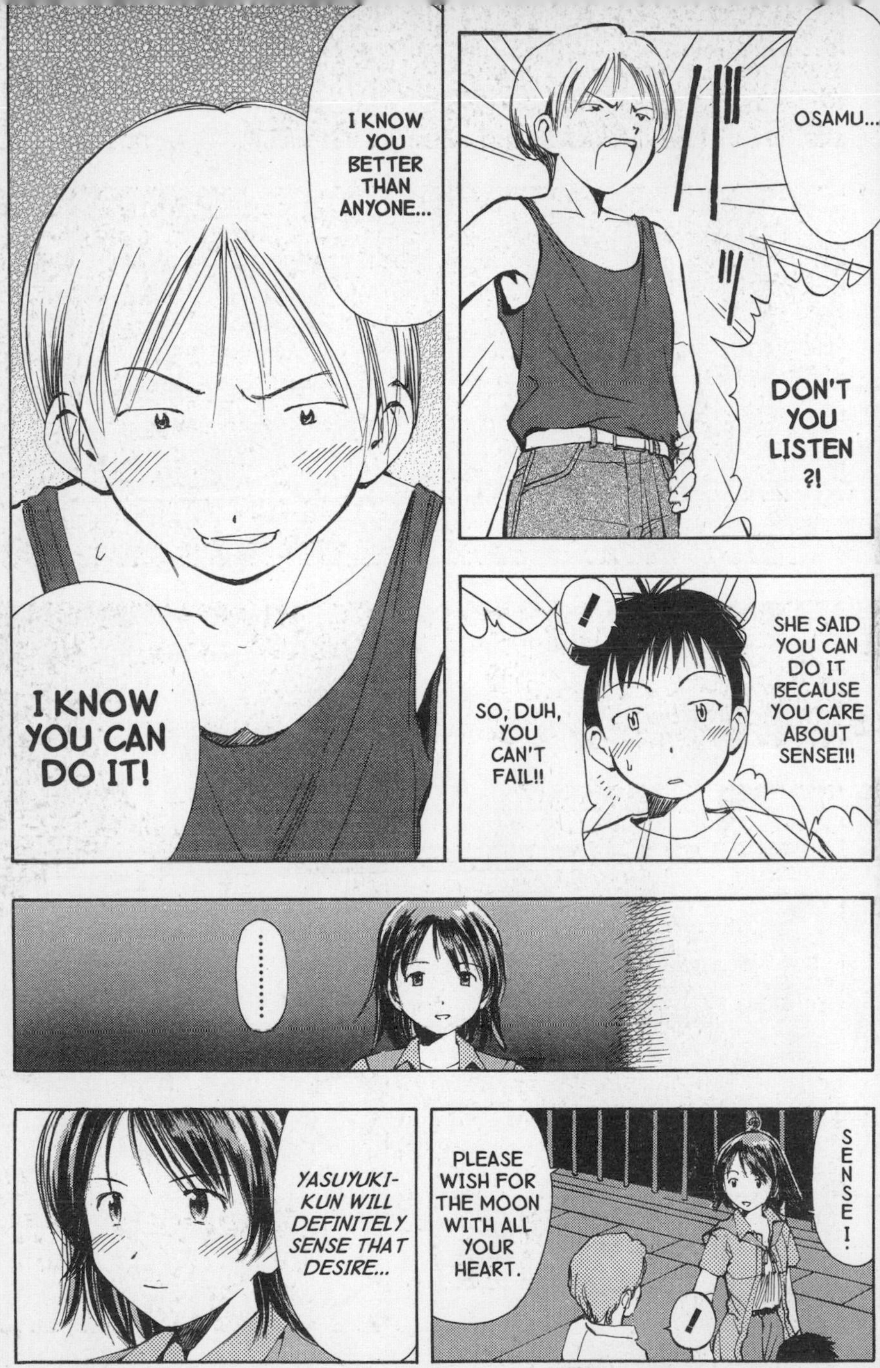
OSAMU...
DON'T YOU LISTEN ?!
SHE SAID YOU CAN DO IT BECAUSE YOU CARE ABOUT SENSEI!!
!
SO, DUH, YOU CAN'T FAIL!!
I KNOW YOU BETTER THAN ANYONE...
I KNOW YOU CAN DO IT!
......
SENSEI!
PLEASE WISH FOR THE MOON WITH ALL YOUR HEART.
!
YASUYUKI-KUN WILL DEFINITELY SENSE THAT DESIRE...

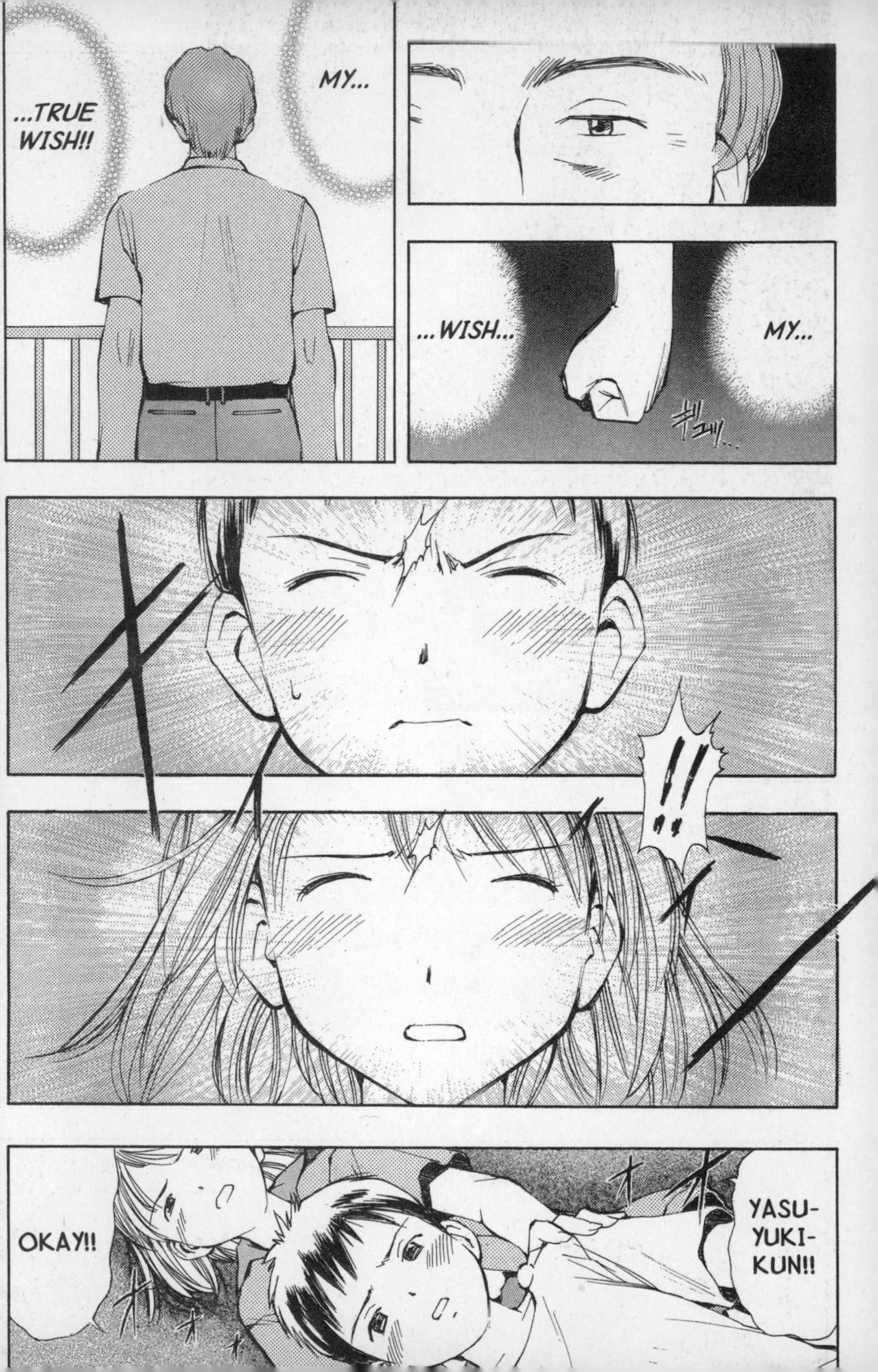
MY...
...WISH...
MY...
...TRUE WISH!!
!!
YASU-YUKI-KUN!!
OKAY!!

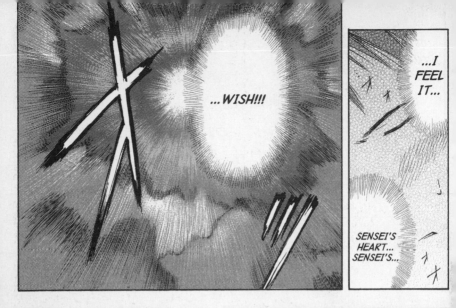

...WISH!!!

...I FEEL IT...

SENSEI'S HEART... SENSEI'S...

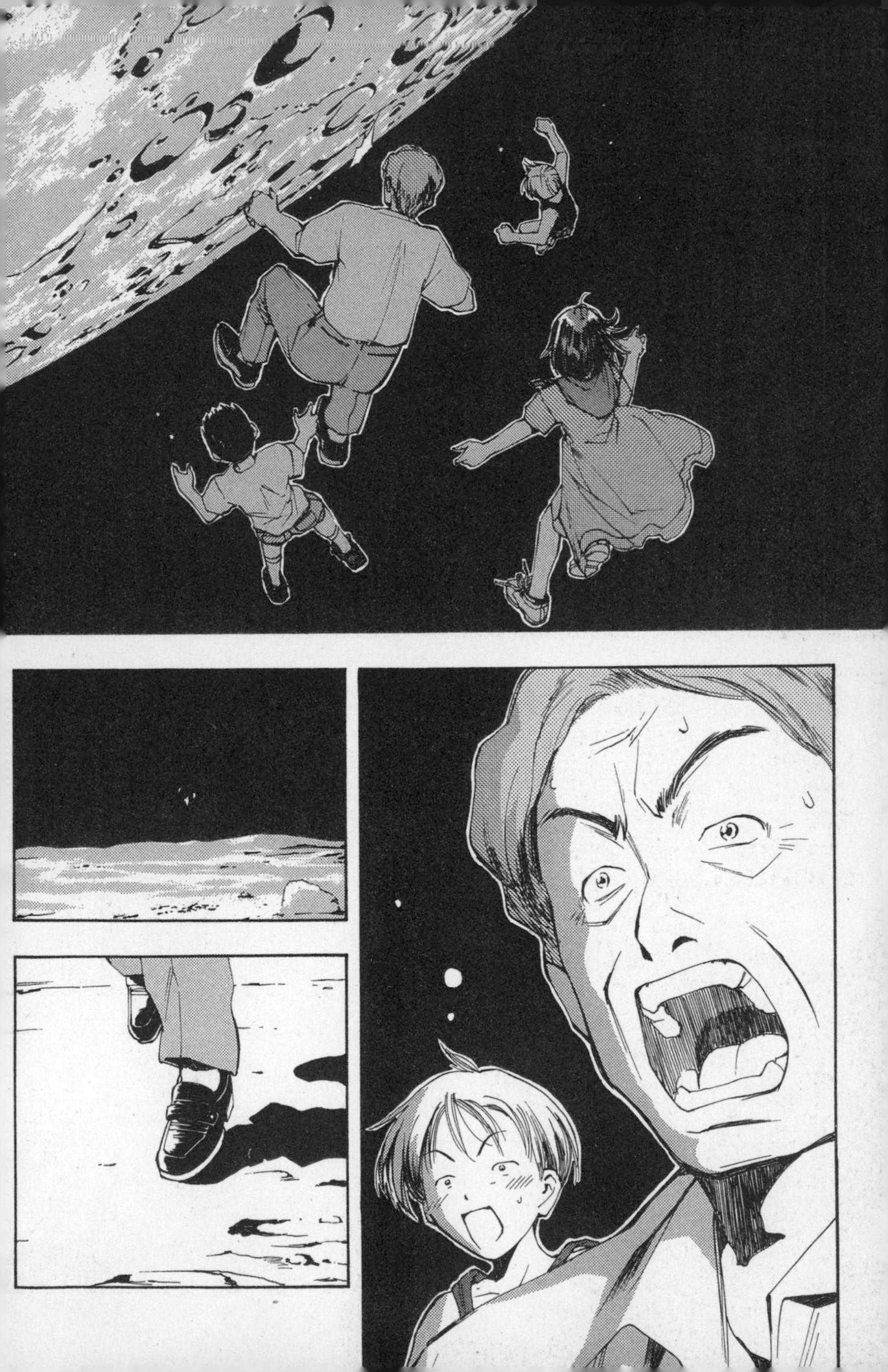

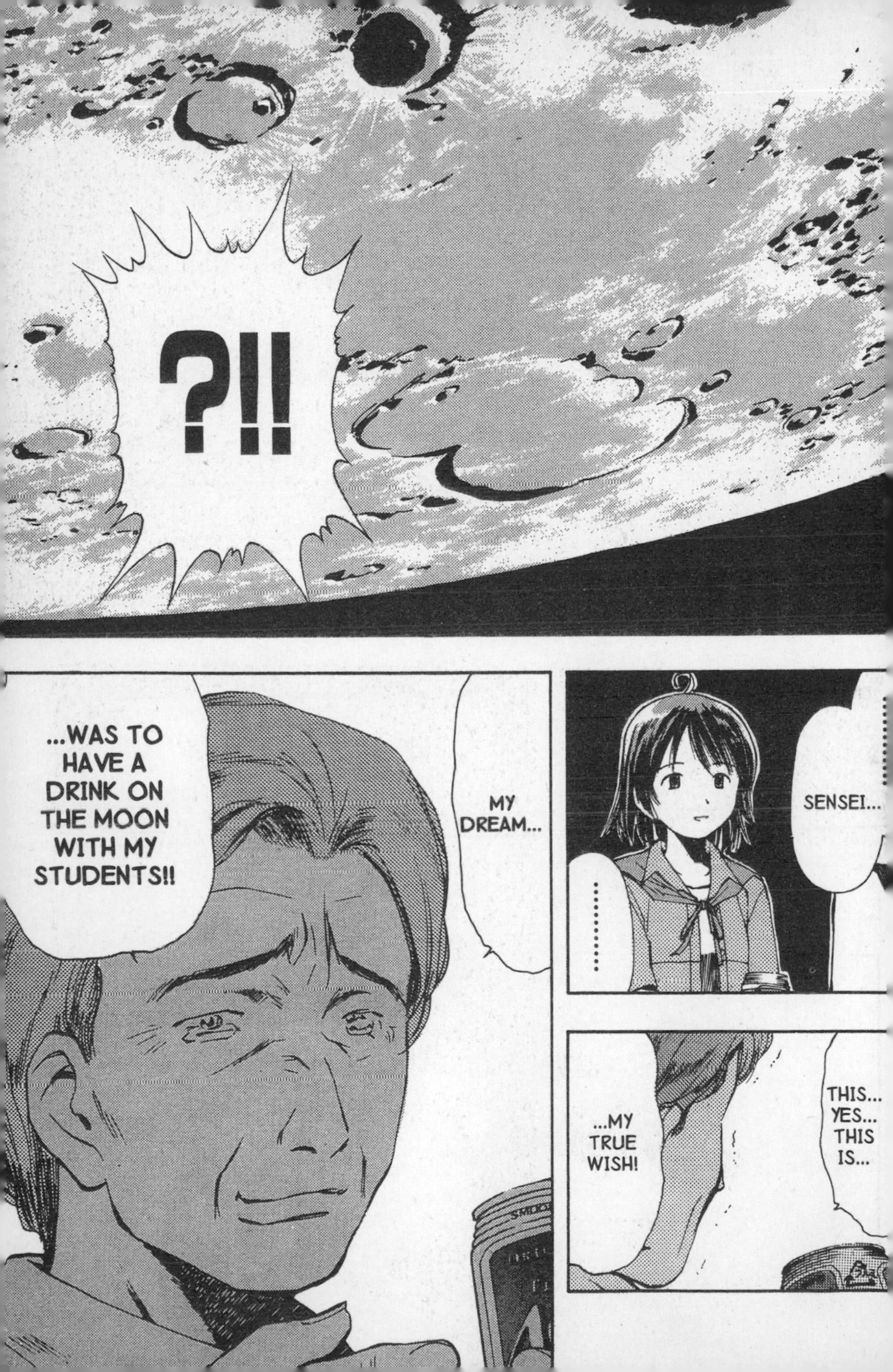
?!!
SENSEI...
......
THIS... YES... THIS IS...
...MY TRUE WISH!
MY DREAM...
...WAS TO HAVE A DRINK ON THE MOON WITH MY STUDENTS!!

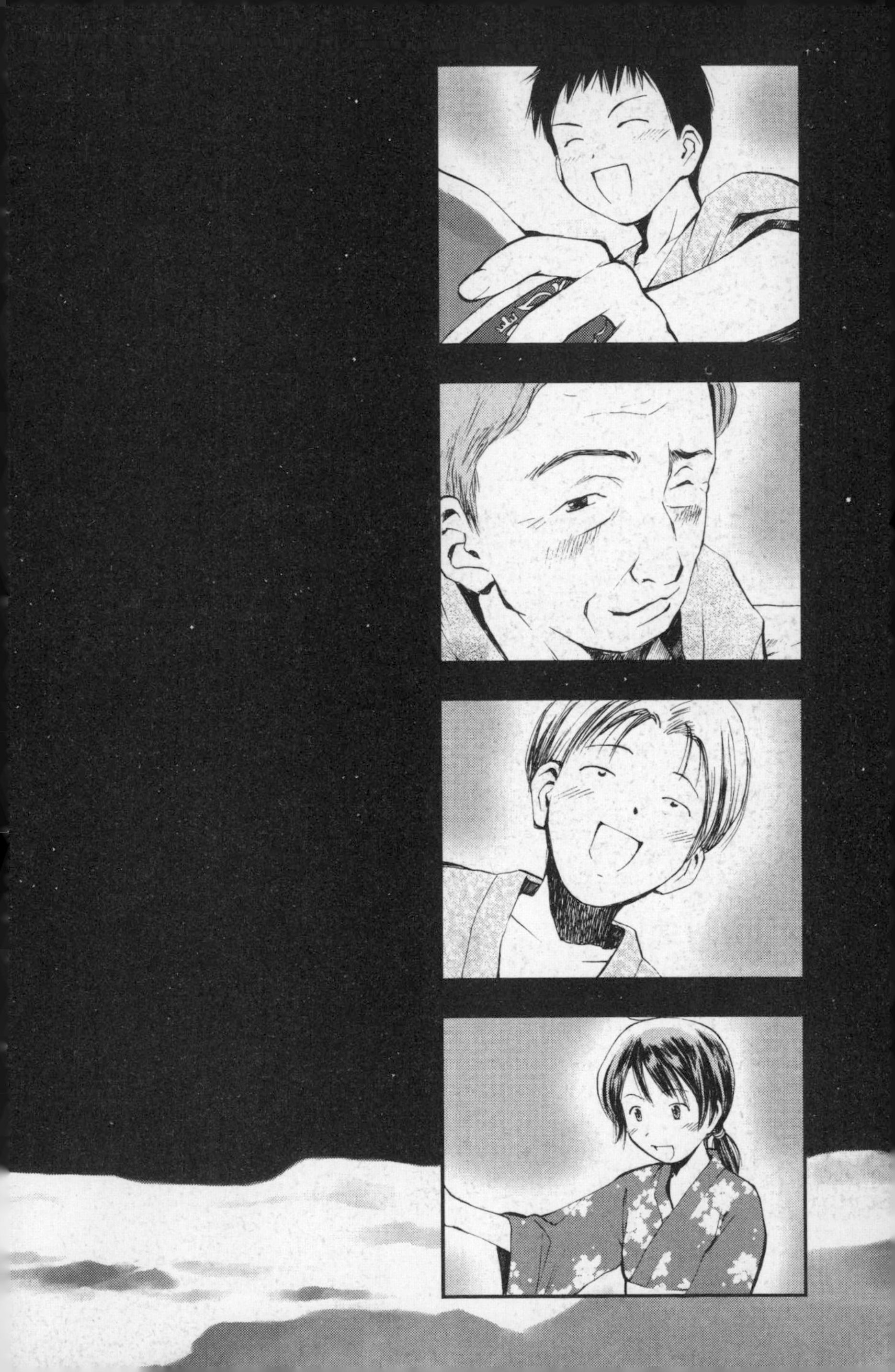

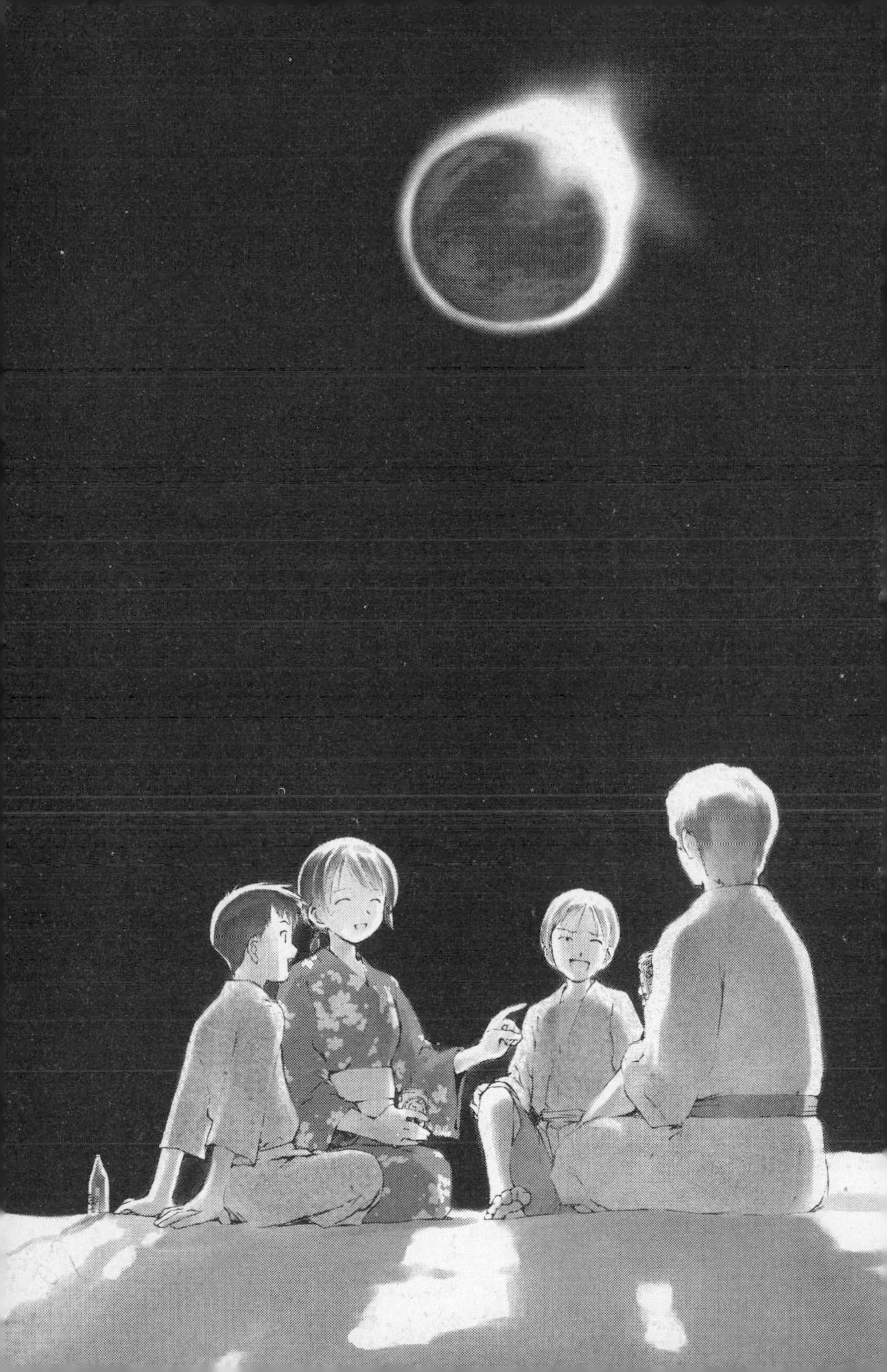

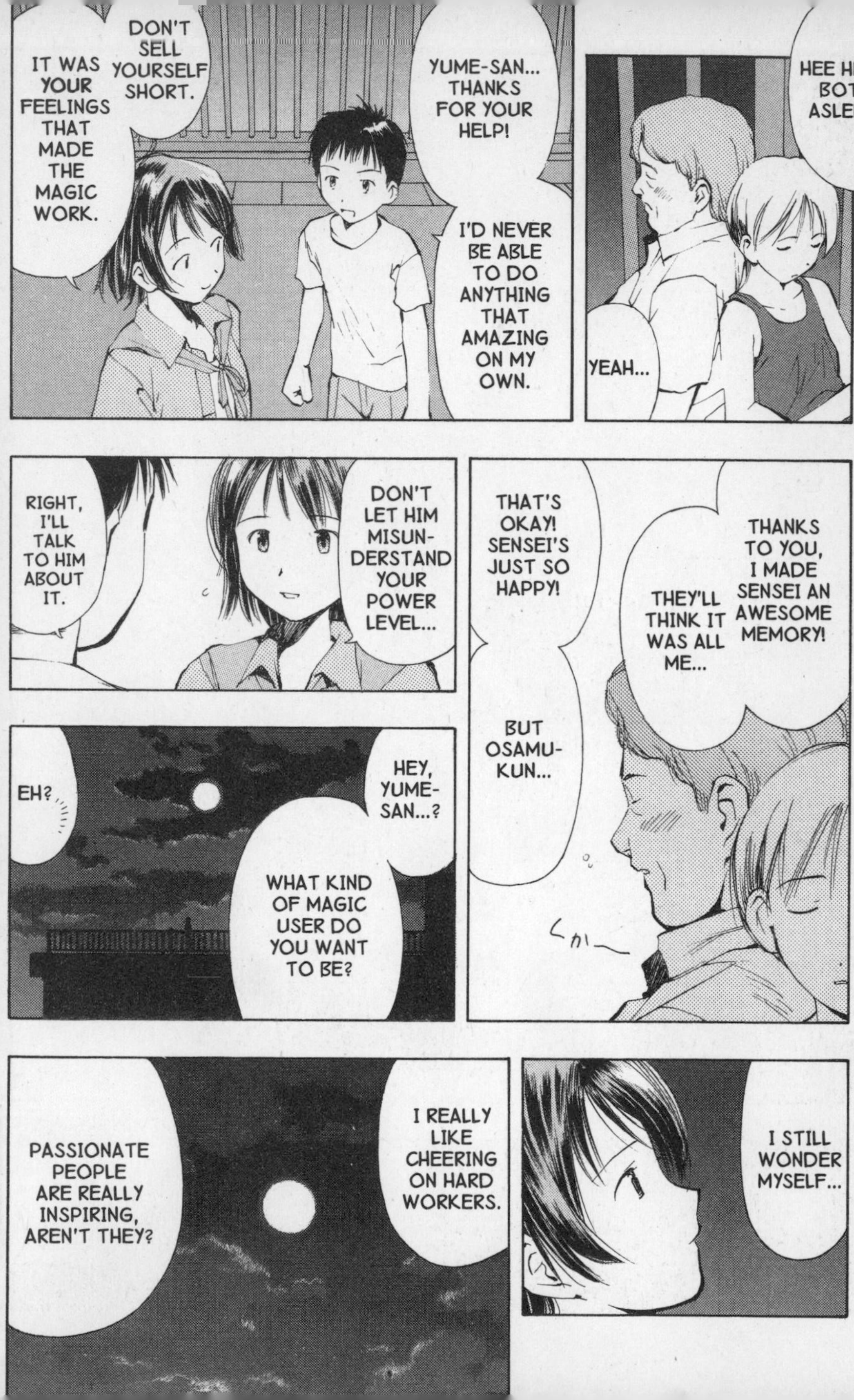
HEE HEE... BOTH ASLEEP.
YEAH...
YUME-SAN... THANKS FOR YOUR HELP!
I'D NEVER BE ABLE TO DO ANYTHING THAT AMAZING ON MY OWN.
DON'T SELL YOURSELF SHORT.
IT WAS YOUR FEELINGS THAT MADE THE MAGIC WORK.
THANKS TO YOU, I MADE SENSEI AN AWESOME MEMORY!
THEY'LL THINK IT WAS ALL ME...
THAT'S OKAY! SENSEI'S JUST SO HAPPY!
BUT OSAMU-KUN...
くかー
DON'T LET HIM MISUNDERSTAND YOUR POWER LEVEL...
RIGHT, I'LL TALK TO HIM ABOUT IT.
HEY, YUME-SAN...?
EH?
WHAT KIND OF MAGIC USER DO YOU WANT TO BE?
I STILL WONDER MYSELF...
I REALLY LIKE CHEERING ON HARD WORKERS.
PASSIONATE PEOPLE ARE REALLY INSPIRING, AREN'T THEY?

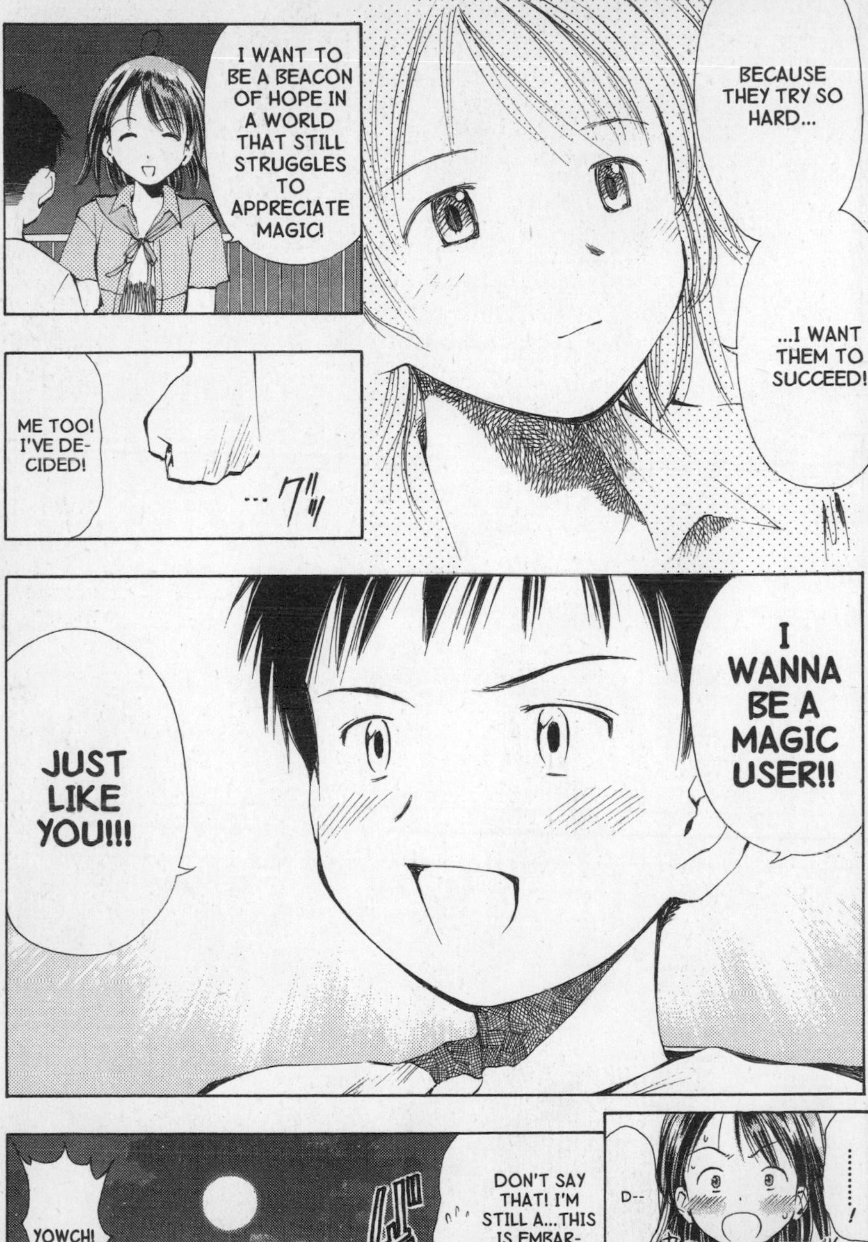
BECAUSE THEY TRY SO HARD...
...I WANT THEM TO SUCCEED!
I WANT TO BE A BEACON OF HOPE IN A WORLD THAT STILL STRUGGLES TO APPRECIATE MAGIC!
ME TOO! I'VE DE-CIDED!
I WANNA BE A MAGIC USER!!
JUST LIKE YOU!!!
......!
D--
DON'T SAY THAT! I'M STILL A...THIS IS EMBAR-RASSING!!
YOWCH!

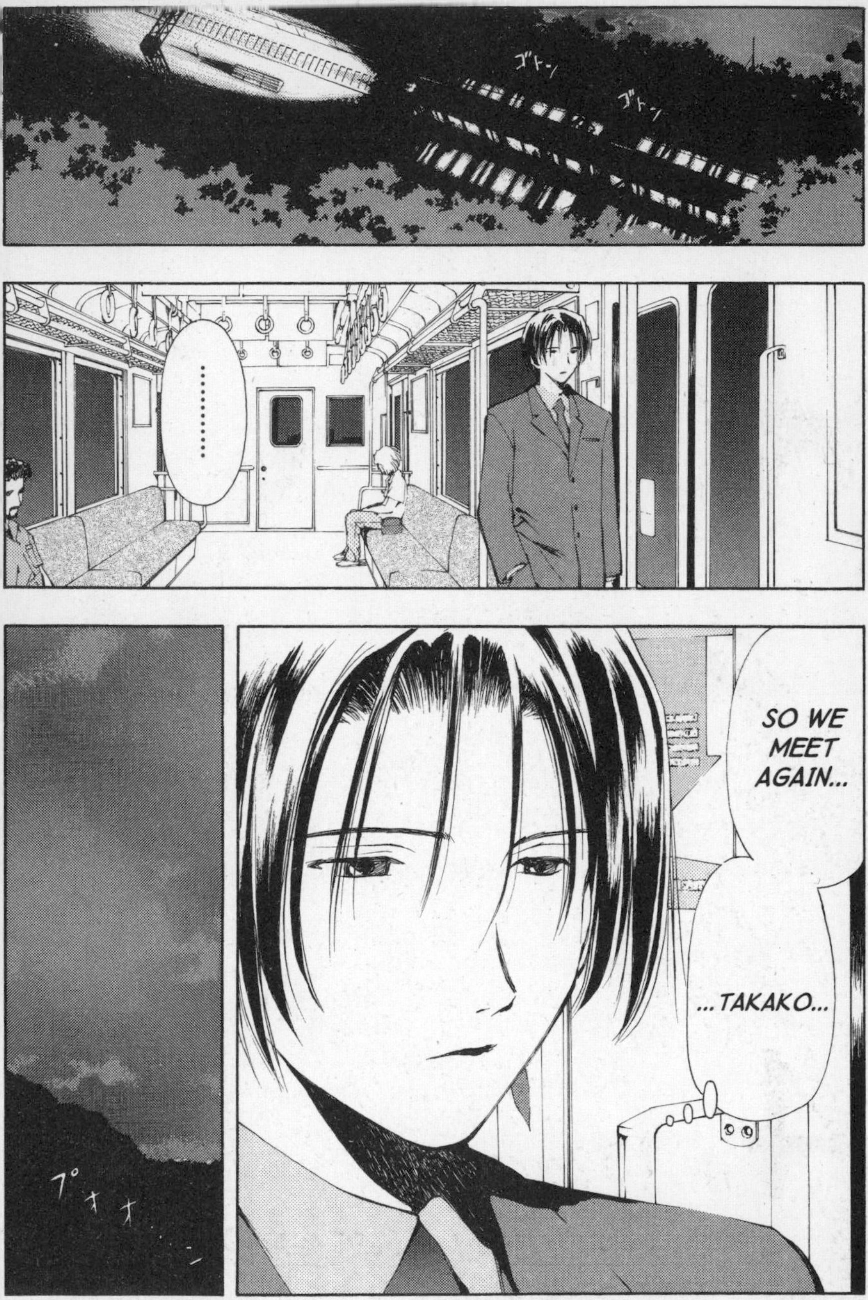
……
SO WE MEET AGAIN...
...TAKAKO...

3rd Dream End

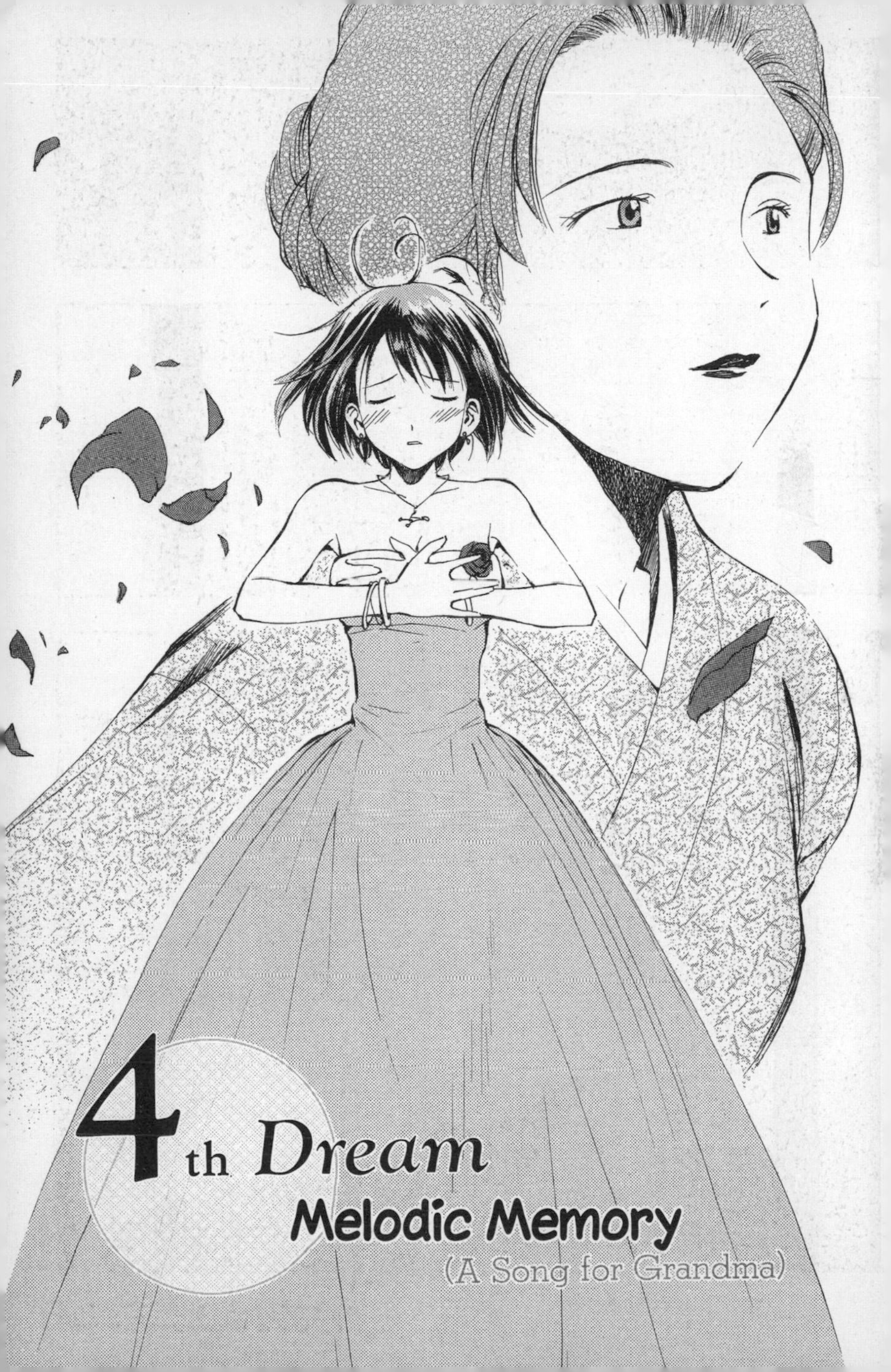
4th Dream
Melodic Memory
(A Song for Grandma)

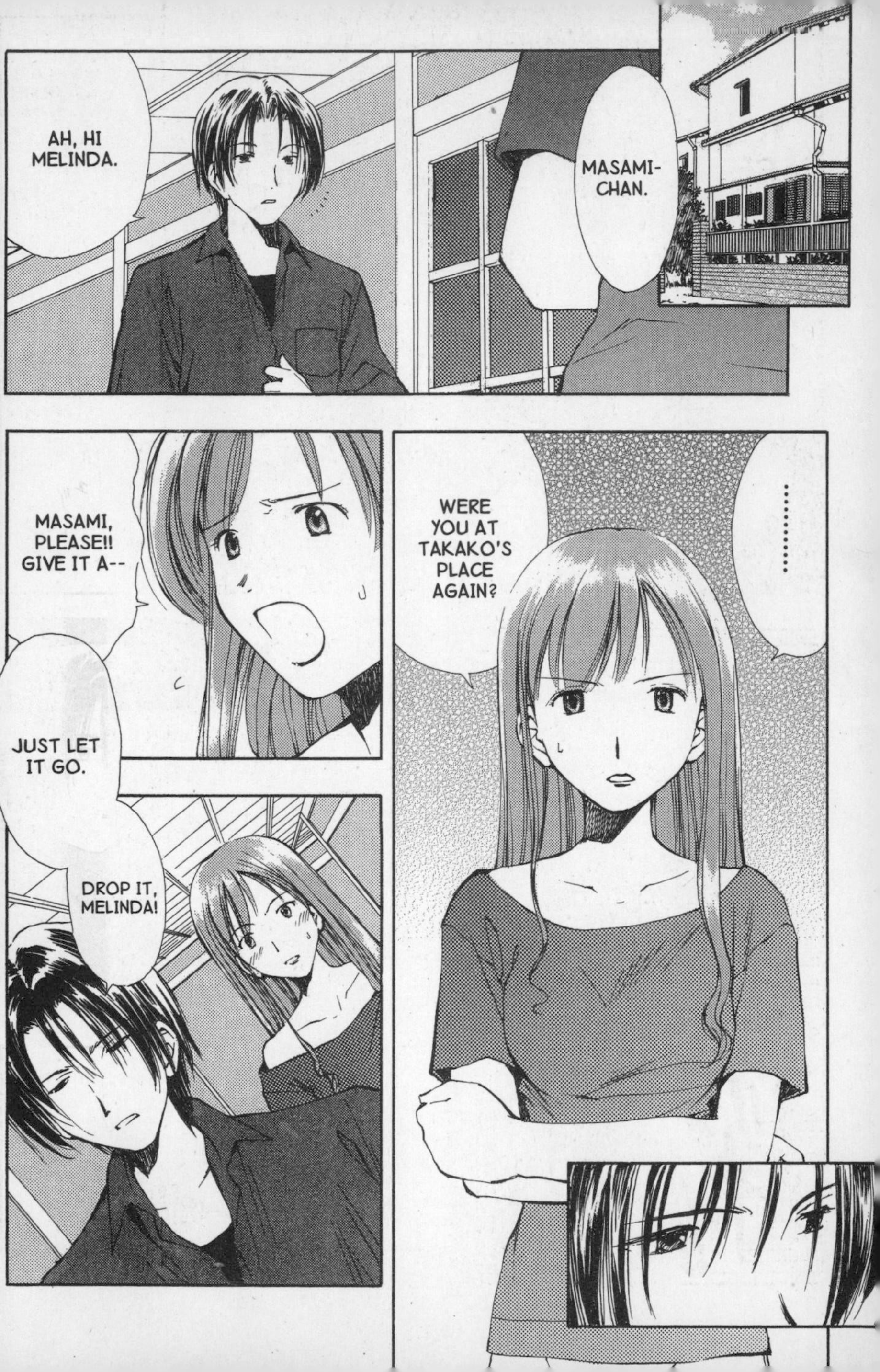
MASAMI-CHAN.
AH, HI MELINDA.
....
WERE YOU AT TAKAKO'S PLACE AGAIN?
MASAMI, PLEASE!! GIVE IT A--
JUST LET IT GO.
DROP IT, MELINDA!

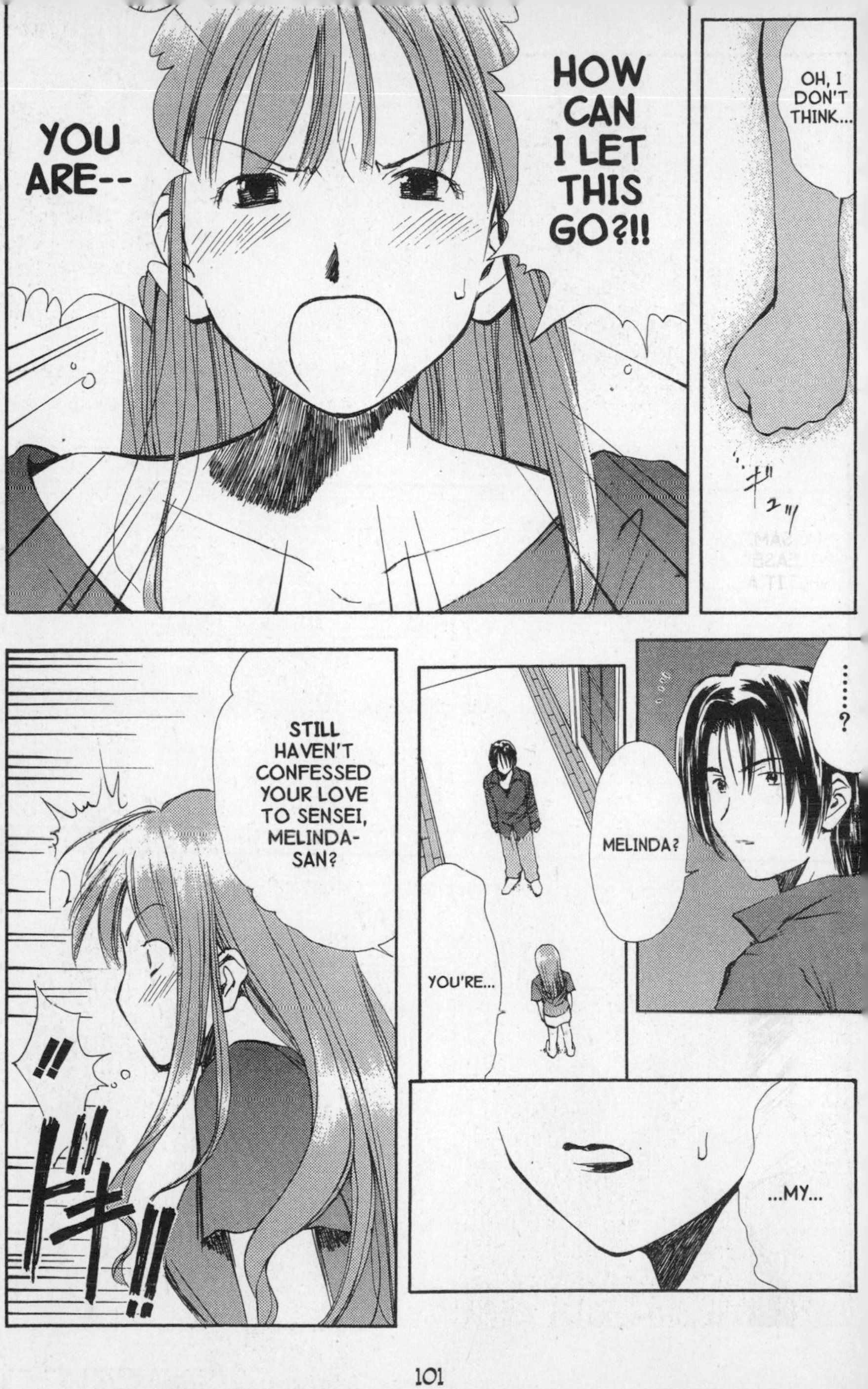
OH, I DON'T THINK...
ギュッ
HOW CAN I LET THIS GO?!!
YOU ARE--
......?
MELINDA?
YOU'RE...
...MY...
STILL HAVEN'T CONFESSED YOUR LOVE TO SENSEI, MELINDA-SAN?
!!
ドキ!!

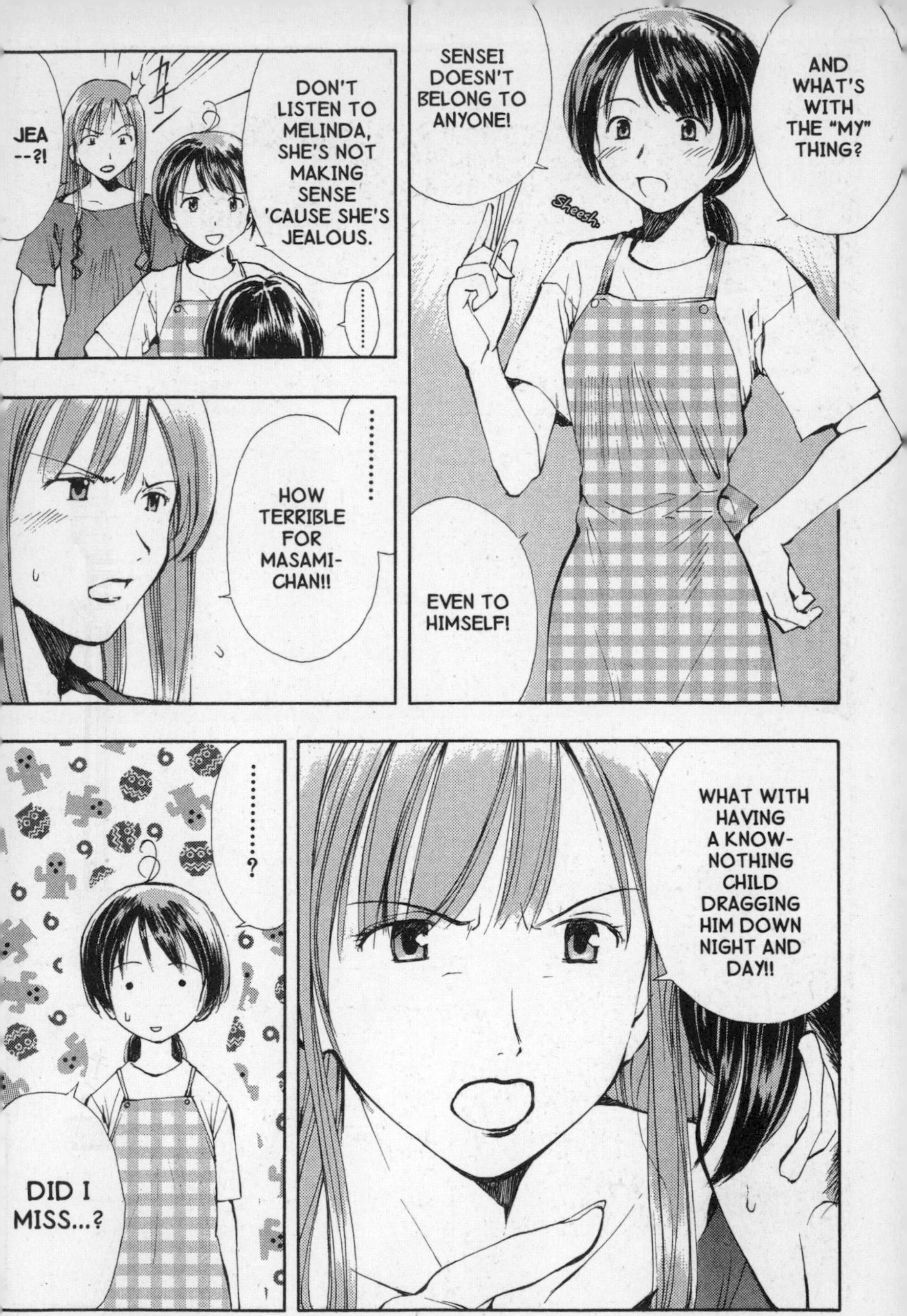
AND WHAT'S WITH THE "MY" THING?
SENSEI DOESN'T BELONG TO ANYONE!
Sheesh,
EVEN TO HIMSELF!
DON'T LISTEN TO MELINDA, SHE'S NOT MAKING SENSE 'CAUSE SHE'S JEALOUS.
......
JEA --?!
......
HOW TERRIBLE FOR MASAMI-CHAN!!
WHAT WITH HAVING A KNOW-NOTHING CHILD DRAGGING HIM DOWN NIGHT AND DAY!!
......?
DID I MISS...?

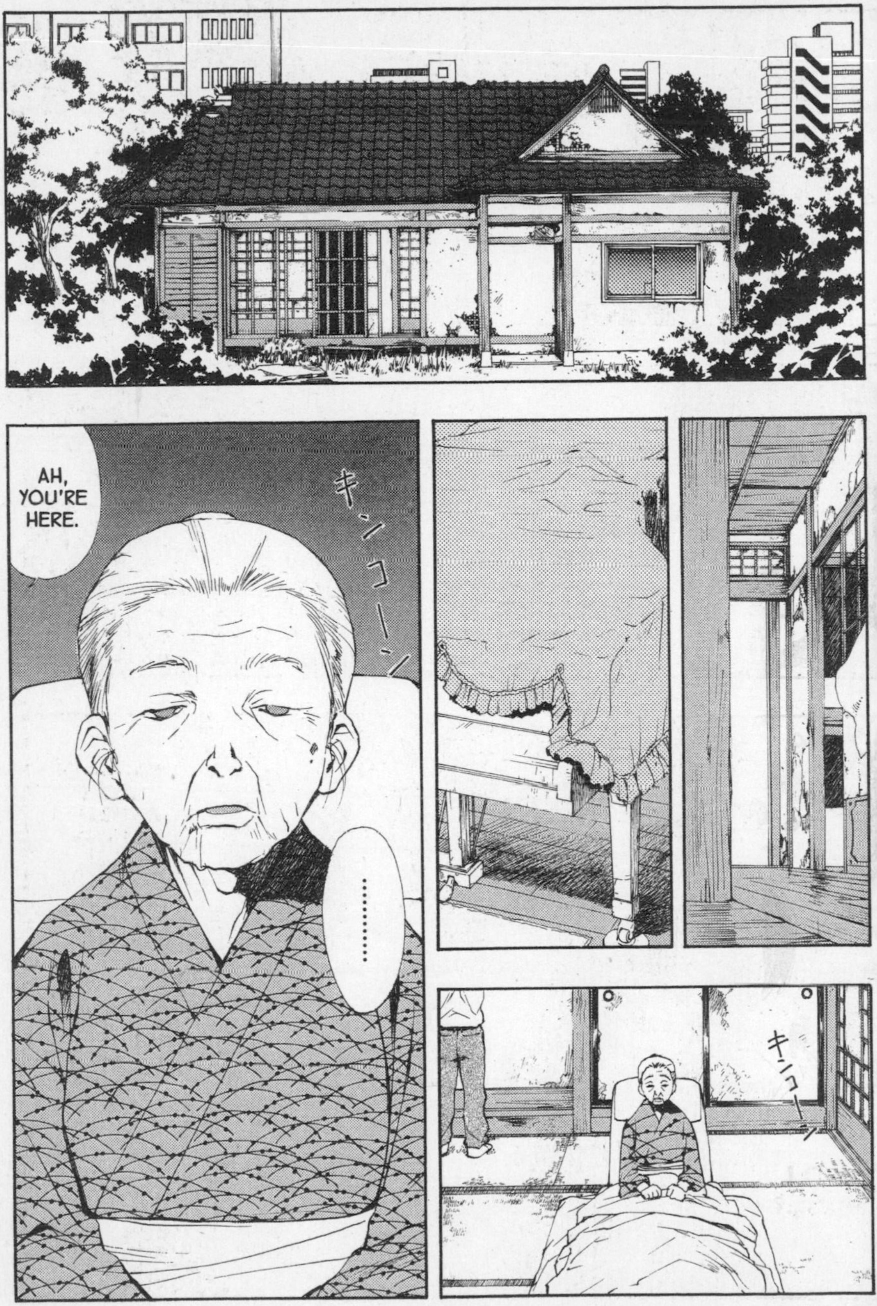
キンコーン
キンコーン
AH, YOU'RE HERE.
……

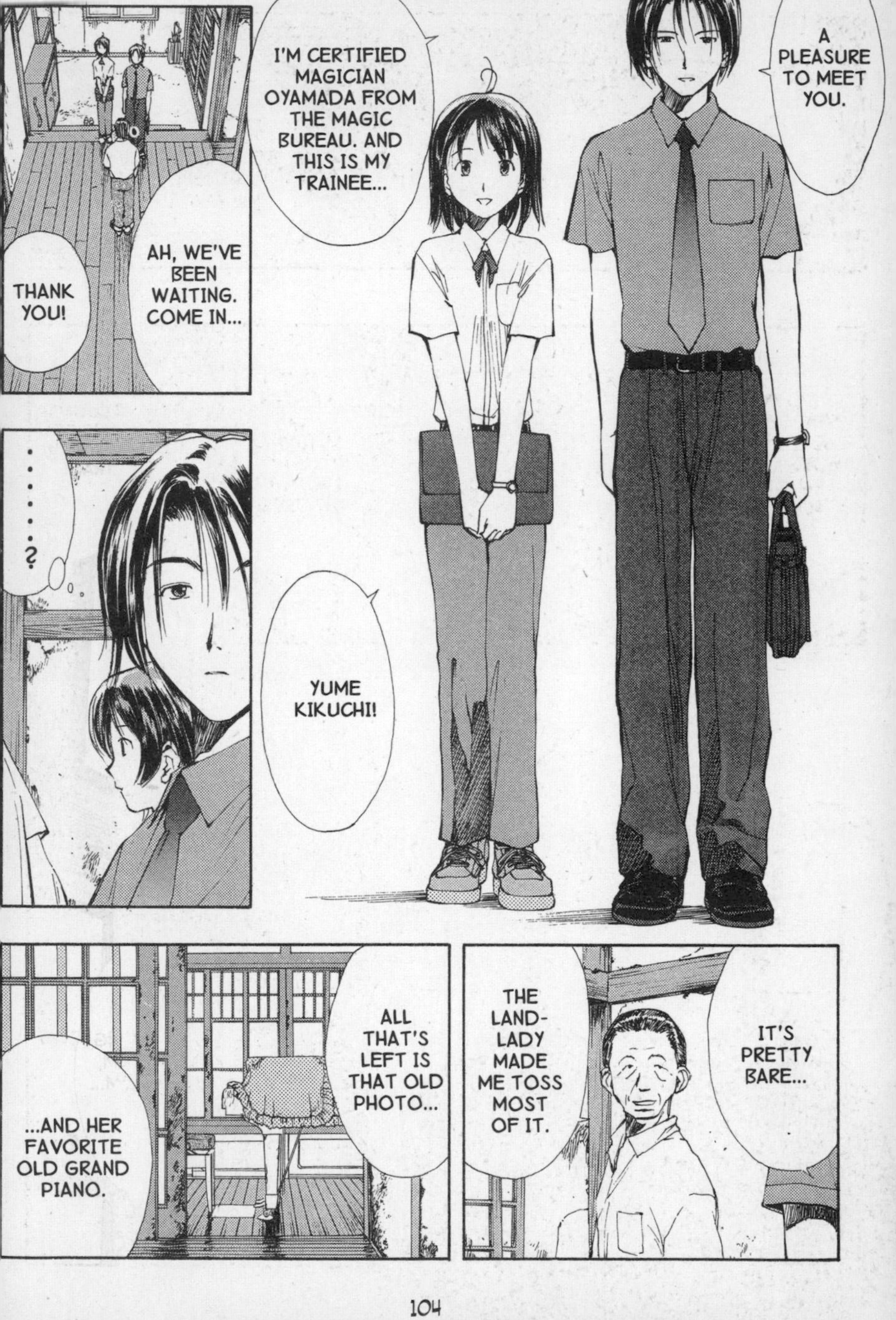
A PLEASURE TO MEET YOU.
I'M CERTIFIED MAGICIAN OYAMADA FROM THE MAGIC BUREAU. AND THIS IS MY TRAINEE...
YUME KIKUCHI!
AH, WE'VE BEEN WAITING. COME IN...
THANK YOU!
......?
IT'S PRETTY BARE...
THE LAND-LADY MADE ME TOSS MOST OF IT.
ALL THAT'S LEFT IS THAT OLD PHOTO...
...AND HER FAVORITE OLD GRAND PIANO.

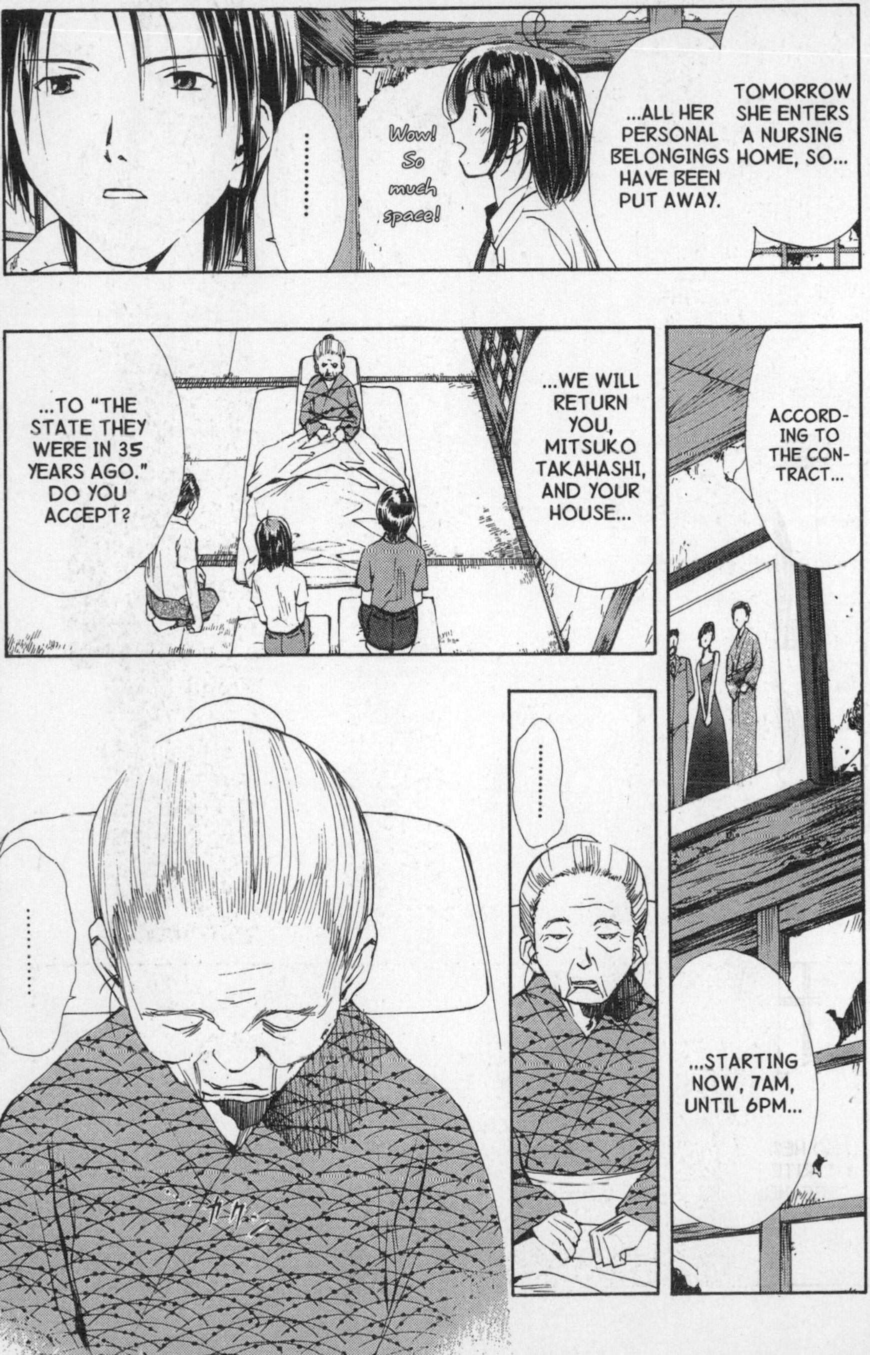
TOMORROW SHE ENTERS A NURSING HOME, SO...
...ALL HER PERSONAL BELONGINGS HAVE BEEN PUT AWAY.
Wow! So much space!
......
ACCORDING TO THE CONTRACT...
...STARTING NOW, 7AM, UNTIL 6PM...
...WE WILL RETURN YOU, MITSUKO TAKAHASHI, AND YOUR HOUSE...
...TO "THE STATE THEY WERE IN 35 YEARS AGO." DO YOU ACCEPT?
......
......
カク

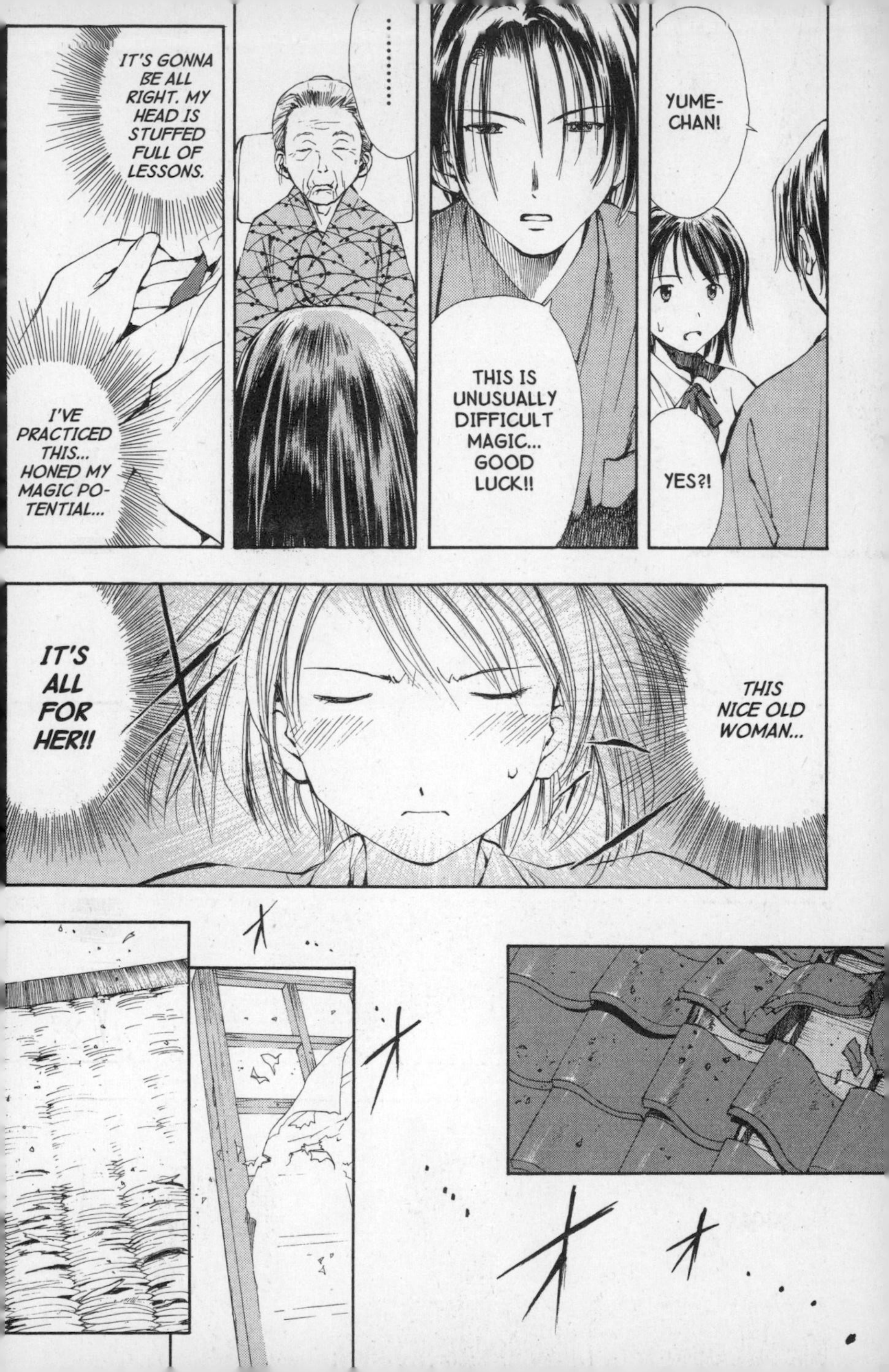
YUME-CHAN!
YES?!
THIS IS UNUSUALLY DIFFICULT MAGIC... GOOD LUCK!!
....
IT'S GONNA BE ALL RIGHT. MY HEAD IS STUFFED FULL OF LESSONS.
I'VE PRACTICED THIS... HONED MY MAGIC PO-TENTIAL...
THIS NICE OLD WOMAN...
IT'S ALL FOR HER!!

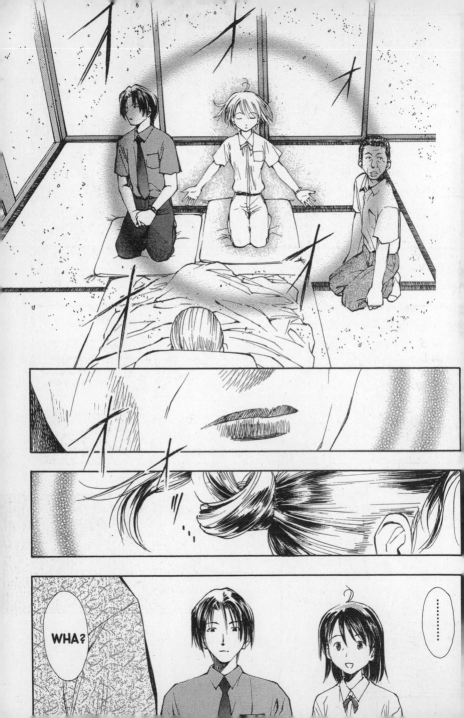

WHA?

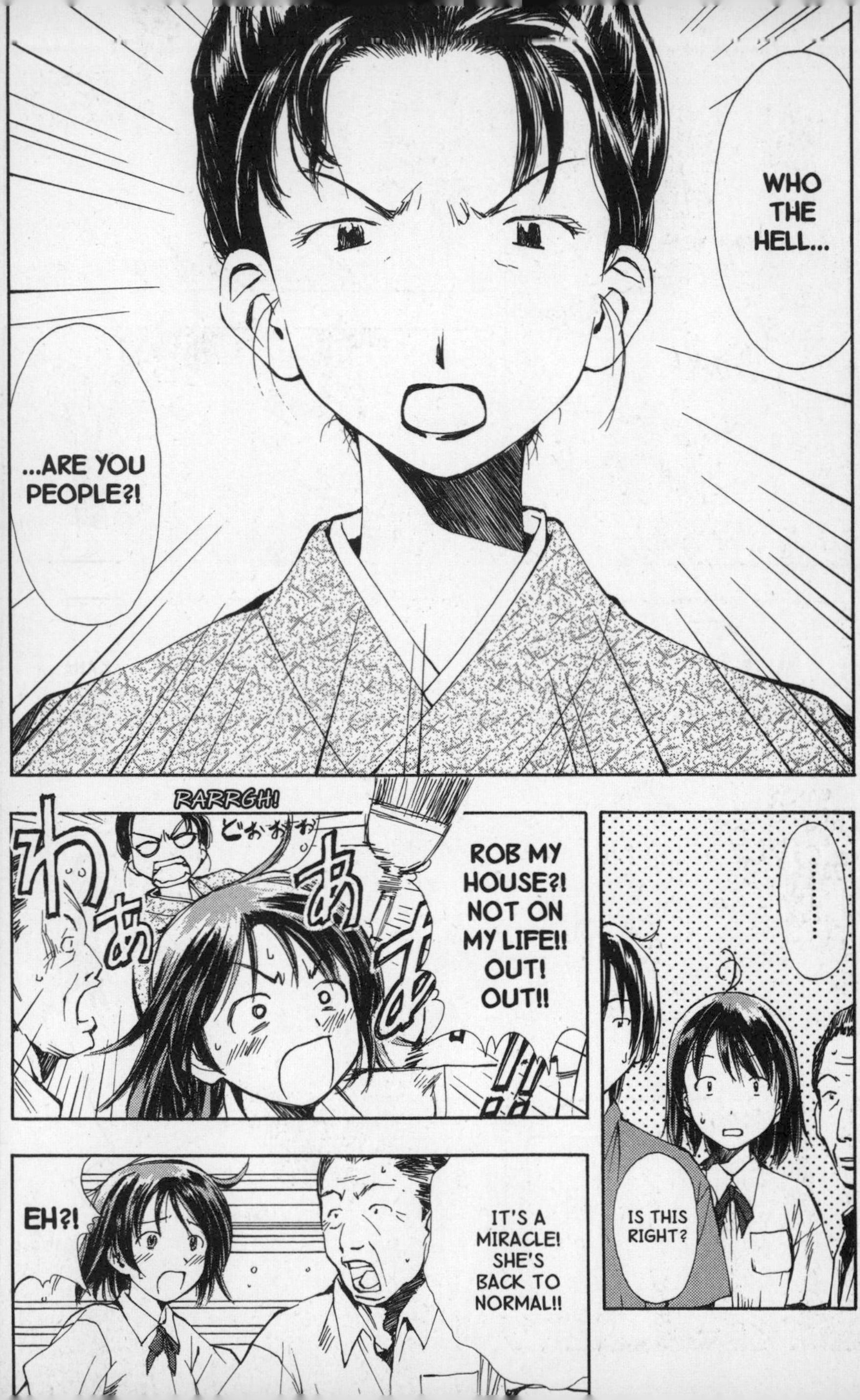
WHO THE HELL...
...ARE YOU PEOPLE?!
......
IS THIS RIGHT?
RARRGH!
ROB MY HOUSE?! NOT ON MY LIFE!! OUT! OUT!!
IT'S A MIRACLE! SHE'S BACK TO NORMAL!!
EH?!

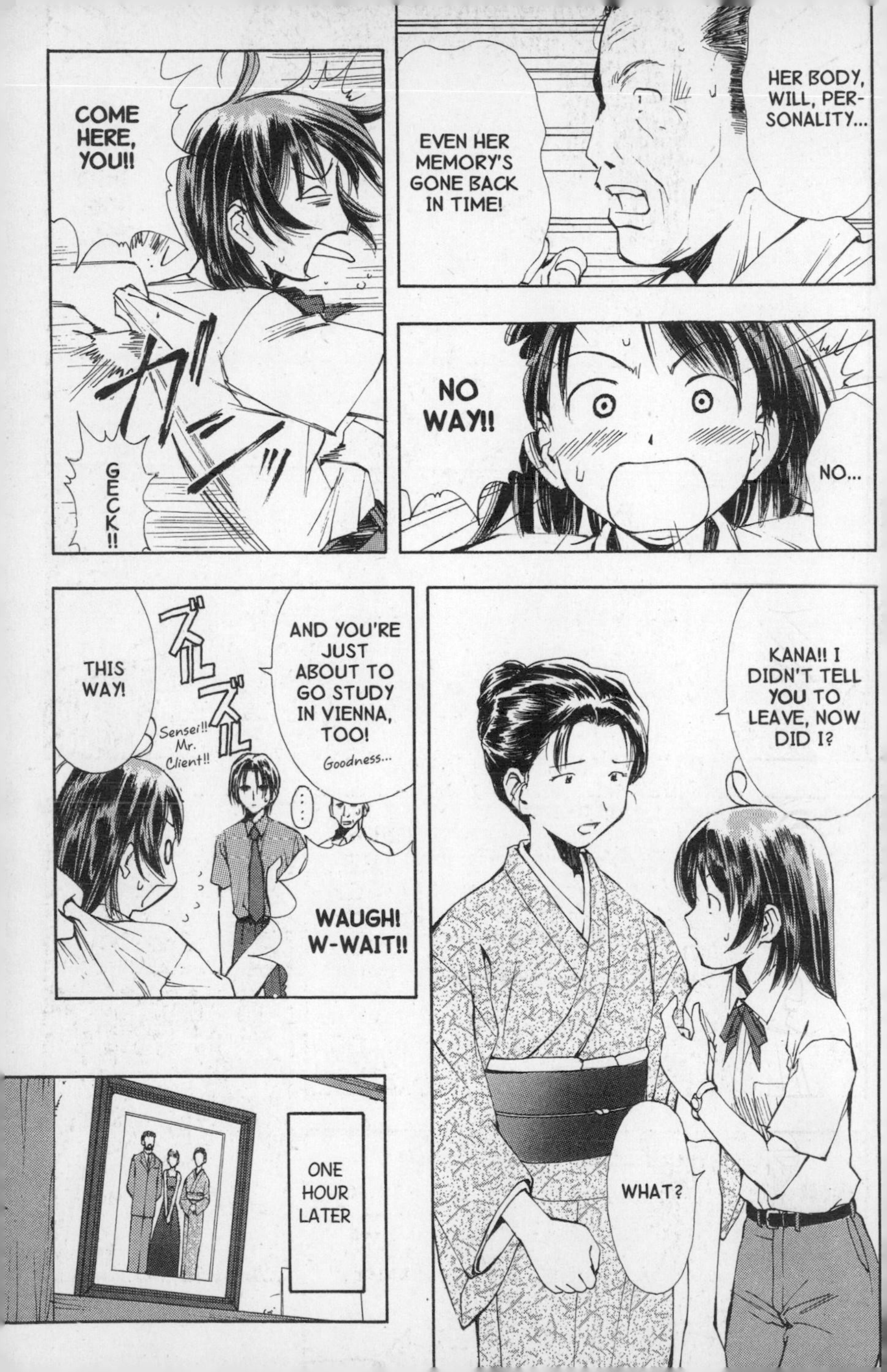
HER BODY, WILL, PER-SONALITY...
EVEN HER MEMORY'S GONE BACK IN TIME!
NO...
NO WAY!!
COME HERE, YOU!!
GECK!!
AND YOU'RE JUST ABOUT TO GO STUDY IN VIENNA, TOO!
Goodness...
THIS WAY!
ズルズル
Sensei!! Mr. Client!!
...
WAUGH! W-WAIT!!
ONE HOUR LATER
KANA!! I DIDN'T TELL YOU TO LEAVE, NOW DID I?
WHAT?

......
WHAT, STARING AT THE PHOTOS?
!
HERE, KANA, THIS IS FOR YOU.
EH? WHAT? THAT DRESS?
I THOUGHT YOU DESERVED TO LOOK PRETTY, TOO.
WOULD YOU LIKE THAT?
IT USED TO BE MINE BUT...
...YOU'VE BLOSSOMED INTO SUCH A FINE VIOLINIST SINCE RETURNING FROM VIENNA.
AH...
Y-YEAH!
I HATE TO ASK THIS, KIKUCHI-SAN, BUT WOULD YOU BE KANA FOR THIS?
KANA...?
THIRY-FIVE YEARS AGO, MITSUKO'S ONLY DAUGHTER, KANA, WENT TO STUDY MUSIC ABROAD.
IN VIENNA, SHE DIED IN A TRAFFIC ACCIDENT...

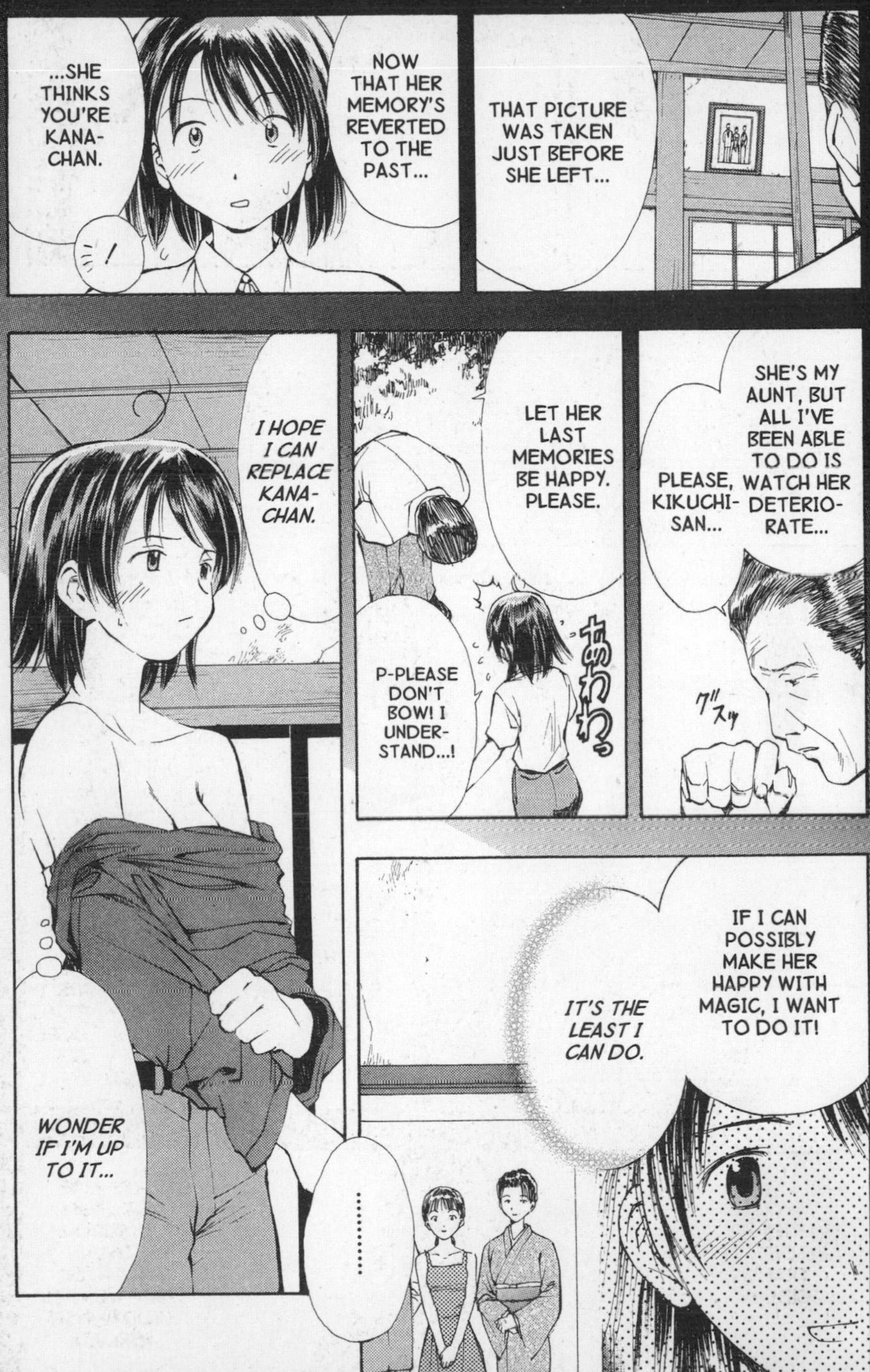
THAT PICTURE WAS TAKEN JUST BEFORE SHE LEFT...
NOW THAT HER MEMORY'S REVERTED TO THE PAST...
...SHE THINKS YOU'RE KANA-CHAN.
!
SHE'S MY AUNT, BUT ALL I'VE BEEN ABLE TO DO IS WATCH HER DETERIORATE...
PLEASE, KIKUCHI-SAN...
グスッ
LET HER LAST MEMORIES BE HAPPY. PLEASE.
あわわっ
P-PLEASE DON'T BOW! I UNDERSTAND...!
IF I CAN POSSIBLY MAKE HER HAPPY WITH MAGIC, I WANT TO DO IT!
IT'S THE LEAST I CAN DO.
......
I HOPE I CAN REPLACE KANA-CHAN.
WONDER IF I'M UP TO IT...

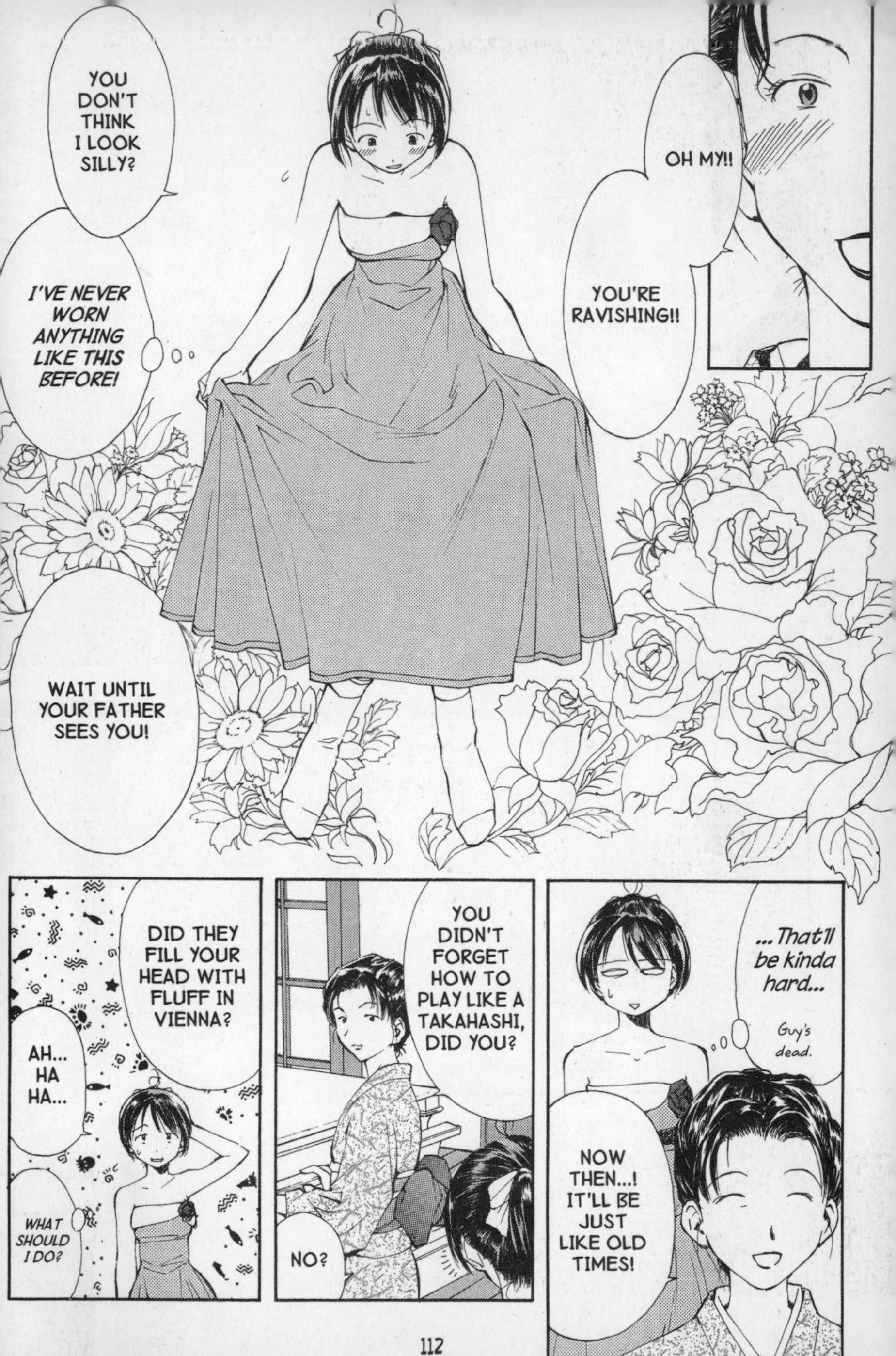
OH MY!!
YOU'RE RAVISHING!!
YOU DON'T THINK I LOOK SILLY?
I'VE NEVER WORN ANYTHING LIKE THIS BEFORE!
WAIT UNTIL YOUR FATHER SEES YOU!
...That'll be kinda hard...
Guy's dead.
NOW THEN...! IT'LL BE JUST LIKE OLD TIMES!
YOU DIDN'T FORGET HOW TO PLAY LIKE A TAKAHASHI, DID YOU?
NO?
DID THEY FILL YOUR HEAD WITH FLUFF IN VIENNA?
AH... HA HA...
WHAT SHOULD I DO?

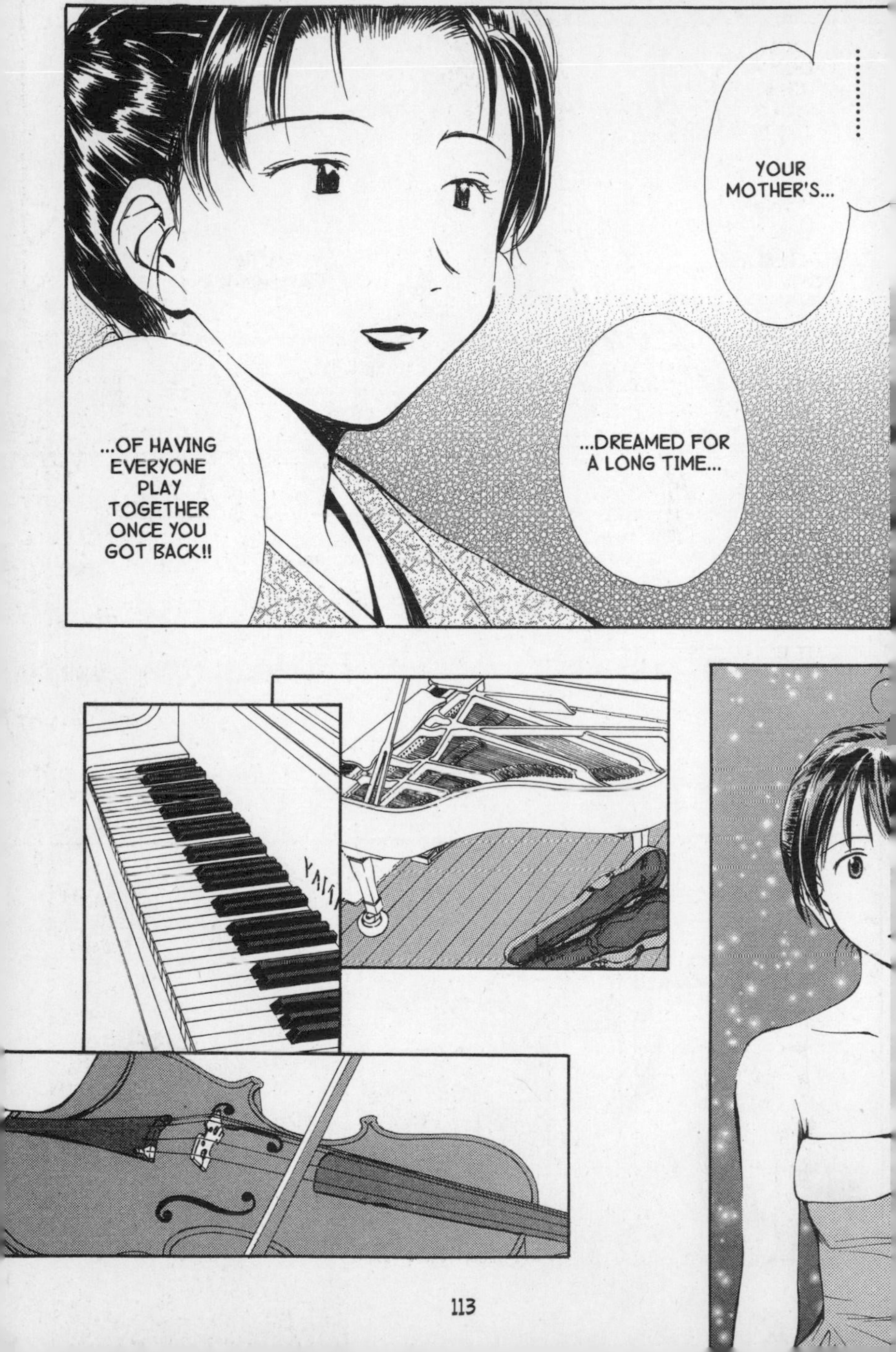
......
YOUR MOTHER'S...
...DREAMED FOR A LONG TIME...
...OF HAVING EVERYONE PLAY TOGETHER ONCE YOU GOT BACK!!

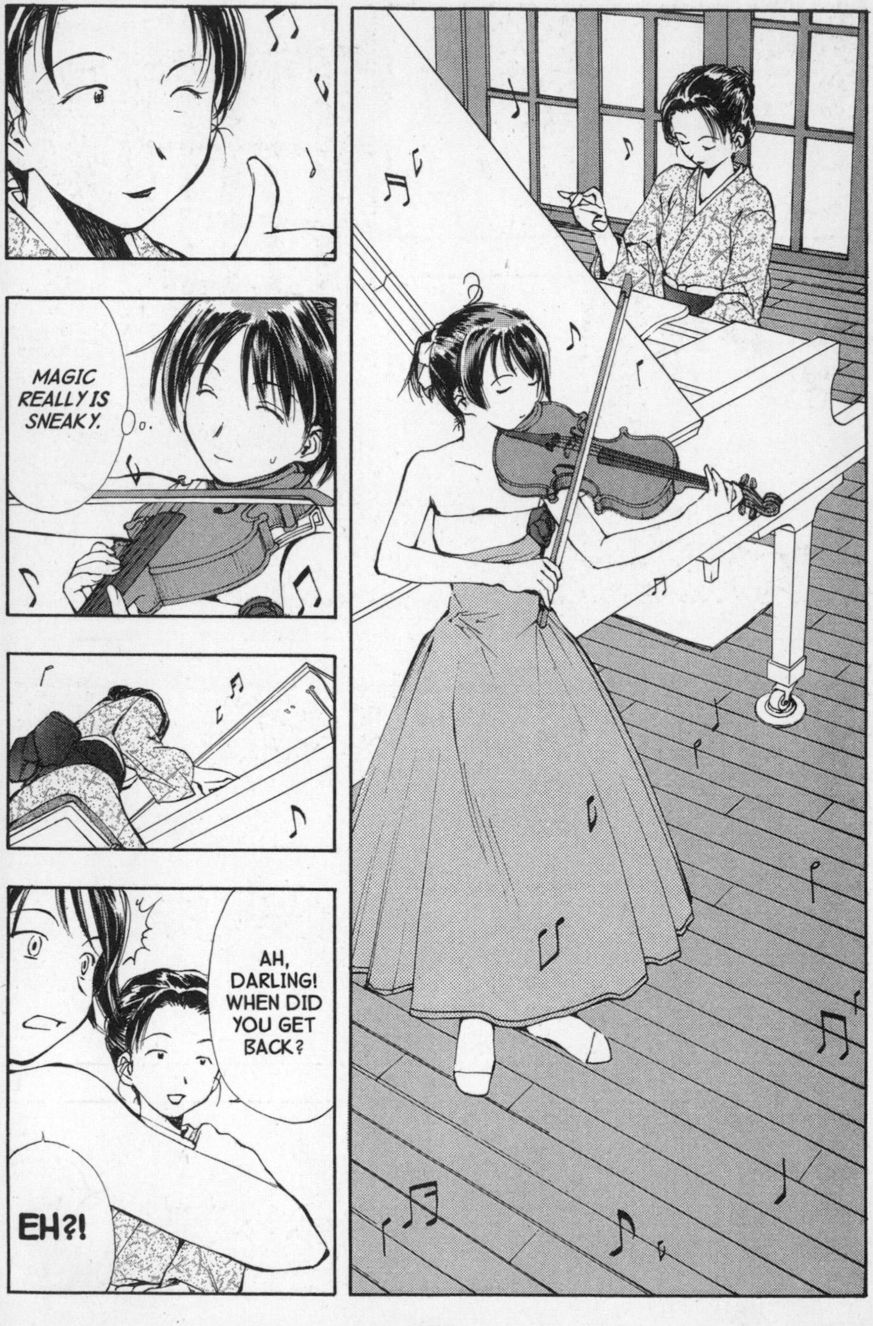
MAGIC REALLY IS SNEAKY.
AH, DARLING! WHEN DID YOU GET BACK?
EH?!

WELL...
SOME-
DAY...

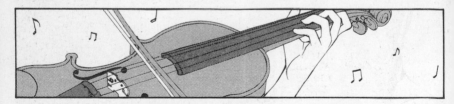

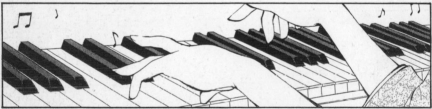

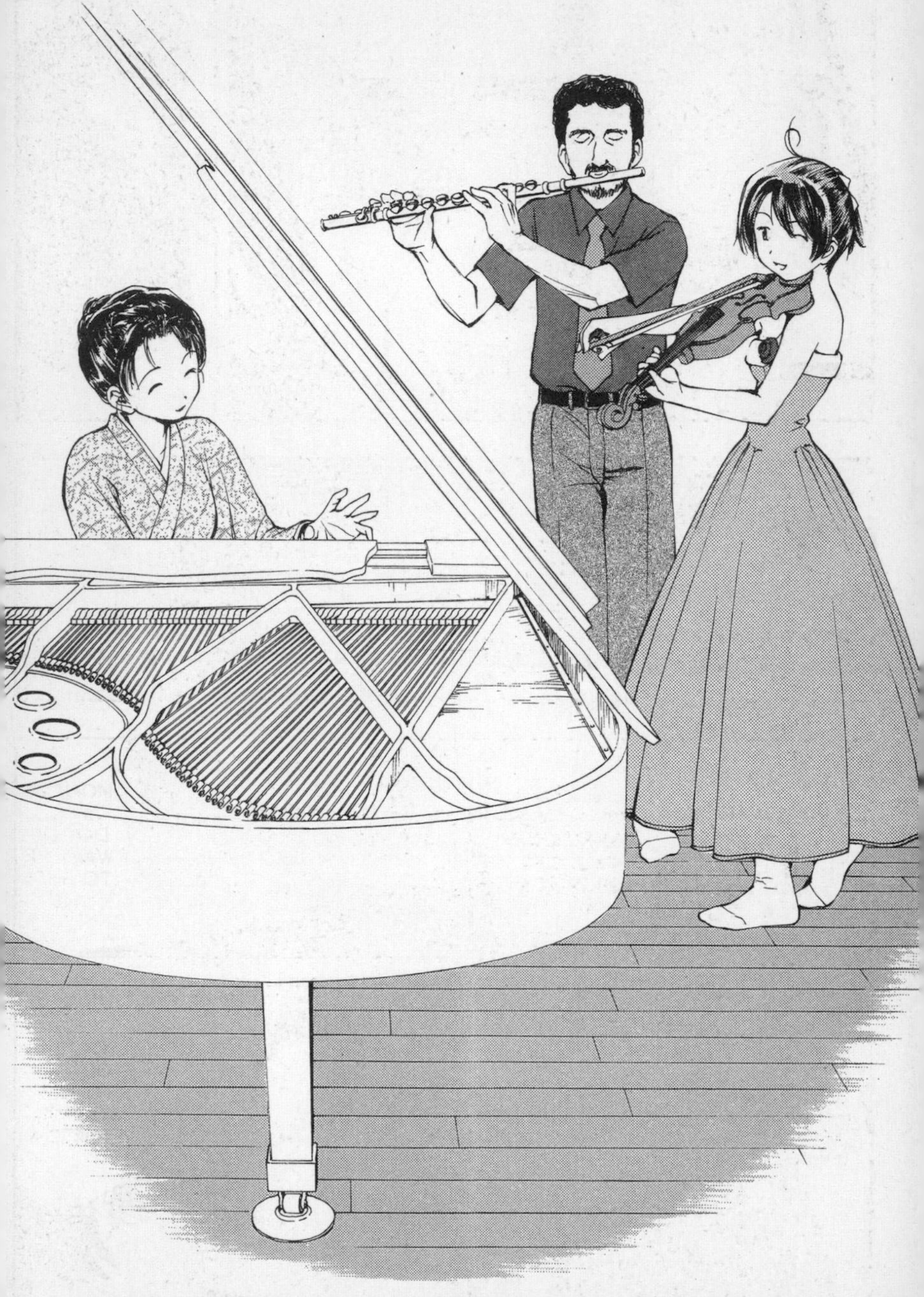

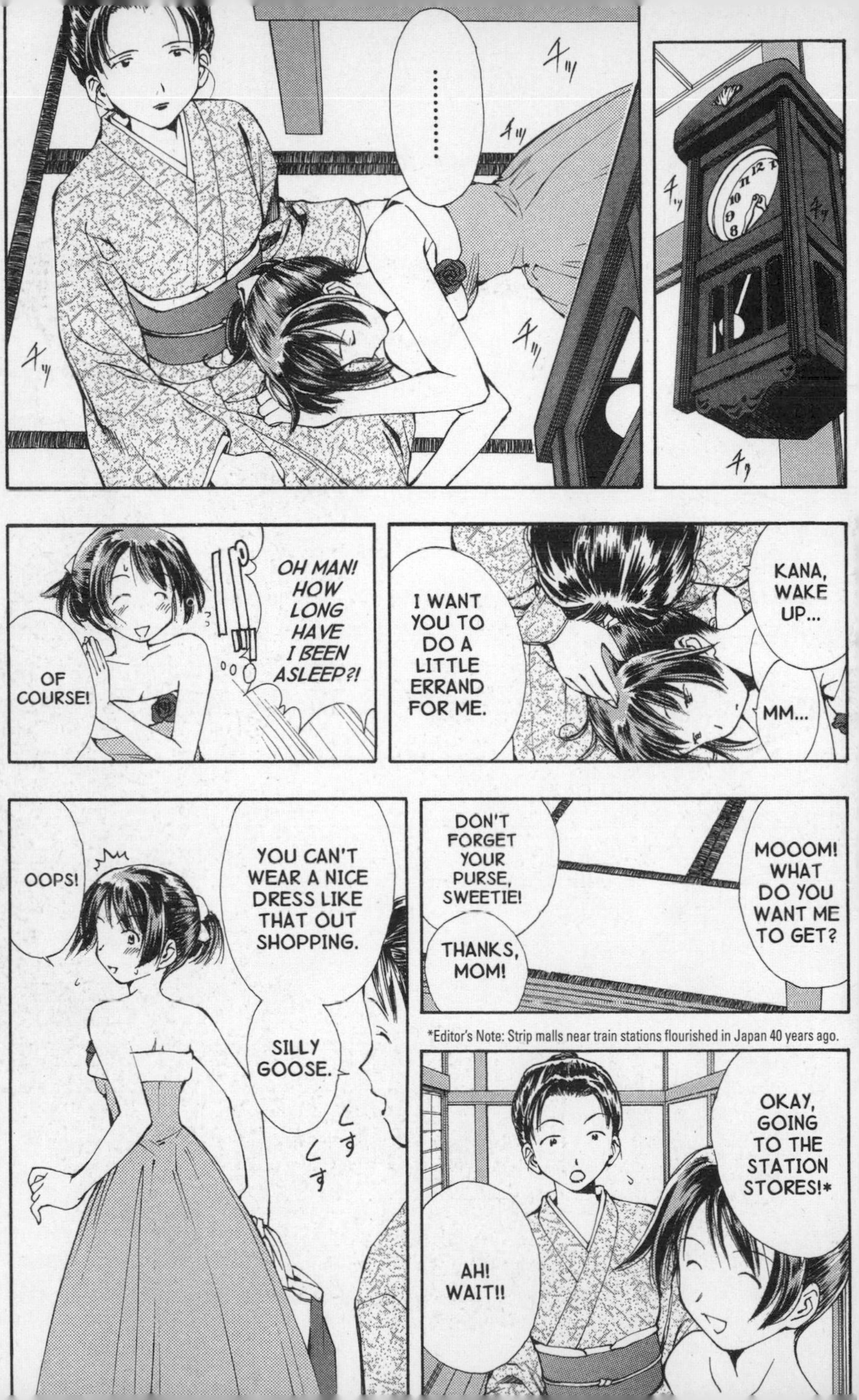
チッ
……
KANA, WAKE UP...
MM...
I WANT YOU TO DO A LITTLE ERRAND FOR ME.
OH MAN! HOW LONG HAVE I BEEN ASLEEP?!
OF COURSE!
MOOOM! WHAT DO YOU WANT ME TO GET?
DON'T FORGET YOUR PURSE, SWEETIE!
THANKS, MOM!
OKAY, GOING TO THE STATION STORES!*
AH! WAIT!!
YOU CAN'T WEAR A NICE DRESS LIKE THAT OUT SHOPPING.
OOPS!
SILLY GOOSE.
くすくす

*Editor's Note: Strip malls near train stations flourished in Japan 40 years ago.

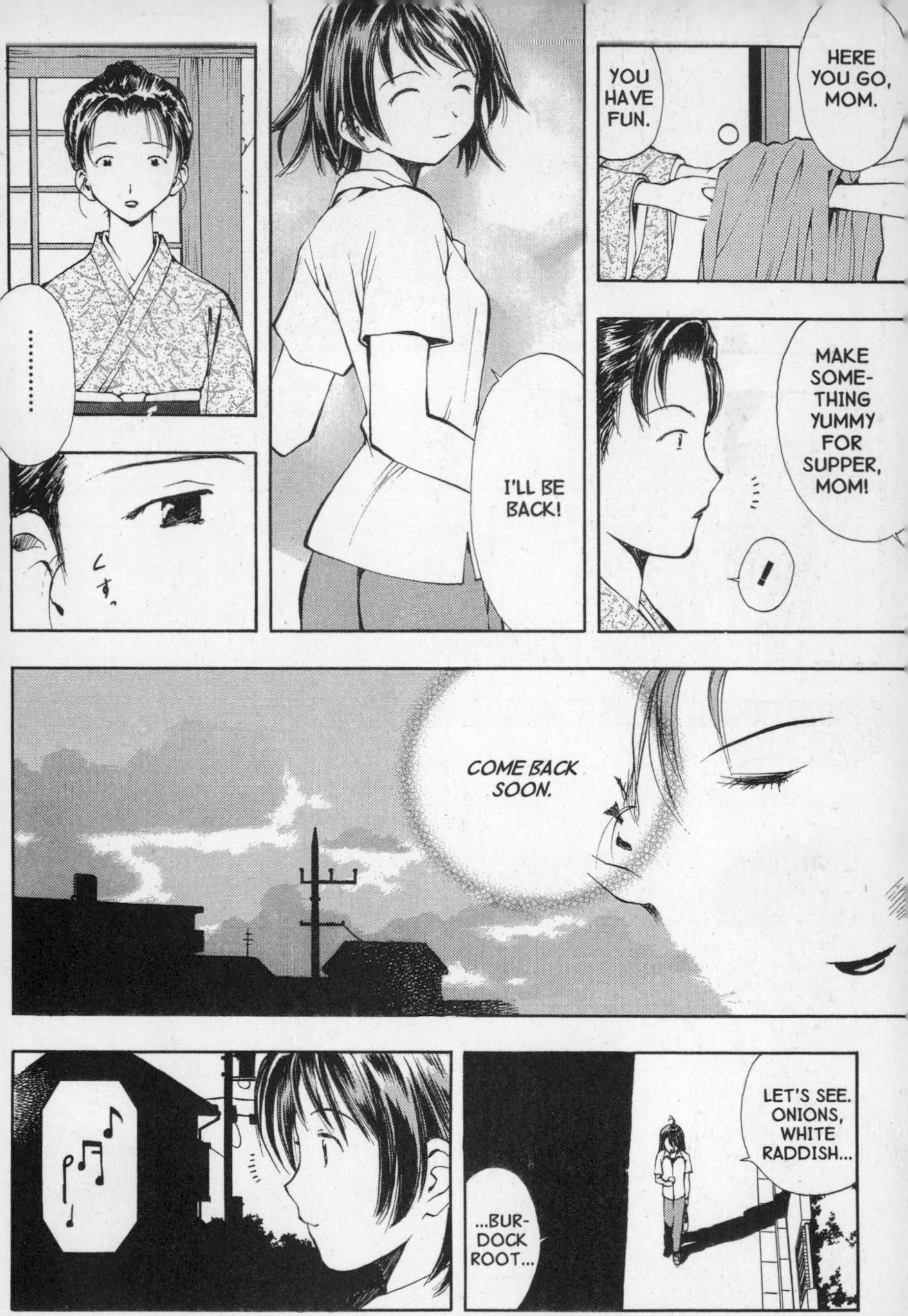
HERE YOU GO, MOM.
YOU HAVE FUN.
MAKE SOME-THING YUMMY FOR SUPPER, MOM!
!
I'LL BE BACK!
......
くすっ
COME BACK SOON.
LET'S SEE. ONIONS, WHITE RADDISH...
...BUR-DOCK ROOT...

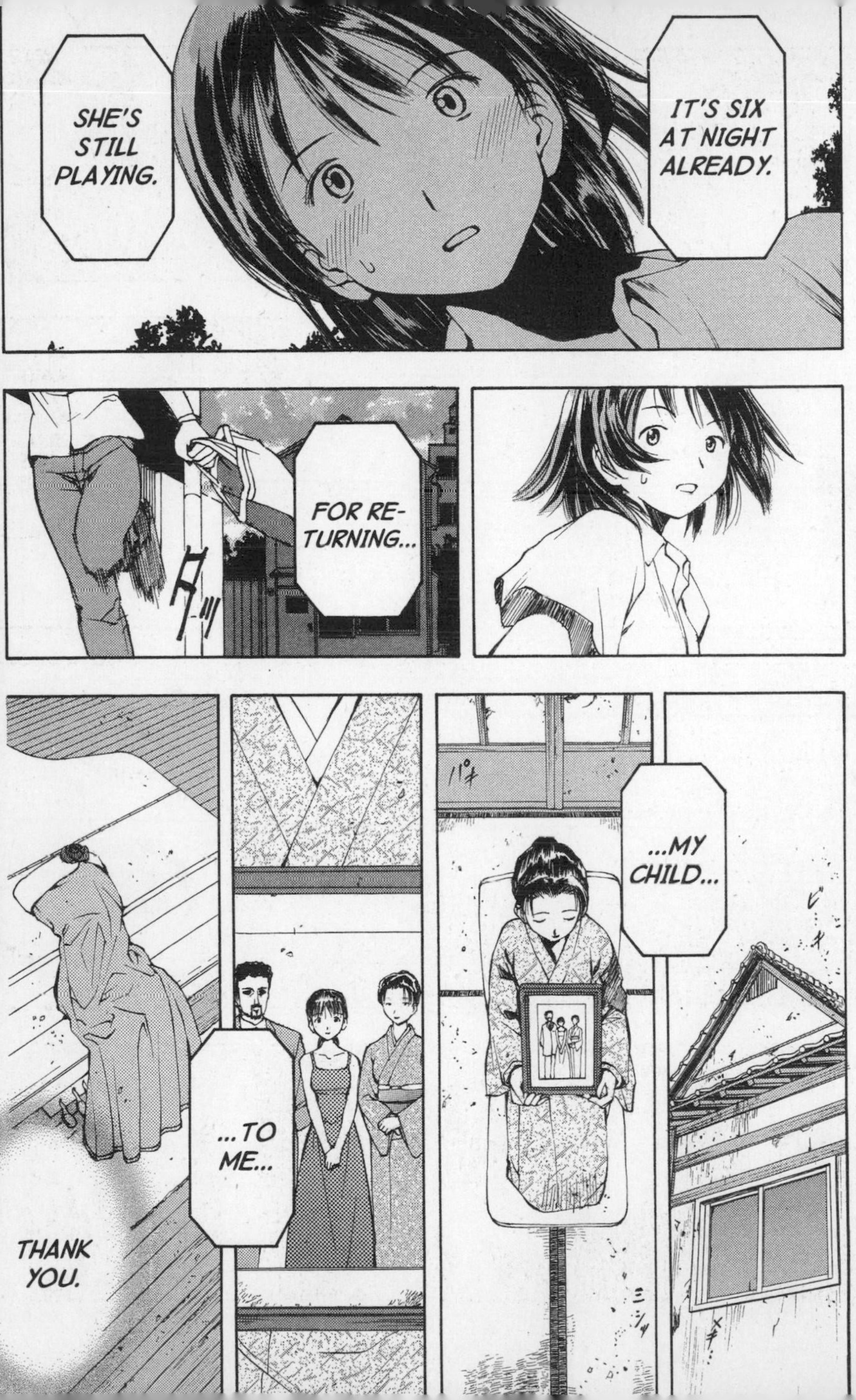
IT'S SIX AT NIGHT ALREADY.
SHE'S STILL PLAYING.
FOR RE- TURNING...
...MY CHILD...
...TO ME...
THANK YOU.

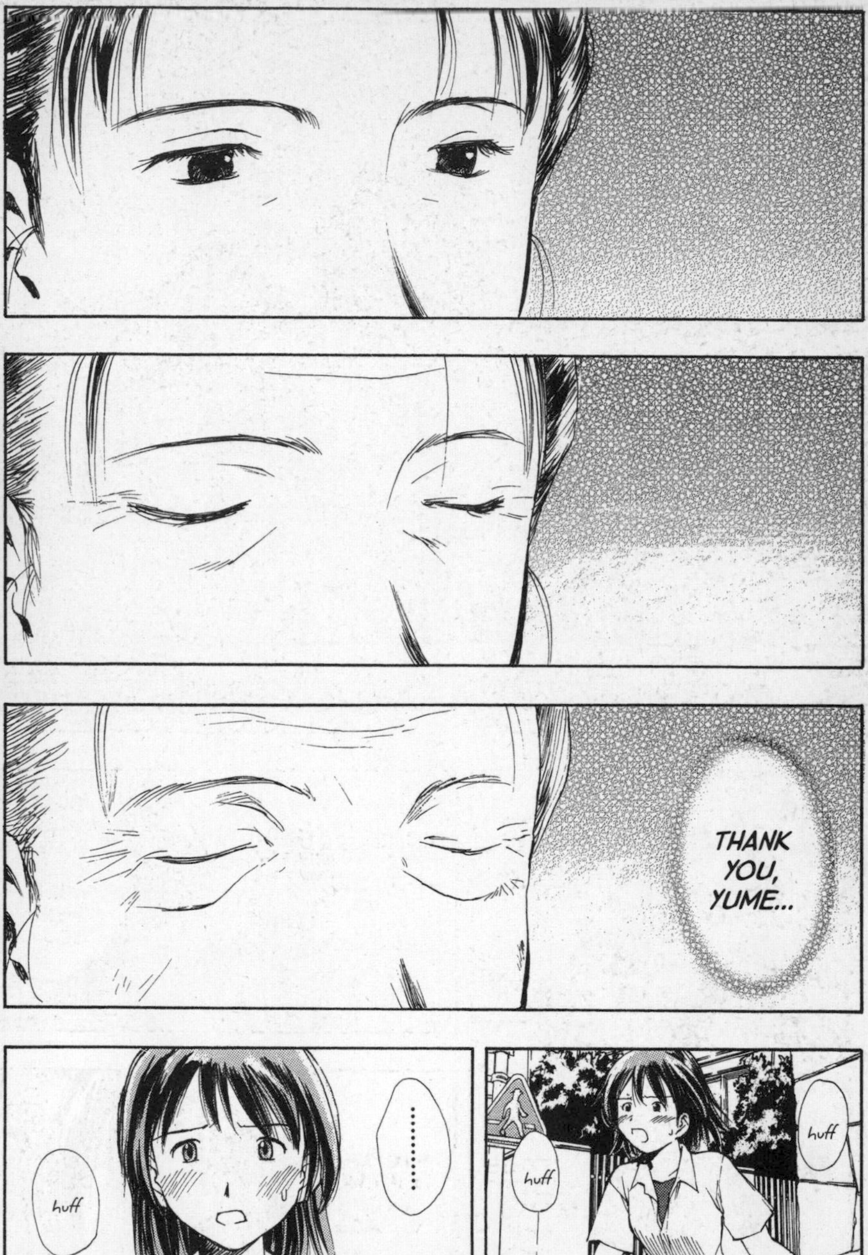
THANK YOU, YUME...
huff
huff
....
huff

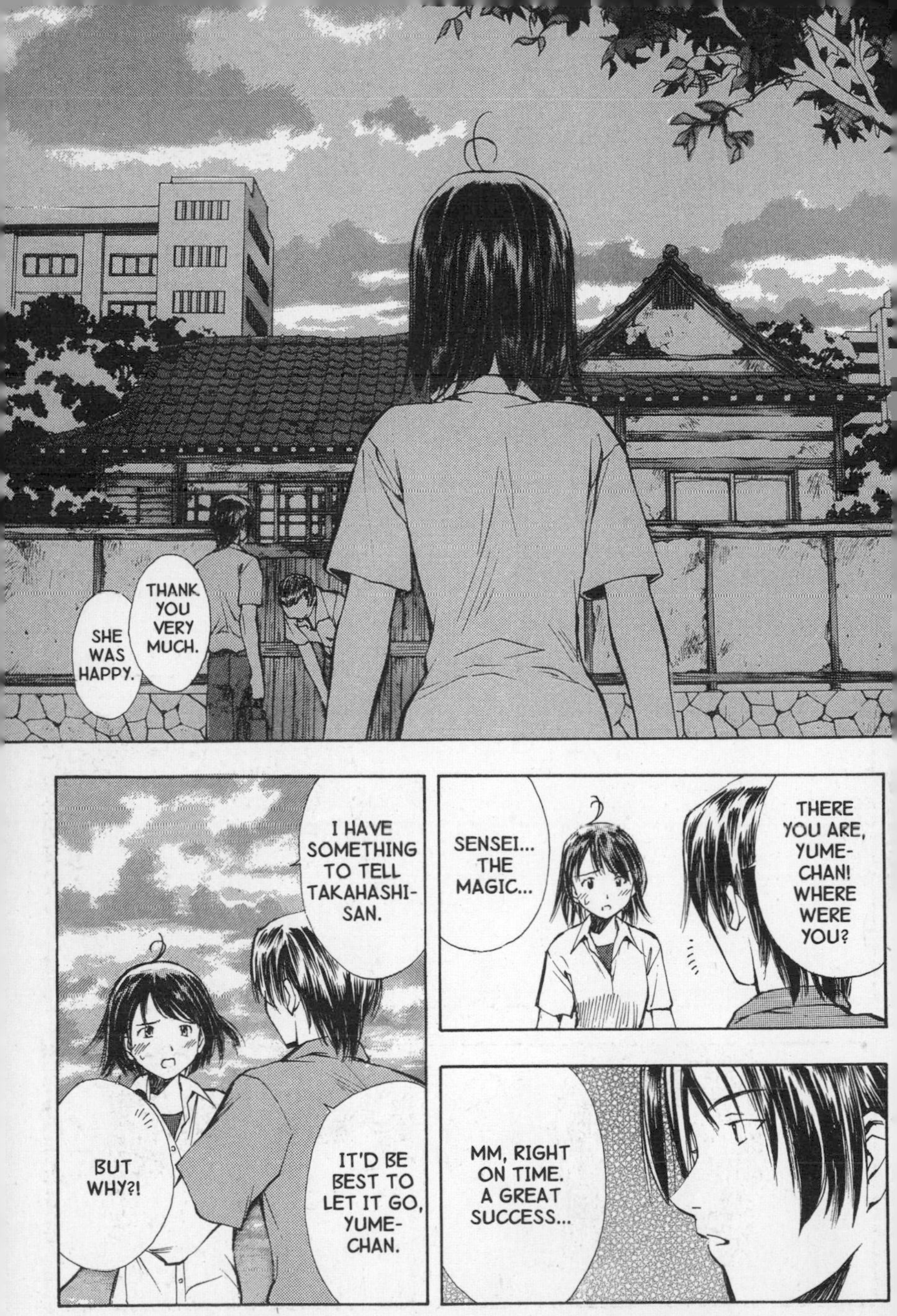
THANK YOU VERY MUCH.
SHE WAS HAPPY.
THERE YOU ARE, YUME-CHAN! WHERE WERE YOU?
SENSEI... THE MAGIC...
MM, RIGHT ON TIME. A GREAT SUCCESS...
I HAVE SOMETHING TO TELL TAKAHASHI-SAN.
IT'D BE BEST TO LET IT GO, YUME-CHAN.
BUT WHY?!

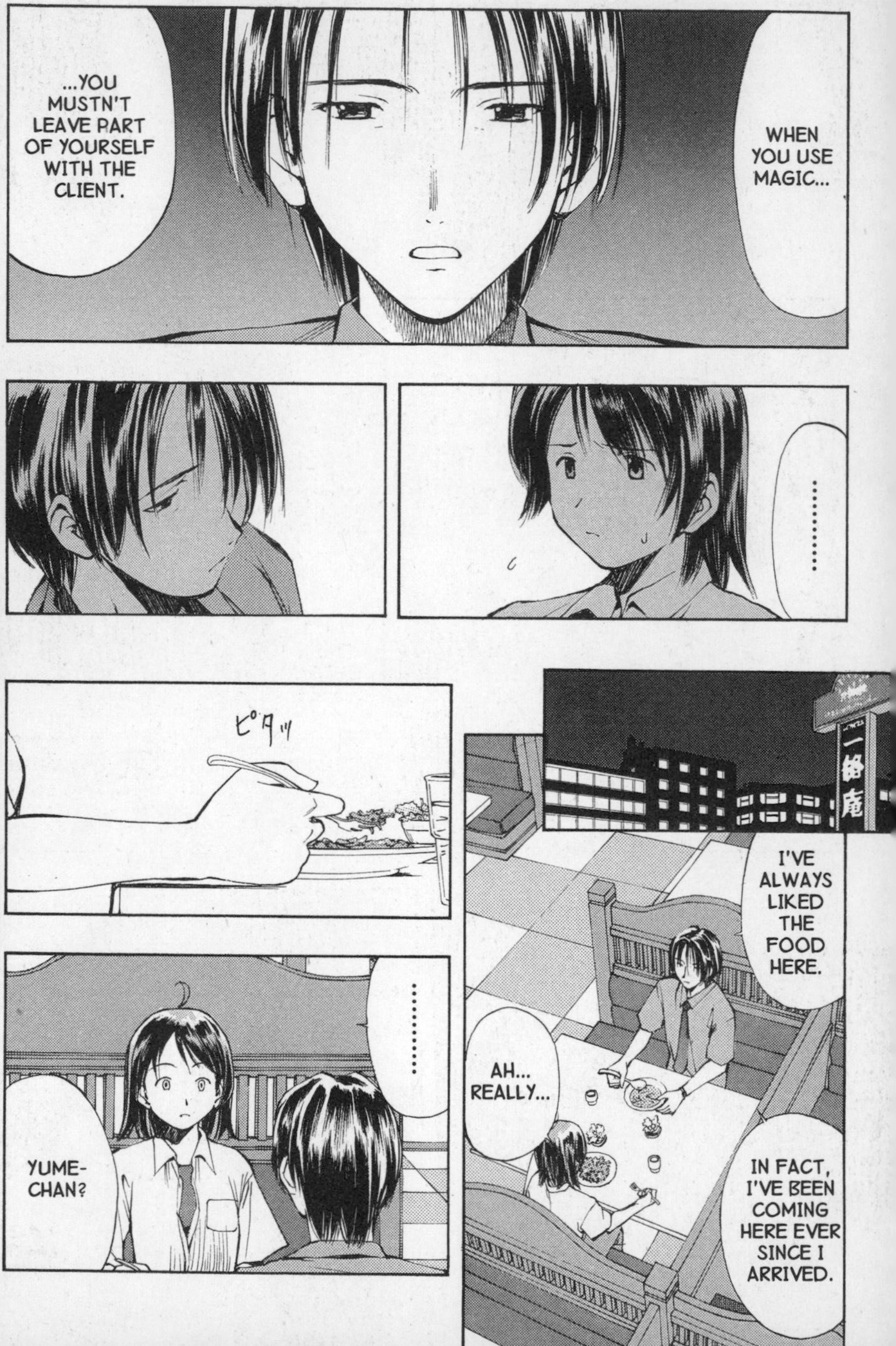
WHEN YOU USE MAGIC...
...YOU MUSTN'T LEAVE PART OF YOURSELF WITH THE CLIENT.
......
I'VE ALWAYS LIKED THE FOOD HERE.
IN FACT, I'VE BEEN COMING HERE EVER SINCE I ARRIVED.
AH... REALLY...
ピタッ
......
YUME-CHAN?

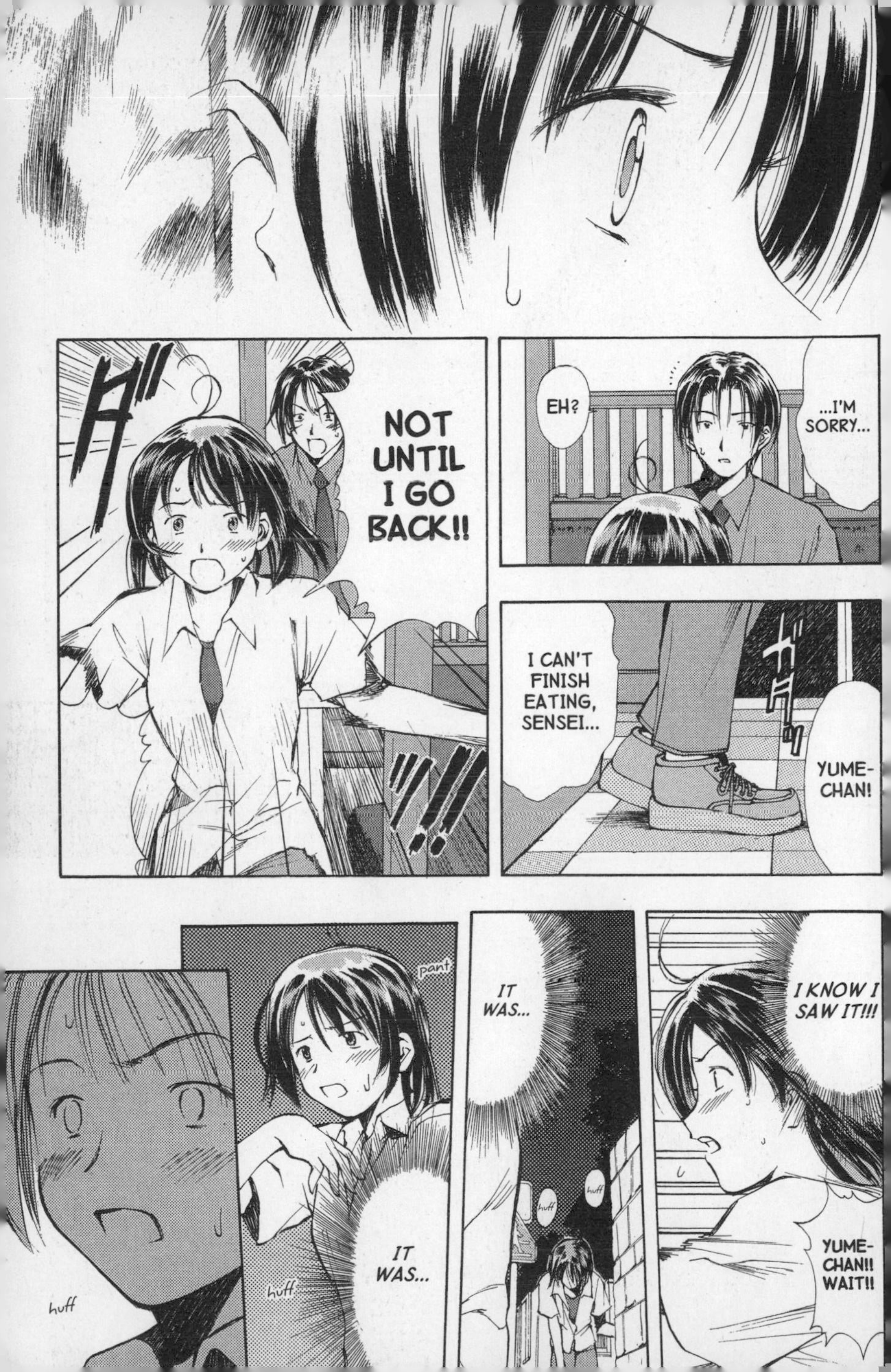
...I'M SORRY...
EH?
YUME-CHAN!
I CAN'T FINISH EATING, SENSEI...
NOT UNTIL I GO BACK!!
I KNOW I SAW IT!!!
YUME-CHAN!! WAIT!!
IT WAS...
huff
huff
pant
IT WAS...
huff
huff

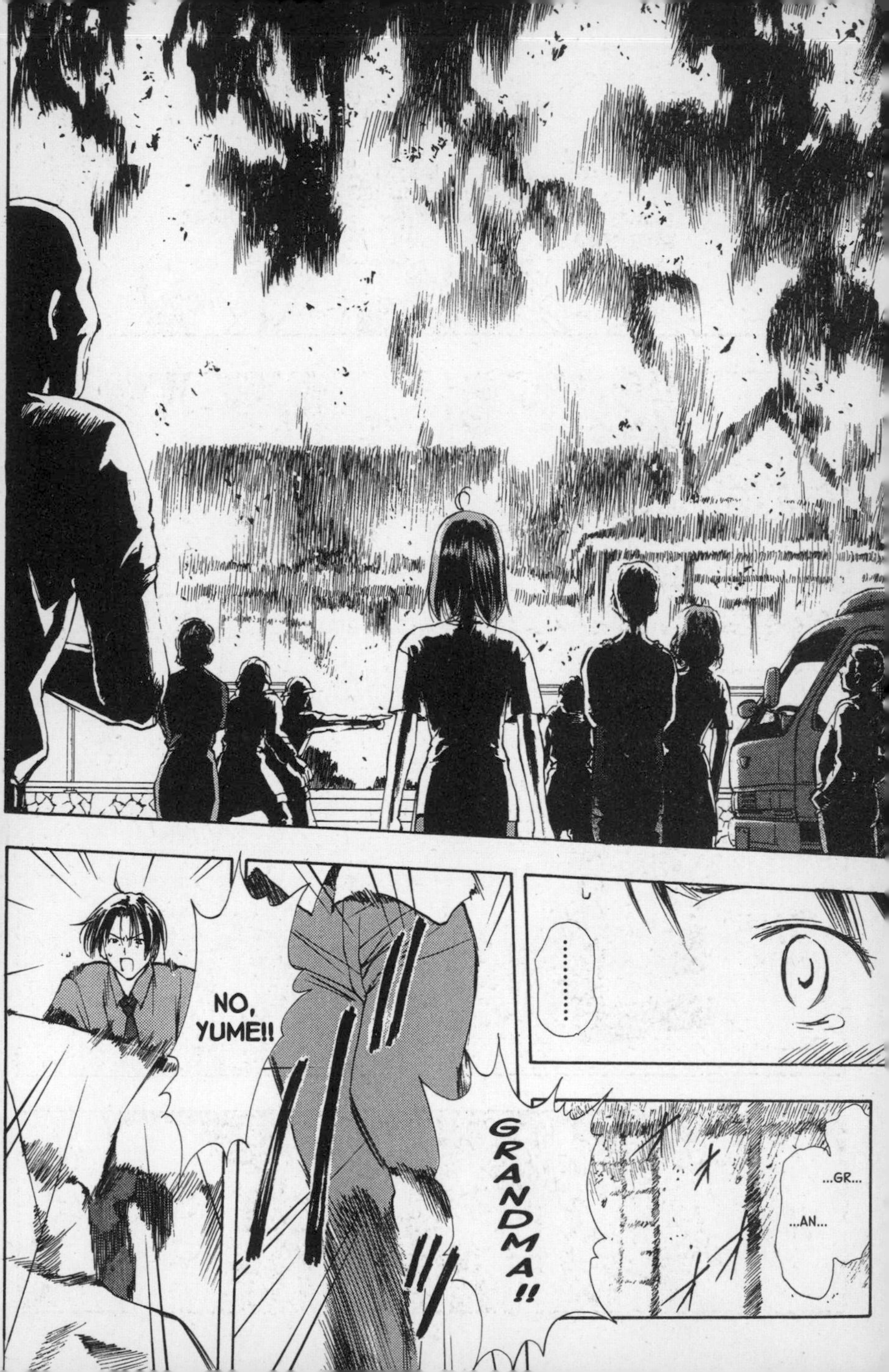

......
...GR...
...AN...
GRANDMA!!
NO, YUME!!

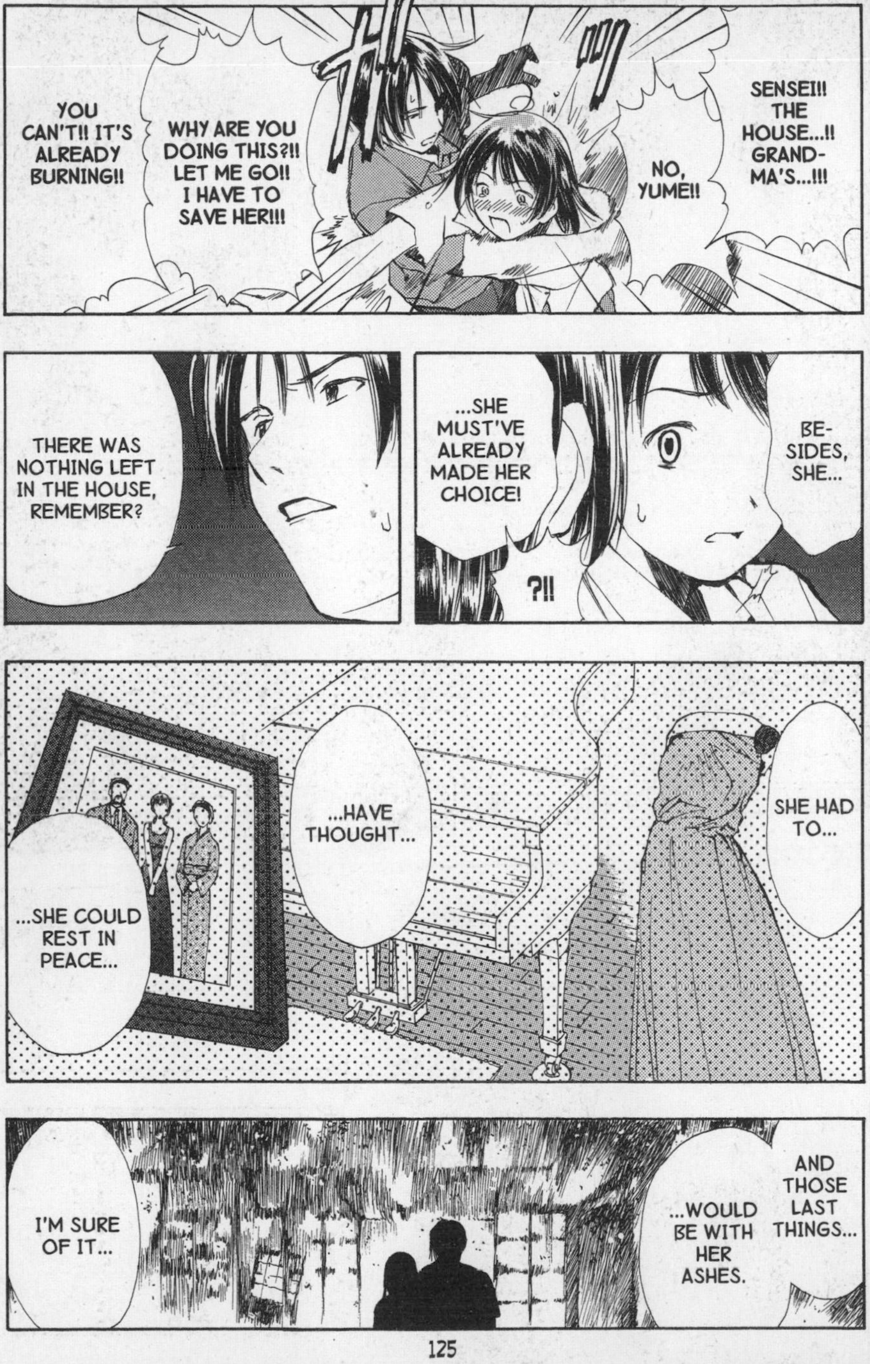
SENSEI!! THE HOUSE...!! GRAND-MA'S...!!!
NO, YUME!!
WHY ARE YOU DOING THIS?!! LET ME GO!! I HAVE TO SAVE HER!!!
YOU CAN'T!! IT'S ALREADY BURNING!!
BE-SIDES, SHE...
...SHE MUST'VE ALREADY MADE HER CHOICE!
?!!
THERE WAS NOTHING LEFT IN THE HOUSE, REMEMBER?
SHE HAD TO...
...HAVE THOUGHT...
...SHE COULD REST IN PEACE...
AND THOSE LAST THINGS...
...WOULD BE WITH HER ASHES.
I'M SURE OF IT...

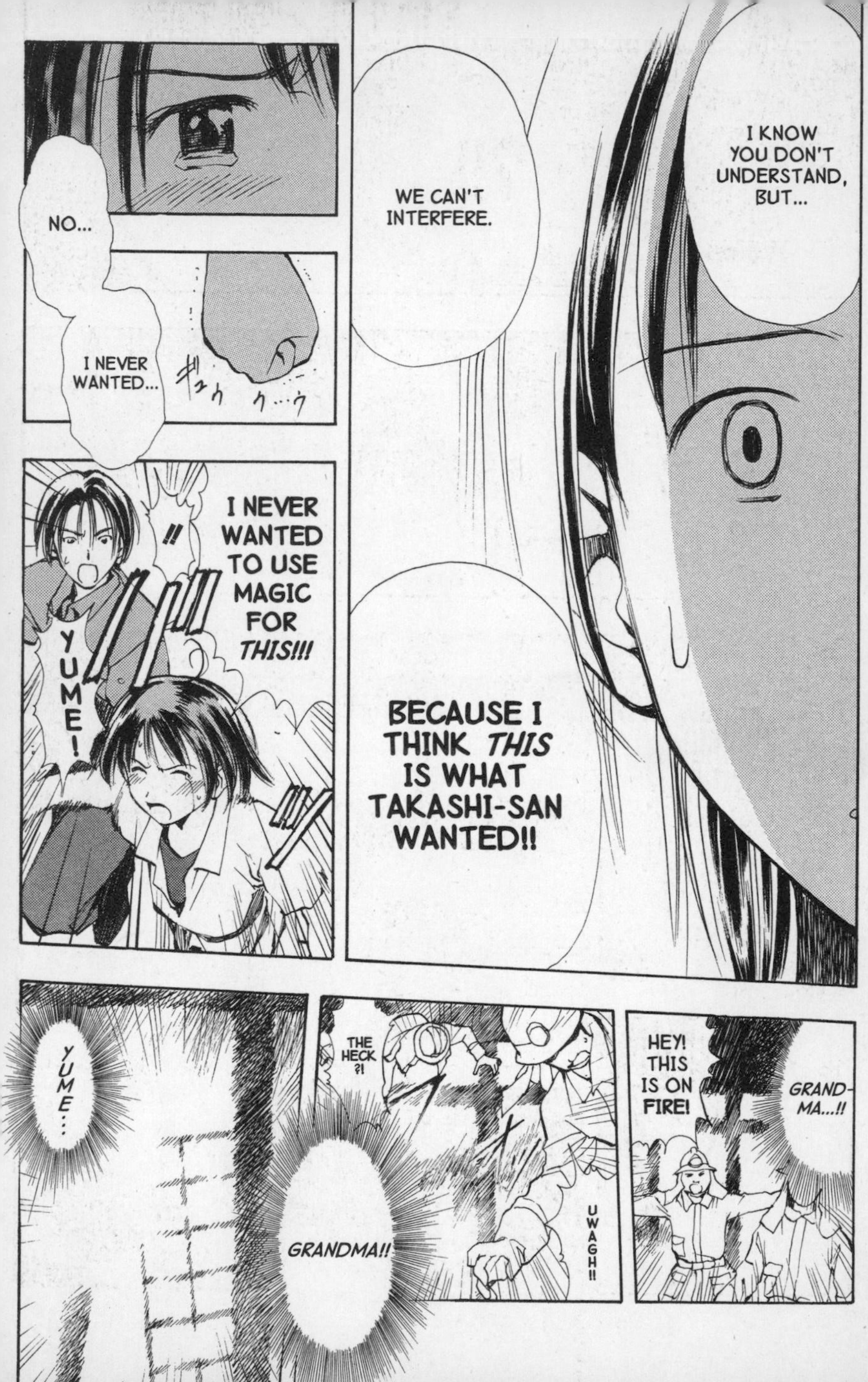
I KNOW YOU DON'T UNDERSTAND, BUT...
WE CAN'T INTERFERE.
BECAUSE I THINK THIS IS WHAT TAKASHI-SAN WANTED!!
NO...
I NEVER WANTED...
I NEVER WANTED TO USE MAGIC FOR THIS!!!
!!
YUME!
GRAND-MA...!!
HEY! THIS IS ON FIRE!
THE HECK?!
UWAGH!!
YUME...
GRANDMA!!

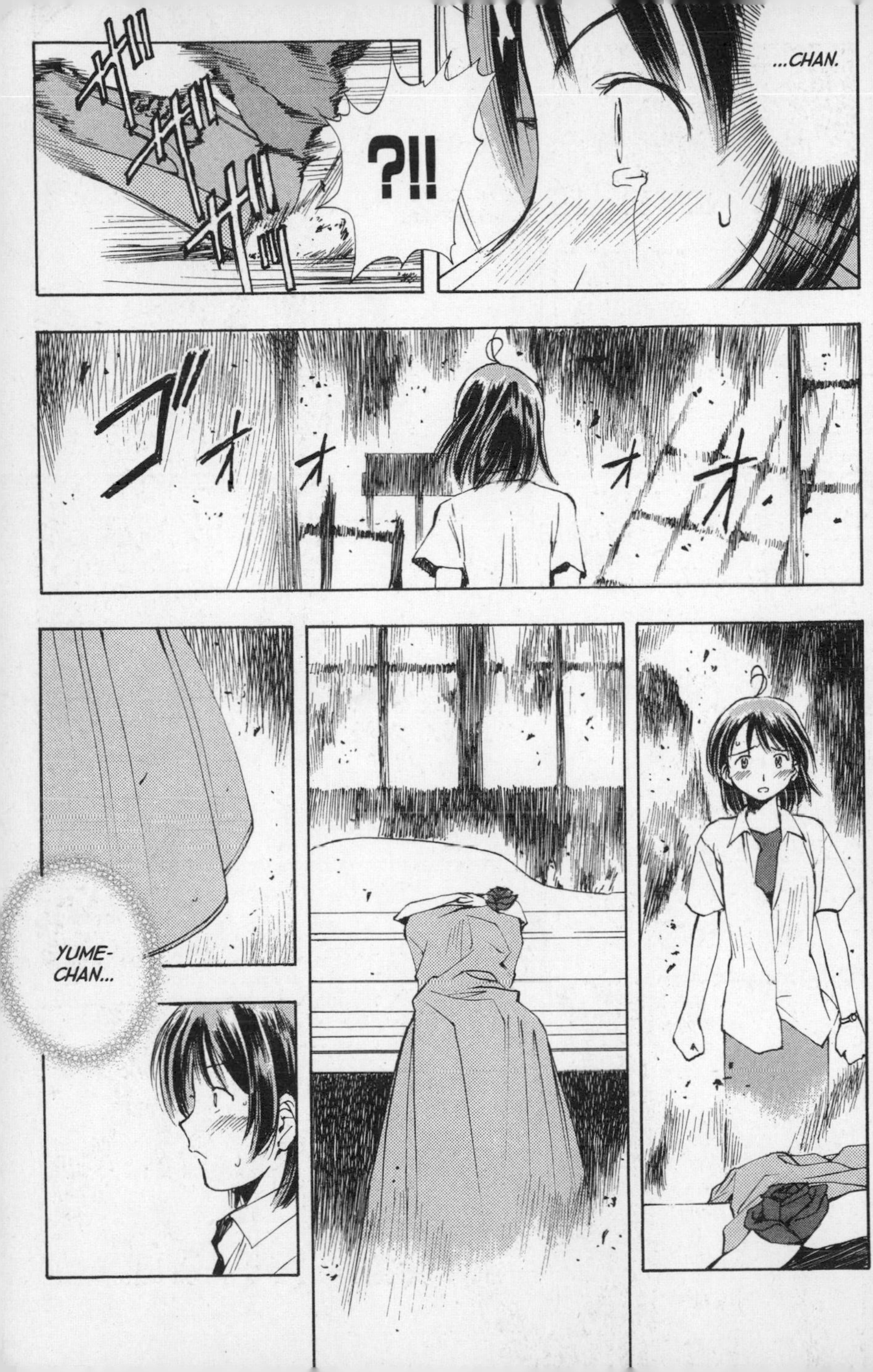

...CHAN.
?!!
ゴオオオオ
YUME-
CHAN...

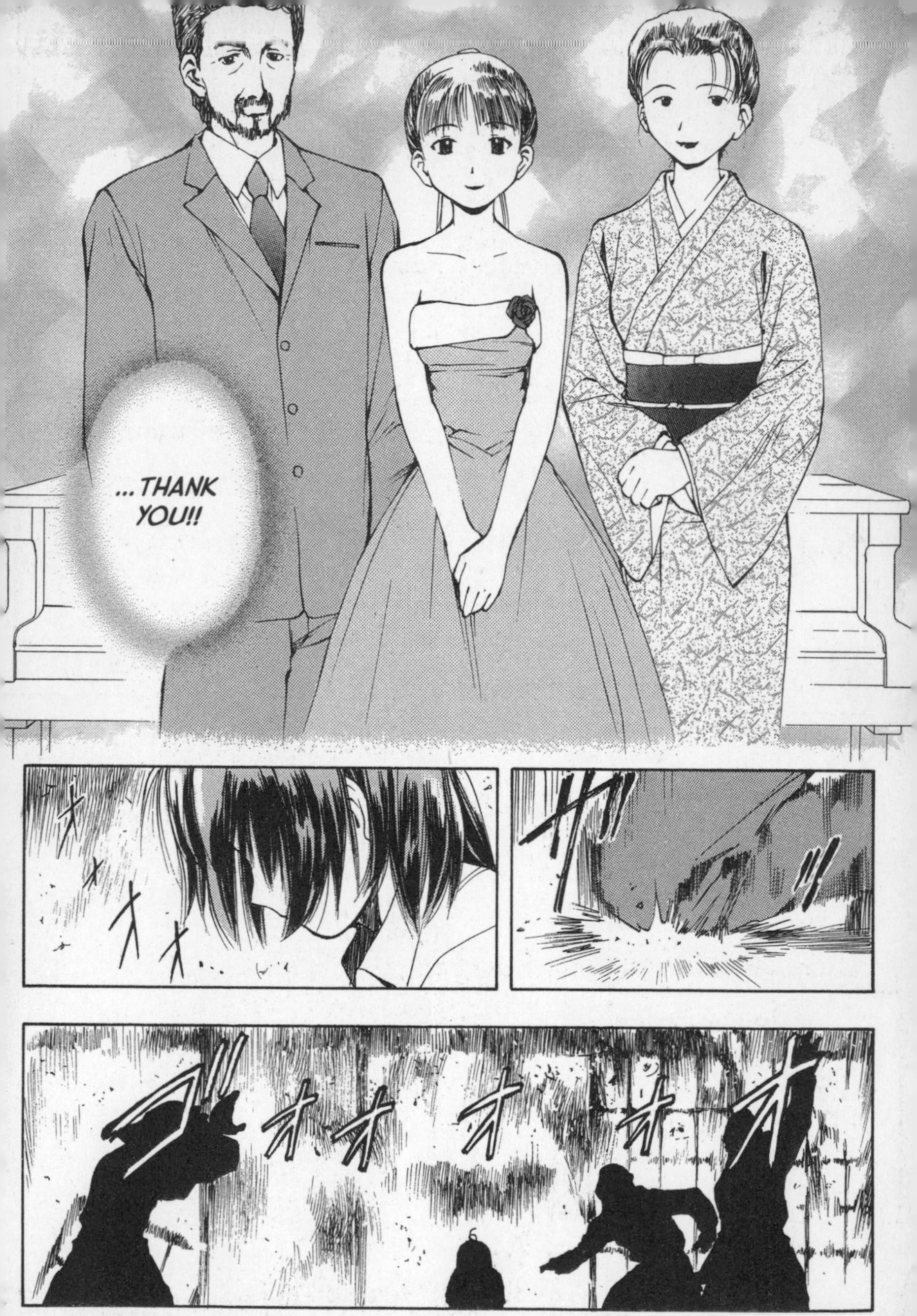
...THANK YOU!!

to be continued...

Drawing Manga is a Very Precious Thing

(A Letter from Kumichi Yoshizuki)

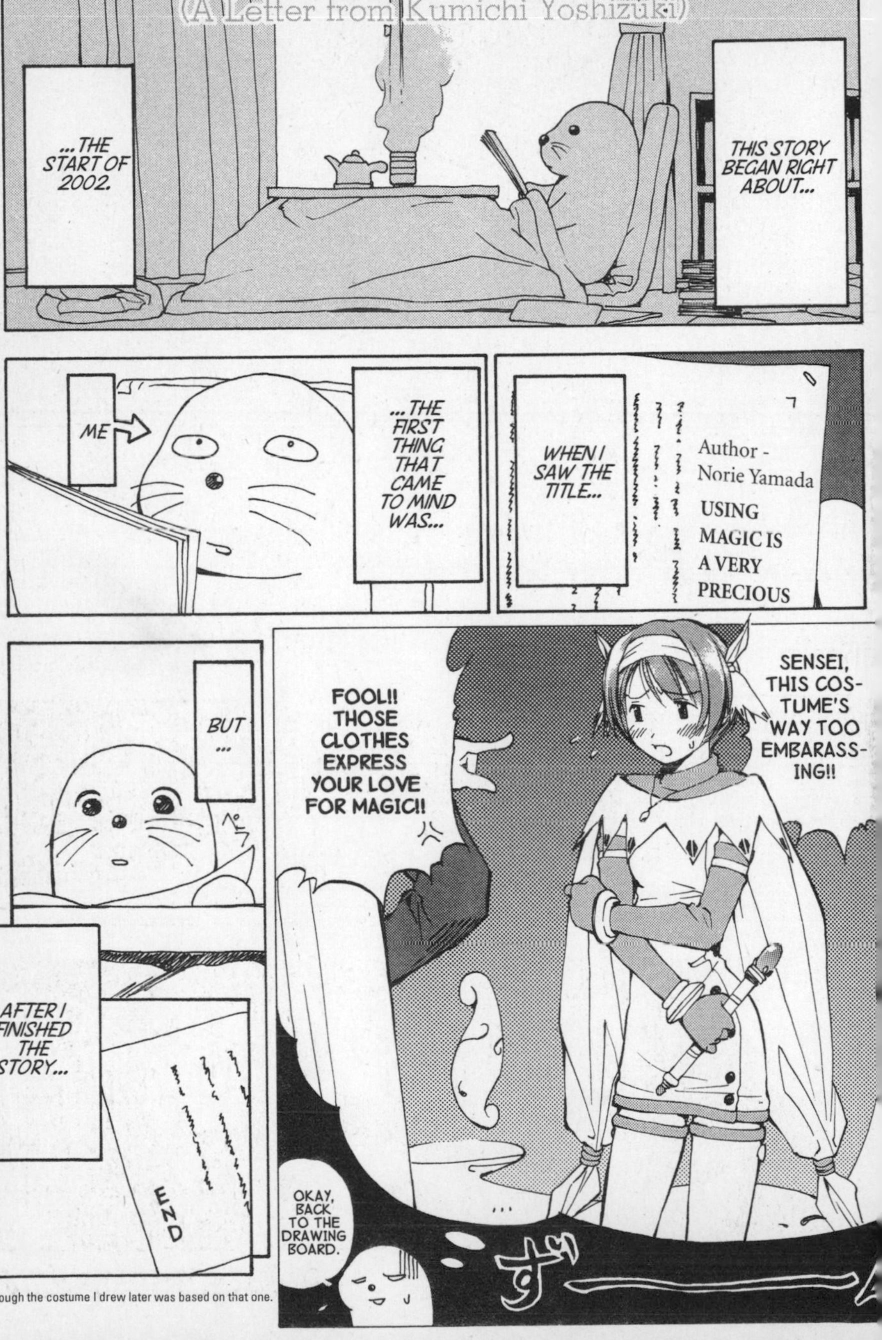
THIS STORY BEGAN RIGHT ABOUT...
...THE START OF 2002.
Author - Norie Yamada
USING MAGIC IS A VERY PRECIOUS
WHEN I SAW THE TITLE...
...THE FIRST THING THAT CAME TO MIND WAS...
ME
SENSEI, THIS COSTUME'S WAY TOO EMBARASSING!!
FOOL!! THOSE CLOTHES EXPRESS YOUR LOVE FOR MAGIC!!
...
OKAY, BACK TO THE DRAWING BOARD.
BUT ...
AFTER I FINISHED THE STORY...
END

*Though the costume I drew later was based on that one.

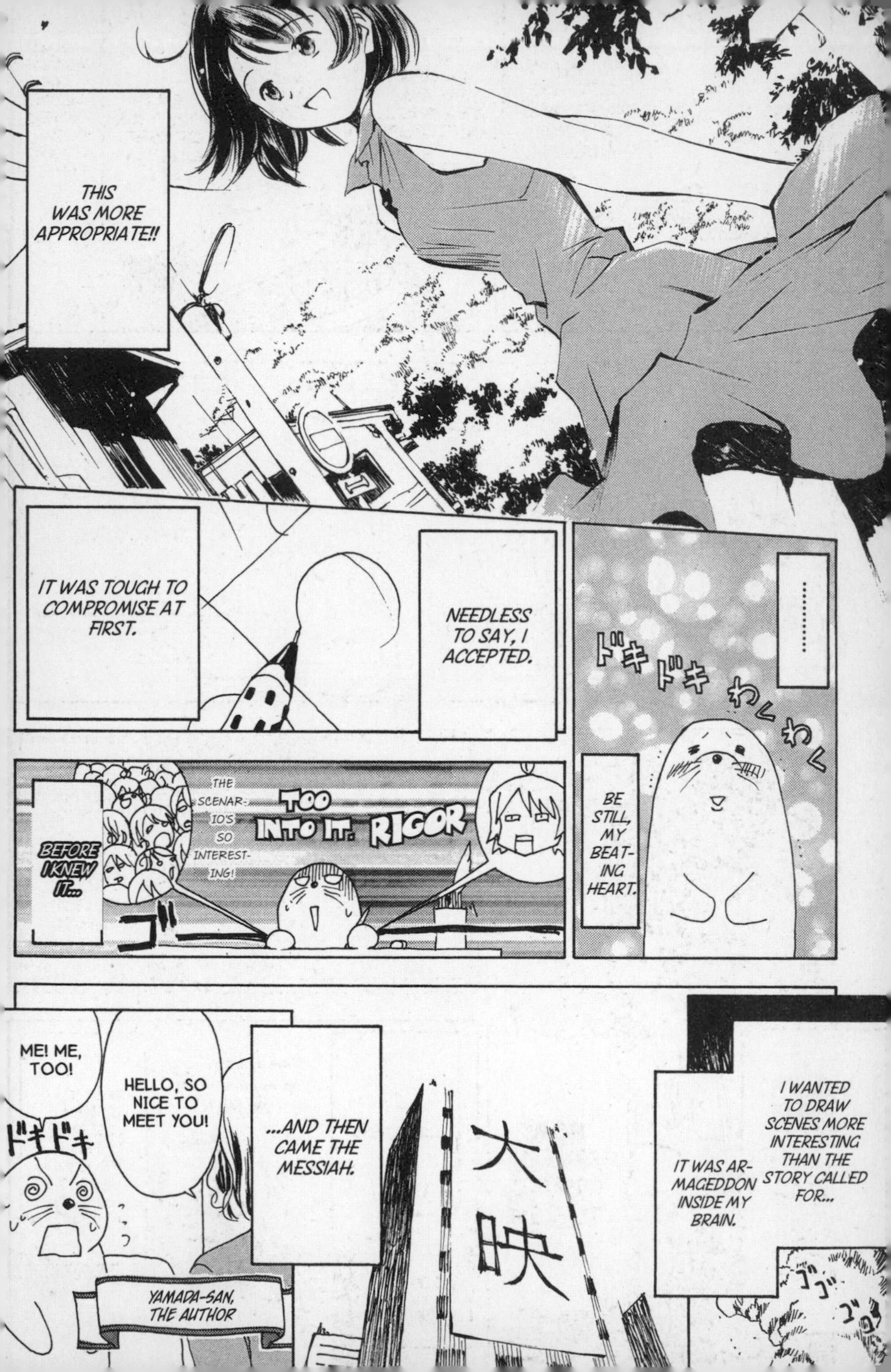
THIS WAS MORE APPROPRIATE!!
……
ドキドキ わくわく
BE STILL, MY BEATING HEART.
NEEDLESS TO SAY, I ACCEPTED.
IT WAS TOUGH TO COMPROMISE AT FIRST.
RIGOR
TOO INTO IT.
THE SCENARIO'S SO INTERESTING!
BEFORE I KNEW IT...
ゴー
I WANTED TO DRAW SCENES MORE INTERESTING THAN THE STORY CALLED FOR...
IT WAS ARMAGEDDON INSIDE MY BRAIN.
ゴゴゴ
...AND THEN CAME THE MESSIAH.
大映
HELLO, SO NICE TO MEET YOU!
ME! ME, TOO!
ドキドキ
YAMADA-SAN, THE AUTHOR

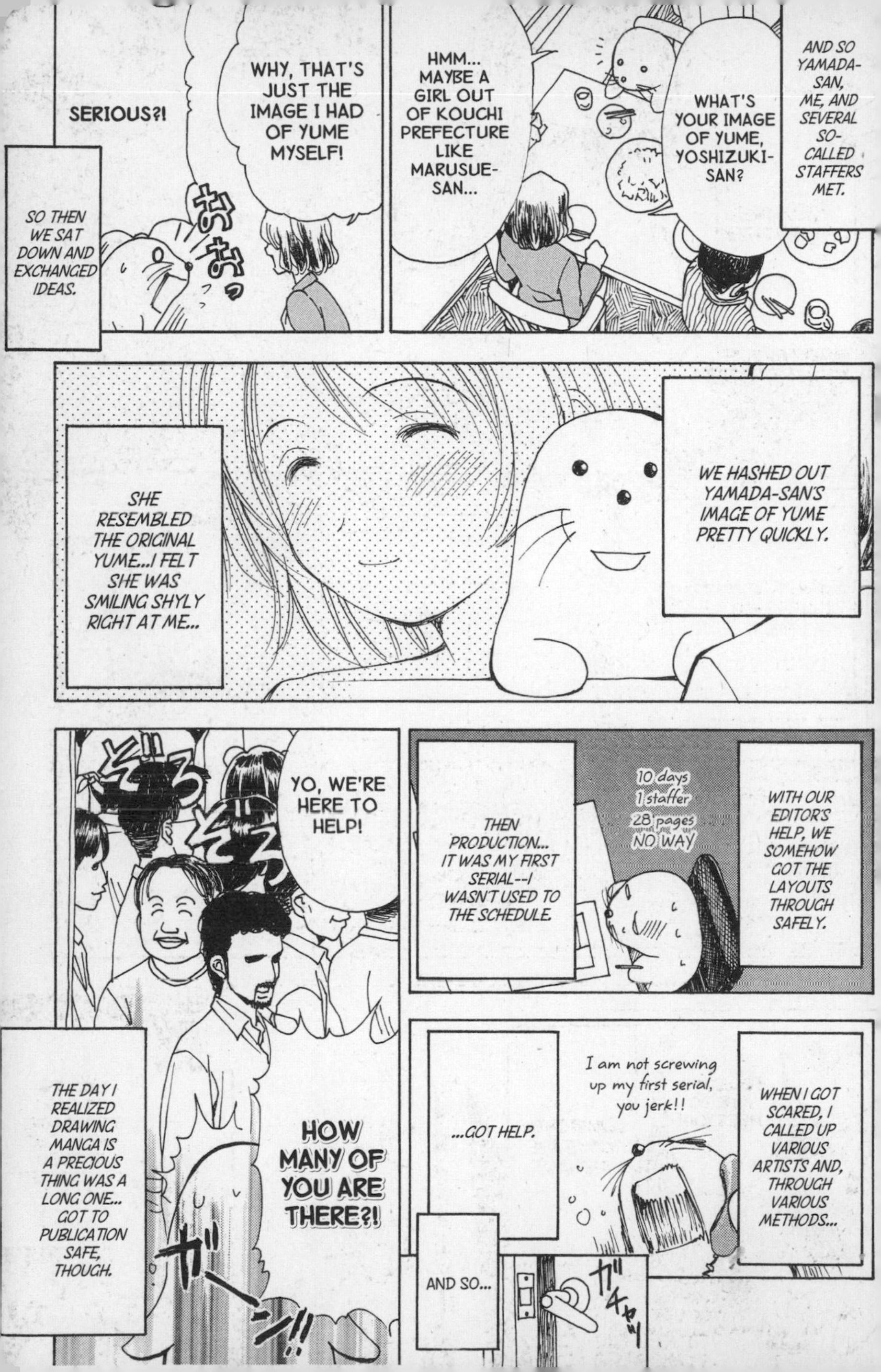
AND SO YAMADA-SAN, ME, AND SEVERAL SO-CALLED STAFFERS MET.
WHAT'S YOUR IMAGE OF YUME, YOSHIZUKI-SAN?
HMM... MAYBE A GIRL OUT OF KOUCHI PREFECTURE LIKE MARUSUE-SAN...
WHY, THAT'S JUST THE IMAGE I HAD OF YUME MYSELF!
SERIOUS?!
おおっ
SO THEN WE SAT DOWN AND EXCHANGED IDEAS.
WE HASHED OUT YAMADA-SAN'S IMAGE OF YUME PRETTY QUICKLY.
SHE RESEMBLED THE ORIGINAL YUME...I FELT SHE WAS SMILING SHYLY RIGHT AT ME...
WITH OUR EDITOR'S HELP, WE SOMEHOW GOT THE LAYOUTS THROUGH SAFELY.
10 days 1 staffer 28 pages NO WAY
THEN PRODUCTION... IT WAS MY FIRST SERIAL--I WASN'T USED TO THE SCHEDULE.
WHEN I GOT SCARED, I CALLED UP VARIOUS ARTISTS AND, THROUGH VARIOUS METHODS...
I am not screwing up my first serial, you jerk!!
...GOT HELP.
AND SO...
YO, WE'RE HERE TO HELP!
HOW MANY OF YOU ARE THERE?!
ガーン!!
THE DAY I REALIZED DRAWING MANGA IS A PRECIOUS THING WAS A LONG ONE... GOT TO PUBLICATION SAFE, THOUGH.

Materials of the Animation①

ORIGINAL CHARACTER DESIGNS!
KUMICHI YOSHIZUKI'S ORIGINAL CHARACTER DESIGNS AND ANIMATION LINEART, UNVEILED FOR THE FIRST TIME! SMILING, HEART-THUMPING AND CRYING FOR THE CAMERA, *SOMEDAY'S DREAMERS* BEAUTIFUL CHARACTERS ARE HERE, INKLESS FOR YOUR VIEWING PLEASURE!

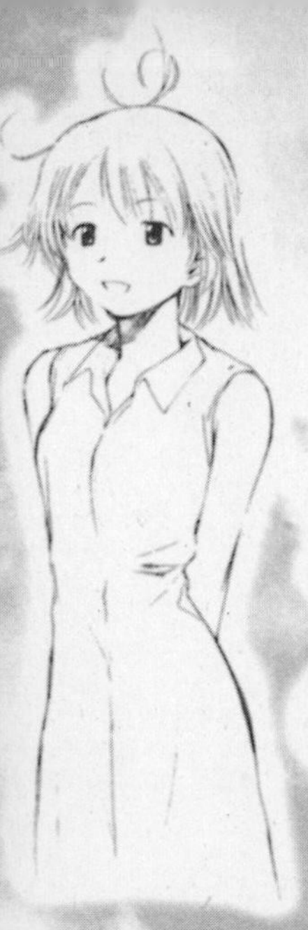

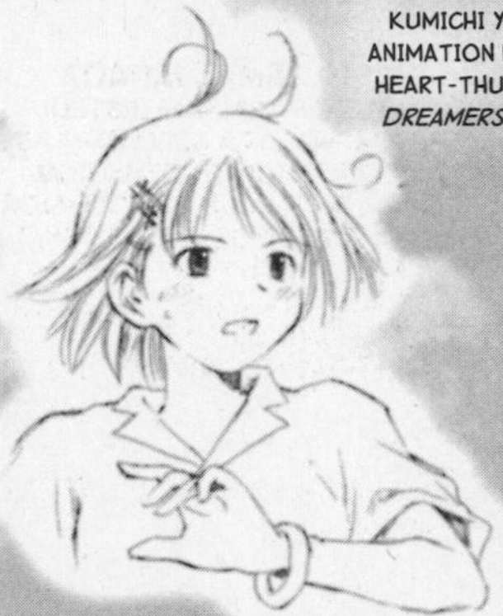

STAFF LIST
CREATOR/SCENARIOS: NORIE YAMADA
SUPERVISOR: MASAMI SHIMODA
CHARACTER CONCEPTS: KUMICHI YOSHIZUKI
CHARACTER DESIGN: MICHINORI CHIBA
OVERALL PROJECT SUPERVISOR: AYAKO KAWASHIMA
AESTHETICS SUPERVISOR: JUNICHIRO NISHIGAWA
COLORIST: MIYUKI ISHIDA
AUDIO SUPERVISOR: HIDEYUKI TANAKA
MUSIC: TAKESHI HAKETA

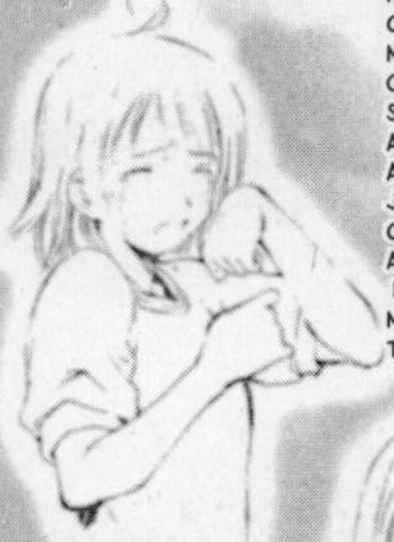

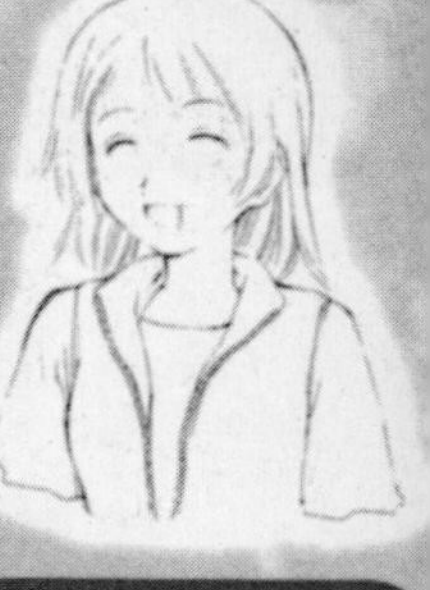

birthday : 29 April/age : 18/
the zodiac : Taurus/
blood type : O/
height : 155/weight : 48/
hometown : Tono Iwate

YUME KIKUCHI
BOTH PARENTS ARE MAGIC USERS. THINKING BECOMING A MAGIC USER WAS ONLY NATURAL, SHE LEFT TONO FOR TOKYO TO UNDERGO TRAINING. THOUGH SHE SHOULD HAVE GREAT TALENT, SHE DOESN'T REALLY SENSE THAT HERSELF. THOUGH SHE'S EIGHTEEN IN THE COMIC, SHE WAS MADE SEVENTEEN FOR THE ANIME VERSION.

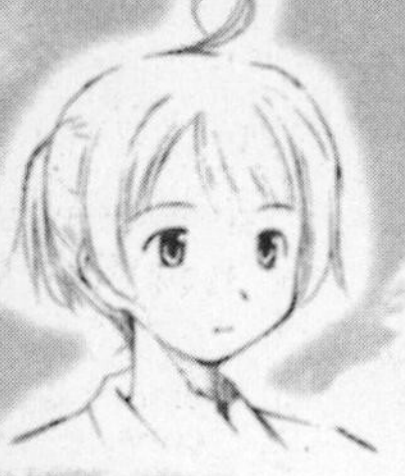

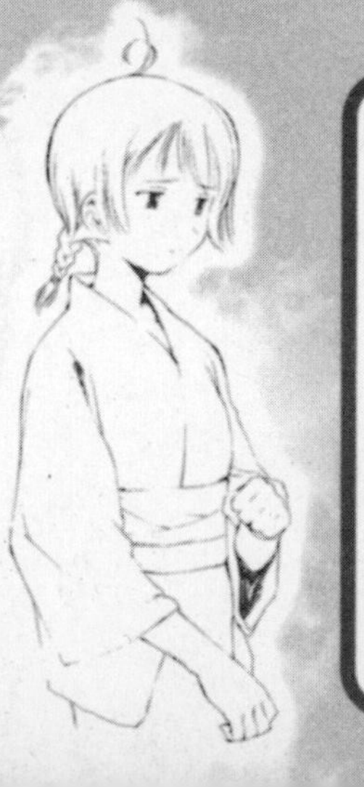

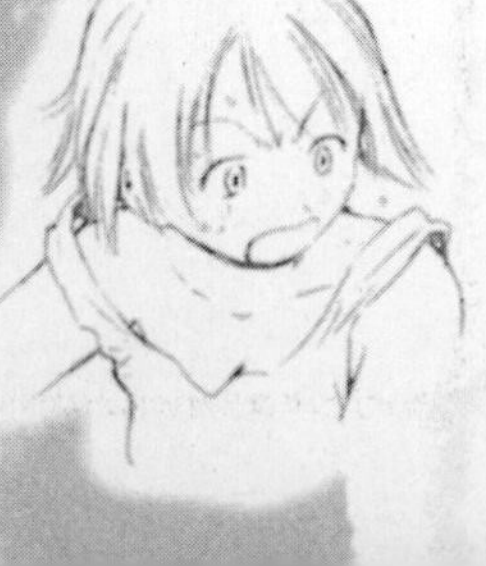

SPACEY AND SOFT YUME. A VERY BUBBLY, LIVELY UPFRONT GIRL. SHE'S ALSO VERY EMOTIONAL UNINTENTIONALLY. HER STANDING HAIR STRAND BECAME HER TRADEMARK FEATURE!

ANIME Ver.

THE MANGA VERSION WAS CUDDLIER. THIS ONE FEELS A LITTLE MORE ADULT AND ANGULAR.

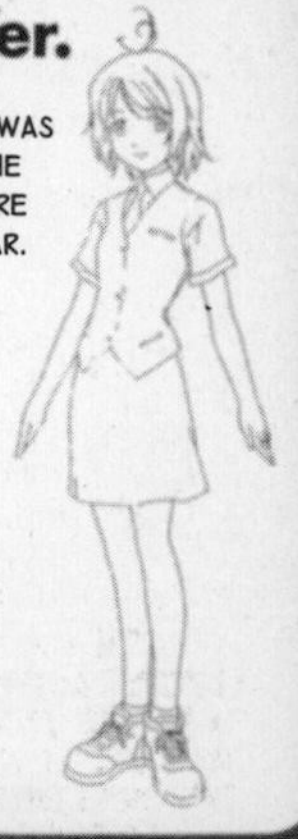

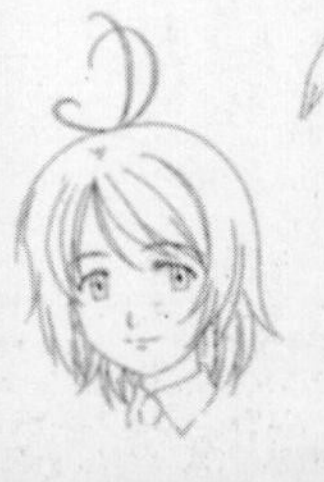

Materials of the Animation②

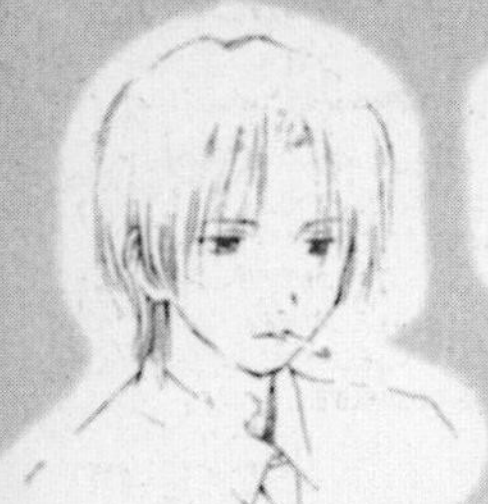
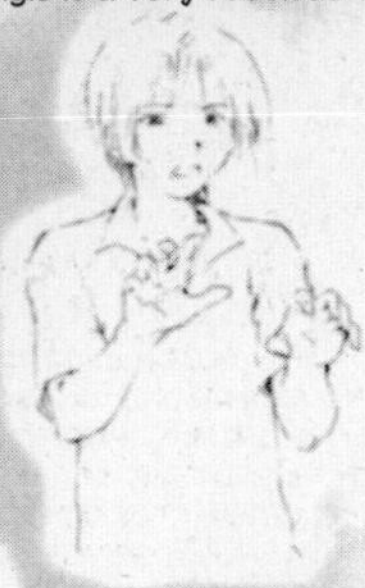
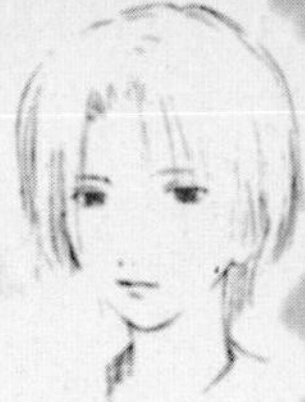
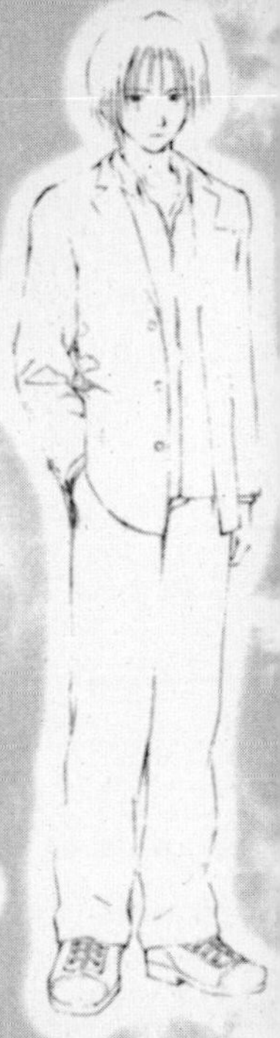

MASAMI OYAMADA
YUME'S TRAINING INSTRUCTOR. HOLDS A SECOND-CLASS CERTIFICATE OF MAGICAL MASTERY. RUNS THE OYAMADA MAGIC OFFICE AND THE SALSA BAR NEXT TO IT. SPEAKS SOFTLY, BUT HAS A SMOLDERING INTENSITY. DOES NOT REVEAL HIS TRUE FEELINGS.

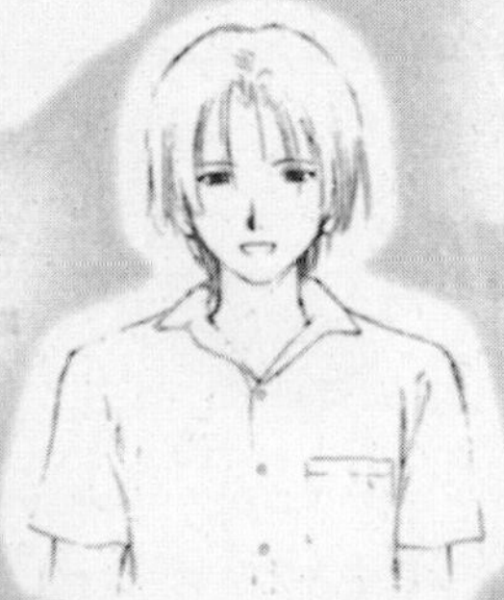

THE COOL, HANDSOME TYPE. THE ORIGINAL DESIGN TRIED TO CONVEY A GENTLER SIDE, BUT IT'S THE ANIME VERSION THAT REALLY CAPTURES THAT.

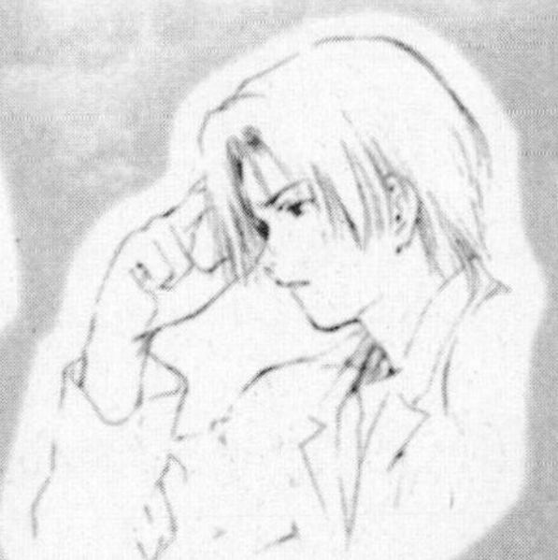

BIRTHDAY: 10 MAY/ AGE: 30/ THE ZODIAC: TAURUS/ BLOOD TYPE: AB/ HEIGHT: 178/ WEIGHT: 67/ HOMETOWN: PARIS, FRANCE

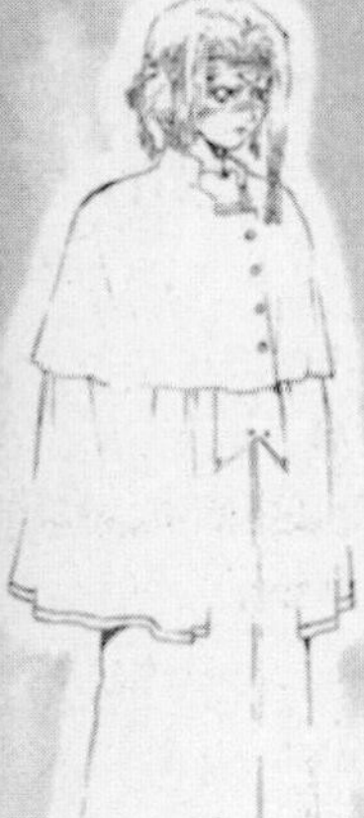

COVERED EYES TO BLOCK OUT THE PHYSICAL WORLD? THE ORIENTAL OUTFIT ADDS TO THE "MYSTERY"

ANIME Ver.

HE SEEMS A LITTLE KINDER AND GENTLER. PERHAPS HE COMES OFF MORE AS A WATCHFUL ADULT.

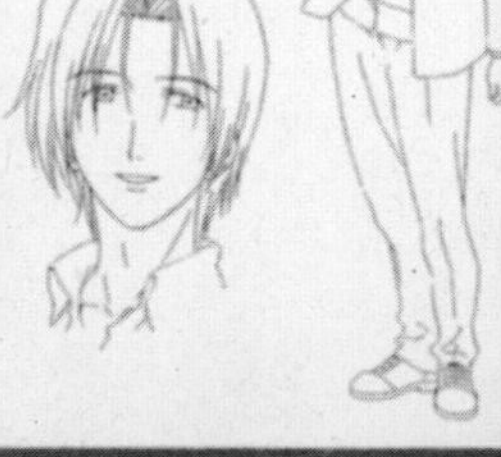

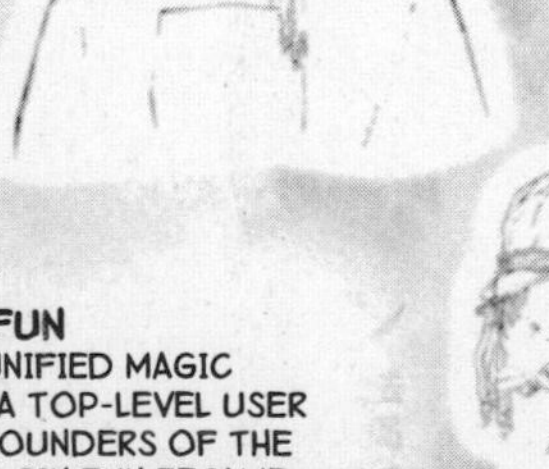
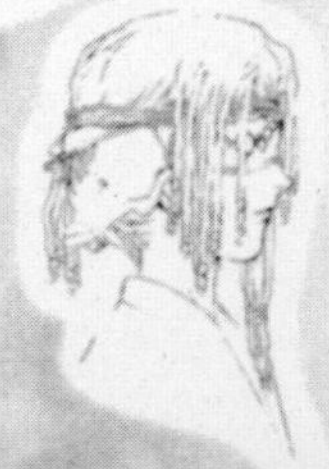

GIN FUN
HEAD OF THE UNIFIED MAGIC LABORERS BUREAU. A TOP-LEVEL USER AND ONE OF THE FOUNDERS OF THE BUREAU OF MAGIC, GIN FUN BECAME ITS FIRST DIRECTOR. ALSO PRESIDES AS EDUCATIONAL DIRECTOR.

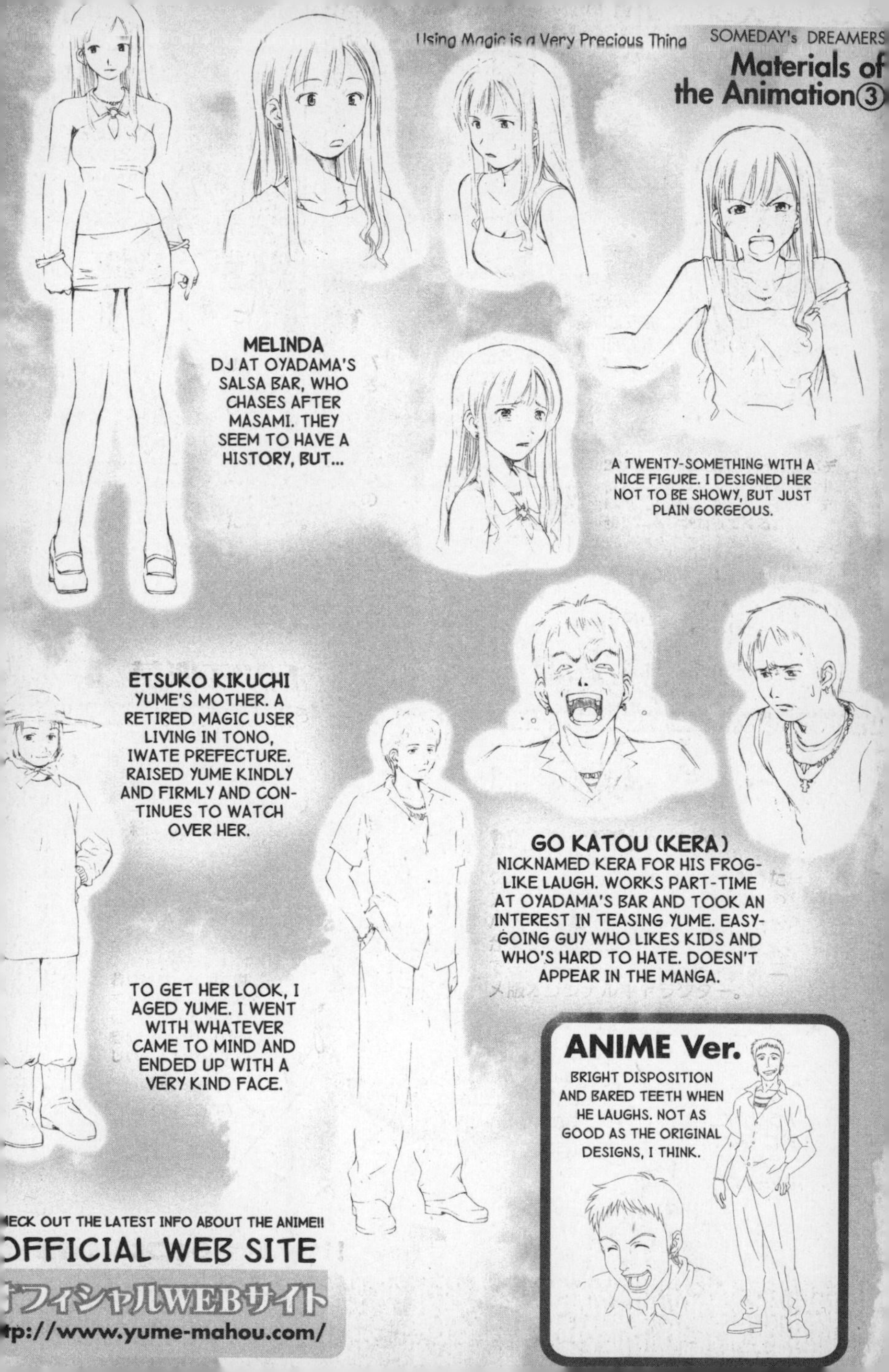
Materials of the Animation③
MELINDA
DJ AT OYADAMA'S SALSA BAR, WHO CHASES AFTER MASAMI. THEY SEEM TO HAVE A HISTORY, BUT...
A TWENTY-SOMETHING WITH A NICE FIGURE. I DESIGNED HER NOT TO BE SHOWY, BUT JUST PLAIN GORGEOUS.
ETSUKO KIKUCHI
YUME'S MOTHER. A RETIRED MAGIC USER LIVING IN TONO, IWATE PREFECTURE. RAISED YUME KINDLY AND FIRMLY AND CONTINUES TO WATCH OVER HER.
TO GET HER LOOK, I AGED YUME. I WENT WITH WHATEVER CAME TO MIND AND ENDED UP WITH A VERY KIND FACE.
GO KATOU (KERA)
NICKNAMED KERA FOR HIS FROG-LIKE LAUGH. WORKS PART-TIME AT OYADAMA'S BAR AND TOOK AN INTEREST IN TEASING YUME. EASY-GOING GUY WHO LIKES KIDS AND WHO'S HARD TO HATE. DOESN'T APPEAR IN THE MANGA.
ANIME Ver.
BRIGHT DISPOSITION AND BARED TEETH WHEN HE LAUGHS. NOT AS GOOD AS THE ORIGINAL DESIGNS, I THINK.
ECK OUT THE LATEST INFO ABOUT THE ANIME!!
OFFICIAL WEB SITE
フィシャルWEBサイト
tp://www.yume-mahou.com/

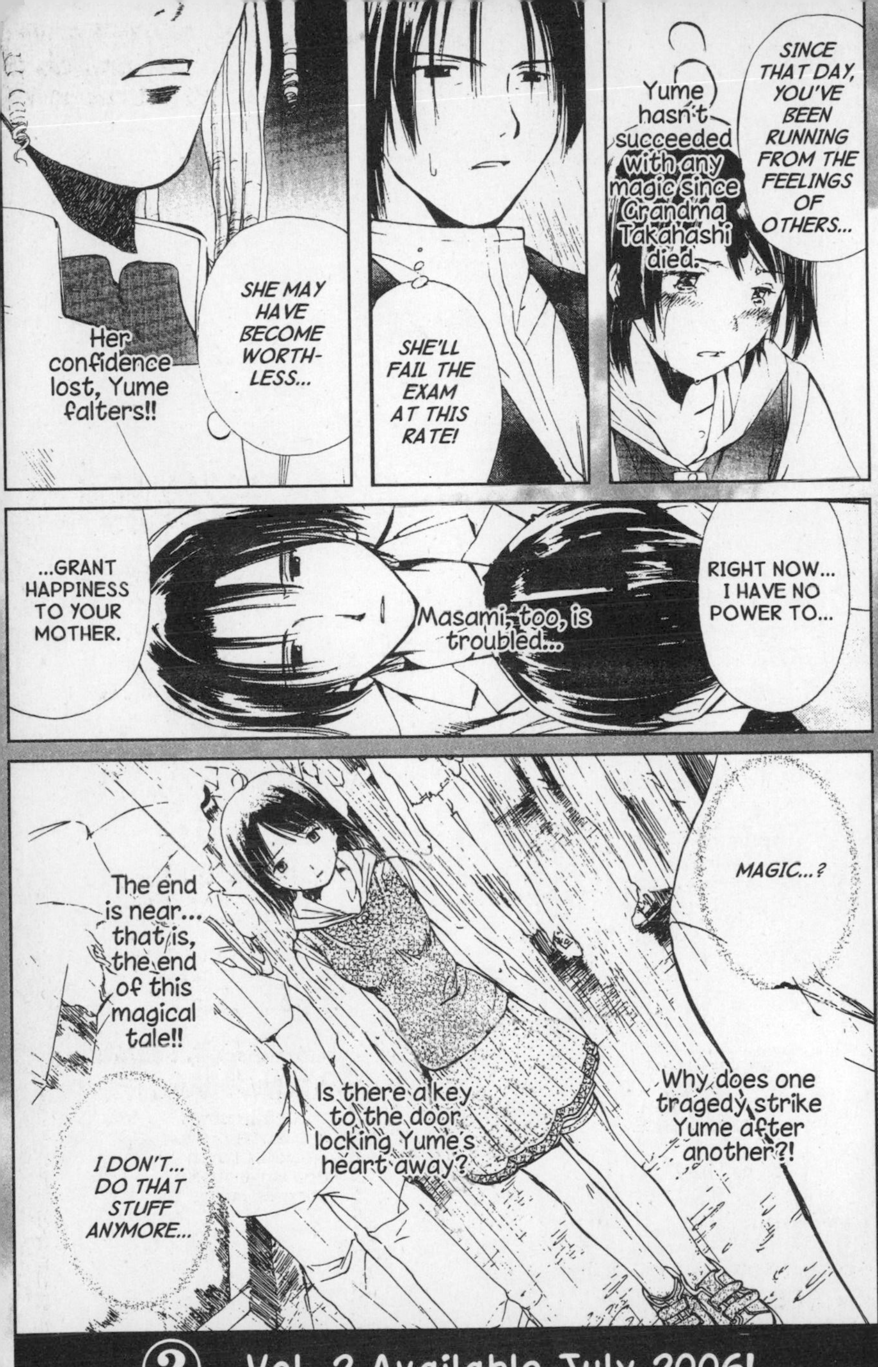
SINCE THAT DAY, YOU'VE BEEN RUNNING FROM THE FEELINGS OF OTHERS...
Yume hasn't succeeded with any magic since Grandma Takahashi died.
SHE'LL FAIL THE EXAM AT THIS RATE!
SHE MAY HAVE BECOME WORTHLESS...
Her confidence lost, Yume falters!!
RIGHT NOW... I HAVE NO POWER TO...
Masami, too, is troubled...
...GRANT HAPPINESS TO YOUR MOTHER.
MAGIC...?
Why does one tragedy strike Yume after another?!
Is there a key to the door locking Yume's heart away?
The end is near... that is, the end of this magical tale!!
I DON'T... DO THAT STUFF ANYMORE...

② Vol. 2 Available July 2006!

TOKYOPOP SHOP

Ayumu struggles with her studies, and the all-important high school entrance exams are approaching. Fortunately, she has help from her best bud Shii-chan, who is at the top of the class. But when the test results come back, the friends are surprised: Ayumu surpasses Shii-chan's scores and gets into the school of her choice—without Shii-chan! Losing her friend is so painful for Ayumu that she starts cutting herself to ease her sorrow. Finally, Ayumu seeks comfort in a new friend, Manami. But will Manami prove to be the friend that Ayumu truly needs? Or will Ayumu continue down a dark path?

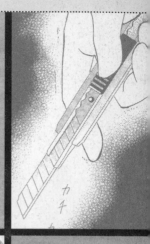

LIFE

Volume 1

Keiko Suenobu

It's about real teenagers...

It's about real high school...

It's about real life.

LIFE
BY KEIKO SUENOBU

Ordinary high school teenagers...
Except that they're not.

LIFE™

OT
OLDER TEEN
AGE 16+

© Keiko Suenobu

READ THE ENTIRE FIRST CHAPTER ONLINE FOR FREE:

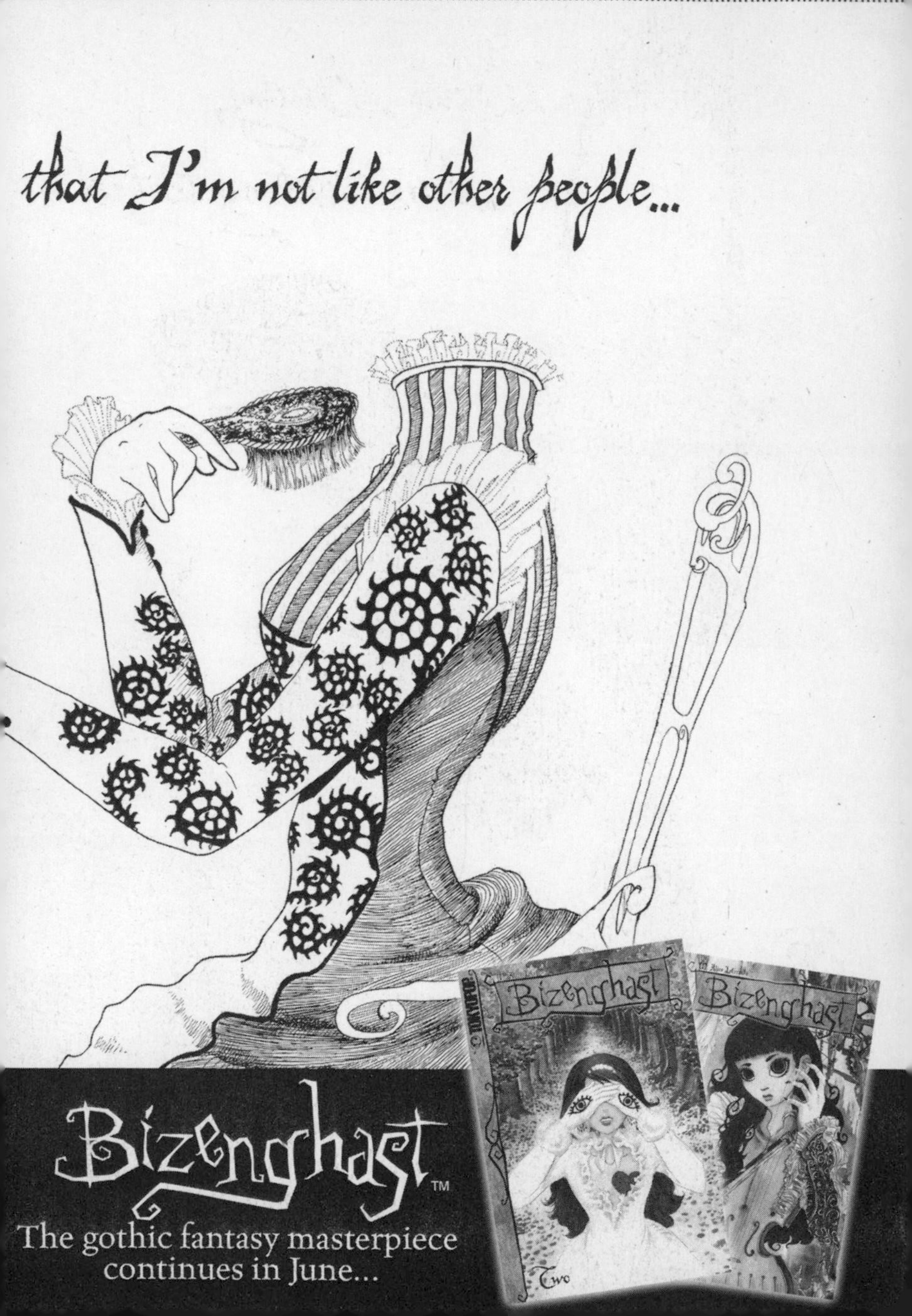

that I'm not like other people...
Bizenghast
Bizenghast
TOKYOPOP
Two
Bizenghast™
The gothic fantasy masterpiece continues in June...

THIS FALL, TOKYOPOP CREATES A FRESH, NEW CHAPTER IN TEEN NOVELS...

For Adventurers...

Witches' Forest:
The Adventures of Duan Surk

By Mishio Fukazawa
Duan Surk is a 16-year-old Level 2 fighter who embarks on the quest of a lifetime—battling mythical creatures and outwitting evil sorceresses, all in an impossible rescue mission in the spooky Witches' Forest!

BASED ON THE FAMOUS
FORTUNE QUEST WORLD

For Dreamers...

Magic Moon

By Wolfgang and Heike Hohlbein
Kim enters the enigmatic realm of Magic Moon, where he battles unthinkable monsters and fantastical creatures—in order to unravel the secret that keeps his sister locked in a coma.

THE WORLDWIDE BESTSELLING FANTASY
THRILLOGY ARRIVES IN THE U.S.!